GLOBALISM AND THE N

THE NEW REGIONALISM

This series summarizes the WIDER international research project on the New Regionalism. Regionalization is seen as a more multidimensional process than in other contemporary analyses. The five volumes in this series are edited by **Björn Hettne**, *Professor, Department of Peace and Development, Göteberg University*, **András Inotai**, *Director-General, Institute for World Economics, Budapest*, and **Osvaldo Sunkel**, *Professor of Economics, Centro de Análisis e Políticas Públicas, Universidad de Chile*.

Titles in the subseries include

Volume 1: GLOBALISM AND THE NEW REGIONALISM

Volume 2: NATIONAL PERSPECTIVES ON THE NEW REGIONALISM IN THE NORTH

Volume 3: NATIONAL PERSPECTIVES ON THE NEW REGIONALISM IN THE SOUTH

Volume 4: THE NEW REGIONALISM AND THE FUTURE OF SECURITY AND DEVELOPMENT

Volume 5: COMPARING REGIONALISMS
Implications for Global Development

*Tables of contents for all these volumes can be found within each book, placed before the index.

Published within the International Political Economy Series
General Editor: Timothy M. Shaw, Professor of Political Science and International Development Studies, and Director, Centre for Foreign Policy Studies, Dalhousie University, Nova Scotia

International Political Economy Series
Series Standing Order ISBN 0–333–71708–2 hardcover
Series Standing Order ISBN 0–333–71110–6 paperback
(*outside North America only*)

You can receive future titles in this series as they are published by placing a standing order. Please contact your bookseller or, in case of difficulty, write to us at the address below with your name and address, the title of the series and the ISBN quoted above.

Customer Services Department, Macmillan Distribution Ltd
Houndmills, Basingstoke, Hampshire RG21 6XS, England

Globalism and the New Regionalism

Volume 1

Edited by

Björn Hettne
Professor
Department of Peace and Development
Göteborg University

András Inotai
Director-General
Institute for World Economics
Budapest

and

Osvaldo Sunkel
Professor of Economics
Centro de Análisis e Políticas Públicas
Universidad de Chile

Foreword by Giovanni Andrea Cornia
Director, UNU/WIDER

 in association with
UNU / WIDER

First published in Great Britain 1999 by
MACMILLAN PRESS LTD
Houndmills, Basingstoke, Hampshire RG21 6XS and London
Companies and representatives throughout the world

A catalogue record for this book is available from the British Library.

ISBN 0–333–68707–8 hardcover
ISBN 0–333–68708–6 paperback

First published in the United States of America 1999 by
ST. MARTIN'S PRESS, INC.,
Scholarly and Reference Division,
175 Fifth Avenue, New York, N.Y. 10010

ISBN 0–312–21563–0

Library of Congress Cataloging-in-Publication Data
Globalism and the new regionalism / edited by Björn Hettne, András
Inotai, and Osvaldo Sunkel ; foreword by Giovanni Andrea Cornia.
p. cm. — (Regionalism (International organization)
Includes bibliographical references and index.
ISBN 0–312–21563–0 (cloth)
1. International economic relations. 2. Regionalism
(International organization) I. Hettne, Björn, 1939– .
II. Inotai, András. III. Sunkel, Osvaldo. IV. Series:
International political economy series. New regionalism.
HF1411.G648 1998
337—dc21   98–19811
                                                                CIP

This book is printed on paper suitable for recycling and made from fully managed and
sustained forest sources.

10   9   8   7   6   5   4   3   2
08   07   06   05   04   03   02   01

Printed & bound by Antony Rowe Ltd, Eastbourne

Contents

List of Abbreviations and Acronyms

ACP	African, Caribbean and Pacific countries associated with the EU
ADB	African Development Bank
AEBR	Assocaition of European Border Regions
AER	Association of European Regions
AERC	African Economic Research Consortium (Nairobi, Kenya)
AFTA	ASEAN Free Trade Area
APEC	Asia Pacific Economic Co-operation
ASEAN	Association of South East Asian Nations
BNU	Mozambique Banco Nacional Ultramarino
BWI	Bretton Woods Institution
CARICOM	Caribbean Common Market
CBI	Crossborder Initiative
CEE	Central and Eastern Europe
CEPR	Centre for Economic Policy Research (London, UK)
CINDE	Corporacion de Investigaciones para el Desarrollo (Santiago, Chile)
CIS	Commonwealth of Independent States
CLRAE	Standing Conference of Local and Regional Authorities of Europe
CMEA	Council for Mutual Economic Assistance
CNN	Cable News Network
COMECON	Council for Mutual Economic Assistance
COMESA	Common Market of Eastern and Southern Africa
DBSA	Development Bank of Southern Africa
EAEC	East Asian Economic Caucus
EC	European Community
ECLAC	UN Economic Commission for Latin America and the Caribbean
ECOWAS	Economic Community of West African States
EEA	European Economic Area
EEC	European Economic Community

EU	European Union
EUI	European University Institute (Florence, Italy)
FDI	foreign direct investment
FONDAD	Forum on Debt and Development (The Hague, the Netherlands)
FSU	former Soviet Union
FTA	free trade area
G-5	Group of Five (France, Germany, Japan, UK, USA)
G-7	Group of Seven (Canada, France, Germany, Italy, Japan, UK, USA)
GATT	General Agreement on Tariffs and Trade
GDP	gross domestic product
IBRD	International Bank for Reconstruction and Development
IED	International Economics Department (World Bank)
IFI	international financial institution
IMF	International Monetary Fund
INGO	international non-governmental organization
IOR	Indian Ocean Rim
IPE	International political economy
IPSA	International Political Science Association
IR	international relations
ISA	International Studies Association
Mercosur	Common Market of the South (Argentina, Brazil, Paraguay, Uruguay)
MFN	most-favoured nation
MUNS	Multilateralism and the United Nations System (UNU)
NAFTA	North American Free Trade Agreement
NATO	North Atlantic Treaty Organization
NGO	non-governmental organization
NIE	newly industrialized/industrializing economy
NIC	newly industrialized/industrializing country
NRA	new regionalism approach
OAPEC	Organization of Arab Petroleum Exporting Countries
OAS	Organization of American States
OAU	Organization of African Unity
OECD	Organization of Economic Cooperation and Development

OPECE	Organization of Petroleum Exporting Countries
OSCE	Organization for Security and Co-operation in Europe
PP21	People's Plan for the Twenty-First Century
PRIO	International Peace Research Institute (Oslo, Norway)
PTA	Preferential Trade Area for Eastern and Southern Africa
R&D	research and development
RIA	regional integration agreement/arrangement
RIIA	Royal Institute for International Affairs (London, UK)
RIPE	Review of International Political Economy
RvM	regionalism versus multilateralism
SAAARC	South Asian Association for Regional Co-operation
SACU	Southern African Customs Union
SADC	Southern African Development Community
SADCC	Southern African Development Co-ordination Conference
SAP	structural adjustment programme
SARCC	South African Rail Commuter Corporation
SREZ	subregional economic zone
SSA	Sub-Saharan Africa
TNC	transnational corporation
TRIP	trade related intellectual property (WTO)
UN	United Nations
UNCTAD	United Nations Conference on Trade and Development
UNCTC	United National Centre on Transnational Corporations
UNPF	United Nations Population Fund
UNU	United Nations University
UNU/WIDER	World Institute for Development Economics Research of the United Nations University (Helsinki, Finland)
UR	Uruguay Round
USAID	United States Agency for International Development
USSR	Union of Soviet Socialist Republics
WEB	World Bank

WEU	Western European Union
WTO	World Trade Organization/Warsaw Treaty Organization

Notes on the Contributors

The Editors

Björn Hettne is Professor at the Department of Peace and Development, Göteborg University. He is the author of a number of books and articles on development theory, international political economy, European integration and ethnic relations, and (in English) of *Development Theory and the Three Worlds*.

András Inotai was Staff member of the World Bank, Washington, DC (1989–91). Since 1991 he has been Director General of the Institute for World Economics, Budapest; Head of the Task Force for Hungary's EU-Integration Strategy (from February 1996); Professor in Political Economy of European Integration and Central and Eastern Europe at the College of Europe, Bruges (Belgium), and Natolin (Poland), author and editor of several books in English, German, Spanish and Hungarian, with more than 300 articles in various professional journals.

Osvaldo Sunkel is Professor of Economics, Faculty of Economics and Business Administration and Co-ordinator, Sustainable Development Program, Centro de Análisis de Políticas Públicas, Universidad de Chile; Special Advisor to ECLAC; President of CINDE; and Director, Pensamiento Económico-Revista de Economía Política, Madrid.

The Contributors

Samir Amin was Director, African Institute for Economic Development and Planning, Dakar 1970–80. Since 1980 he has been Director, African Office of the Third World Forum, and author of a number of books, including *The Empire of Chaos* and *Re-reading the Post War Period: An Intellectual Itinerary*.

Richard Falk is Albert G. Milbank Professor of International Law at Princeton University. He was founding member of the World Order Models Project and his most recent book is *On Human Governance: Toward a New Global Politics*.

Helge Hveem is Professor of International Politics at the Department of Political Science, University of Oslo, and Research Director at the Centre for Development and the Environment of the same university. He has published extensively in the field of international political economy and international development studies, including *The Political Economy of Third World Producer Associations*, *International Relations and World Images* and (in Norwegian) *Power and Welfare in the Global Society: Theories of International Political Economy*. He has worked as a consultant with UNCTAD and several other UN institutions.

Jyrki Käkönen is Research Director at Tampere Peace Research Institute, specializing in international politics in the Arctic, sustainable development, regionalization and the role of civil society in international relations.

Kaisa Lähteenmäki is Researcher (graduate school) at the University of Turku. She is preparing her PhD dissertation on the role of subnational regions in the EU and the relationship between regionalization and globalization. She is the editor of *Dimensions of Conflict and Cooperation in the Baltic Sea Rim*.

Percy S. Mistry is Chairman of the Oxford International Group, and serves on the boards of several corporations, including Oxford International Finance, Synergy Power Corporation, and the Industrial Credit and Investment Corporation of India. He was formerly Chief-of-Staff in the Finance Complex of the World Bank. He has been an adviser on matters of debt, macroeconomic management and structural adjustment to several governments in Africa, Asia, and Europe, as well as a consultant for a variety of multilateral organizations. He was Chief Consultant of a three-volume study on economic integration in Southern Africa, and author of *Regional Integration Arrangements in Economic Development: Panacea or Pitfall?*

James H. Mittelman is Professor of International Relations in the School of International Service, American University, Washington, DC. (Previously he served as Professor and Dean of the Graduate School of International Studies, University of Denver, and Professor and Dean, Division of the Social Sciences, Queens College of the City University of New York.) His most recent books are *Globalization: Critical Reflections*, of which he is editor and a contributing author, and *Out from Underdevelopment Revisited: Changing Global Structures and the Remaking of the Third World*, co-authored by Mustapha Kamal Pasha.

Bertil Odén is Senior Researcher at the Nordic Africa Institute in Uppsala, Sweden, where he conducts a research programme on regionalization in Southern Africa. He holds a licentiate degree from Göteborg University. He has edited a number of books from the Uppsala Institute, among which is *Southern Africa after Apartheid*. In the UNU/WIDER series on World Development Studies, he has published *Regionalization in Southern Africa*

Ralph Pettman holds the Foundation Chair of International Relations at the Victoria University of Wellington, New Zealand. He has worked in government in Australia and has taught world affairs there, as well as in the UK, the US and Japan. He is the author and editor of several academic monographs, the most recent of which is *Understanding International Political Economy, with readings for the fatigued*.

Foreword

It is a great pleasure to introduce to the reader the results of this innovative research project. UNU/WIDER is deeply concerned with ongoing global transformations; and in particular, with the ways these affect development, overall inequality and security. The close relationship between these issues is today widely recognized, but the more precise inter-relationships have not been systematically researched, particularly not in a global setting.

The approach to the new regionalism taken in this UNU/WIDER research project is fundamentally different from the dominant one spearheaded by the Bretton Woods institutions. According to these institutions, the new regionalism is mainly an economic phenomenon, reflecting a trade promotion policy built on regional arrangements rather than on the multilateral framework. As such, this approach can constitute a threat to multilateralism, reduce global welfare, and be considered only as a 'second-best' solution. Regionalism today is often considered 'new' only in the sense that it is a revival of protectionism.

Without denying the relevance of this analysis, the 'UNU/WIDER approach' defines the new regionalism as a comprehensive, multi-dimensional, political phenomenon including economics, security, environment and other issues which challenge the nation states today. It is thus 'new' in a qualitative sense as it is an integral part of current global transformation, often called globalization, and it can only be understood in that context, and within an interdisciplinary framework.

From a normative point of view, it represents a way of tackling problems which cannot be dealt with efficiently at the national level. The new regionalism is still 'new' enough to raise many questions, and I hope that these five volumes will provide a base line for more new research in the years to come. I thus strongly recommend this excellent and provocative analysis to the readers.

GIOVANNI ANDREA CORNIA
Director, UNU/WIDER

The New Regionalism: A Prologue

The research project on new regionalism was born a few years ago at the UNU/WIDER research centre in Helsinki, where the initial participants in a brain-storming seminar concluded that the recent wave of regionalization throughout the world warranted a new type of analysis which went beyond classical integration theory and emphasized the social, political and cultural dimensions, apart from the economic which traditionally had been the focus. In searching for its own distinctive and appropriate approach, the project could fall back on two earlier UNU programmes: first the *Regional Perspectives Programme*, dating back to the mid-eighties, and second the more recent programme on *Multilateralism and the UN System* (MUNS). The first of these, strongly associated with former UNU vice-rector Kinhide Mushakoji, pointed to the 'world region' as an important research object *cum* political subject in its own right. The second, intellectually fathered by Robert Cox, raised new issues regarding the future world order, and argued in normative terms in favour of a 'new multilateralism' in which a more symmetrical relationship between the regions of the world would be possible.

Similarly, the focus of this particular project is not so much on the region *per se* but rather on the *role* of supranational or 'world' regions in the current global transformation.

Regions in this sense are not 'given', neither are they formal organizations. Rather they are created and recreated in the process of global transformation. Thus the project participants have been programmatically open-minded as far as *definitions* are concerned, although many would agree: (1) that regions are territorially based subsystems of the international system, and (2) that there are many varieties of regional subsystems with different degrees of 'regionness'; that is, the degree to which a particular region in various respects constitutes a coherent unit.

There is also a variety of *theoretical approaches* to the study of such subsystems ranging from neorealism to postmodernism. Most analysts would, however, say that a post-Westphalian situation warrants a post-realist approach. In this regard as well the

project has remained eclectic, perhaps with some bias in favour
of systemic approaches; that is, theorizing about the larger
systemic context of regionalization rather than with regions as such.
The region can thus only be understood as forming part of something
larger.

As in most internationally organized research undertakings, participants in the New Regionalism project have over the years carried
out their discussions at different meeting places, and have shared
experiences which also form part of the research agenda, thus bestow-
ing their own distinct flavour to the discourse. The workshop venues,
symbolizing the evolution of this particular project, happened to be
Berlin, Jerusalem and Kathmandu, and the best way of presenting its
intellectual history is therefore to use these places as its relevant
'milestones', as it were. The three major issues can be described as
the *global context*, the *dynamics* and the *consequences* of regionalism.
This way of structuring the argument also underlies the way the series
of five project publications (see pp. 251–4 for their tables of contents)
have been organized. First, however, the overall theme will be briefly
outlined.

THE THEME

The starting point of the project was the realization that regionalism
over the last decade has 'been brought back in', albeit in a different
form compared to the debate on regional integration some thirty
years ago. Thus it was assumed that we were dealing with a 'new'
regionalism. This discovery has, of course, been made in many quarters and given birth to a number of more or less compatible definitions and perceptions, some alarmist, some more enthusiastic. For the
critics, often representing the international financial institutions (IFIs)
and taking a globalist view, the regionalist trend constitutes a threat to
the multilateral system. By contrast, for the enthusiast, the new wave
of regionalism forms the basis for an improved and better functioning
multilateral system – a 'new multilateralism'.

The new regionalism was within this project tentatively defined as a
multidimensional form of integration which includes economic, political, social and cultural aspects and thus goes far beyond the goal of
creating region-based free trade regimes or security alliances. Rather,
the political ambition of establishing regional coherence and identity
seems to be of primary importance.

Some notable differences between 'old' and 'new' regionalism are thus that current processes of regionalization are more from 'below' and 'within' than before, and that not only economic, but also ecological and security imperatives push countries and communities towards co-operation within new types of regionalist frameworks. The actors behind regionalist projects are no longer states only, but a large number of different types of institutions, organizations and movements. Furthermore, today's regionalism is extroverted rather than introverted, which reflects the deeper interdependence of today's global economy. 'Open regionalism' is thus one way of coping with global transformation, since an increasing number of states realize that they lack the capability and the means to manage such a task on the 'national' level.

One of the defining characteristics of the new regionalism is, finally, that it takes place in a multipolar global order, whereas the old regionalism was marked by bipolarity. The decline of US hegemony and the breakdown of the communist subsystem created a room-for-manoeuvre in which this new regionalism could develop. This type of regionalism would not have been consistent with the cold-war system since the 'quasi-regions' of that system tended to reproduce the dualist bipolar structure within themselves. This pattern of *hegemonic regionalism* was of course most evident in Europe, but was discernible also in other world regions at the height of the cold war. Purely economic regions – that is, regional free trade arrangements, customs unions and so on – similarly, ultimately reproduced centre–periphery tensions within themselves, which made them either disintegrate or fall into slumber.

For more than a decade, there has been a new trend towards regionalism in all parts of the world. In the approach of this project no determinism or monocausal approach was involved. Regions can only be defined *post factum,* so there are many different regionalisms, supported or challenged by many different ideological arguments and reflecting various positions in the world economy as a whole. Regionalism is one approach to dealing with various global problems, but its content will be conditioned by the nature of these problems.

As mentioned, the regional frame represents one way of understanding the emerging global structure. A rough distinction can here be made between *core regions* and *peripheral regions*. The former are politically stable and economically dynamic and organize for the sake of being better able to control the world. The latter are defined as being politically more turbulent and economically more stagnant;

consequently they organize in order to arrest a process of marginalization, at the same time as their regional arrangements are fragile and ineffective. They are necessarily more introverted. Their overall situation makes 'security regionalism' and 'developmental regionalism' more important than the creation of free trade regimes.

The core thus constitutes those regions which are economically dynamic and politically capable, whether this capability is expressed in a formal political organization or not. So far only one of the three core regions, namely Europe, aspires to build such an organization. The other two, North America and Asia–Pacific, are economically strong, but, for reasons that will be discussed below, lack a regional political order.

Intermediate regions are also in the processes of being incorporated into the core: Central Europe, waiting for membership in the European Union, Latin America and the Caribbean, in the process of becoming 'North Americanized', and South East Asia, the European Pacific (Australia, New Zealand) and South Pacific, being drawn into the East Asia economic space.

Remaining in a peripheral position are thus the following areas: the former Soviet Union, the major parts of which are now in the process of being reintegrated in the form of the Commonwealth of Independent States; the Balkans, where the countries have lost whatever tradition of co-operation they once might have had; the Middle East, with an unsettled regional structure; South Asia, with a very low level of regionness because of the 'cold war' (sometimes getting hot) between the major powers India and Pakistan; and Africa, where even the political structures called 'states' are falling apart.

Thus, peripheral regions are peripheral because they are economically stagnant, politically turbulent and war-prone, and the only way for them to become less peripheral is to become more regionalized: that is, to increase their level of regionness. The alternative is further disintegration and the complete disappearance of the most fragile states, whose territories will be absorbed by stronger neighbours.

From a normative point of view the project has thus been dealing with the oft-discussed 'new world order' with particular focus on the regional factor, as against the more common assumption of globalization; that is, the process of homogenization of the world, driven by market expansion. Current regionalism also becomes 'new' to the extent that the process of internationalization has acquired a qualitatively new, 'global', dimension.

No strict terminology was imposed on the contributors, but nevertheless a certain consensus gradually appeared. By 'regionalism' one can imply both the general phenomenon as well as the ideology of regionalism; that is, the urge for a regionalist order, either in a particular geographical area, or as a type of world order. Regionalization generally denotes the process, and, furthermore, normally implies an activist element, a strategy of regionalization. As was emphasized above, such a strategy may transform a peripheral geographical region from a passive object, that at the most could create problems for more organized core regions ('chaos power'), to a subject with capacity to articulate the interests of the emerging region, as well as resolving conflicts internal to the region. This process is described in terms of increasing levels of 'regionness'.

The degree of 'regionness' of particular areas can increase or decrease depending on regional dynamics, in which global as well as national/local forces of course have an impact. Regionalization takes place at many levels of the world system: the system as a whole, the level of interregional relations, and the internal structure of the single region (including nation states, subnational ethnic groups and microregions). It is not possible to state which of these levels comes first or which is the more important, since changes on the various levels interact, and the relative importance of them differs from one region and one period to another. When everything depends on everything else, it is a difficult methodological problem to find a viewpoint. In our research it was found that the most appropriate approach to the new regional dynamics was to explore the options of single states and the underlying power structures determining their external orientations.

THE BERLIN AGENDA: GLOBALISM VERSUS REGIONALISM

In the early process of conceptualization it was soon realized that the project had to grapple with the intricate relationship between regionalization and *globalization,* the much discussed 'stepping-stone or stumbling-block' controversy. Compared to 'regionalism', with an impressive theoretical tradition behind it, 'globalism' is a more recent concept in social science; and it is often, whether its implications are seen as catastrophic or as the ultimate unification of the world, used in a rather loose sense. Normally it indicates a qualitative deepening of the internationalization and/or transnationalization processes, thus strengthening the functional and weakening the territorial dimension of development (sometimes called the 'end of geography'). In cultural terms it refers to objective (compression of the world) as well as subjective (planetary consciousness) processes.

Without disregarding other important aspects, globalism is here taken to be primarily an economic phenomenon. We are concerned with a process (globalization) rather than a condition, which partly explains the difference between various perceptions. It implies the growth of a world market, increasingly penetrating and dominating subordinate 'national' economies, which in the process thus lose some of their 'nationness'.

There is a variety of perceptions and opinions on globalization, and a global awareness may thus also lead to negative expectations, for instance regarding the desirability of the dominance of the world market over the structure of local production, as well as the excessive prevalence of Western-type consumerism. Following from this, there may emerge a political will to halt or to reverse the process of globalization in order to safeguard a degree of territorial control and diversity of cultures.

One way of achieving such a change in the course of events could be through a new regionalism, which in that case must be sufficiently distinguishable from globalism. It cannot simply be a 'stepping-stone' in a linear process, but this does not necessarily mean that it consti- tutes a 'stumbling block' either. This new regionalism, although not necessarily inward-orientated, cannot therefore be a purely neoliberal project like, for instance, APEC and the 'open regionalism' of the Pacific, and now also Latin America. This is to say that activities which are organized regionally but essentially imply globalization do not come under the category of regionalism.

The two processes of economic globalization and political regiona- lization are going on simultaneously. They deeply affect the stability of the Westphalian state system; and therefore they at the same time contribute to both disorder and, possibly, a future order. The question raised at the Berlin workshop (and at a simultaneous panel of the 1994 IPSA World Congress) was: how do they actually relate? To what extent are they distinct processes? Are they mutually supporting and reinforcing each other, or are they incompatible and contradictory? The two processes are articulated within the same larger process of global structural transformation, the outcome of which depends on a dialectical rather than linear development. The latter cannot therefore be readily extrapolated or easily foreseen. But rather it expresses the relative strength of contending social forces involved in the two processes, taking different forms in different parts of the world. Regions are emerging phenomena, ambiguously forming part of and driving, but also reacting against and modifying the process of globalization. Regionalism can, then, intentionally or unintentionally, also be a road to globalism. If so, the question arises whether this would imply a globalism different from the 'direct route' from the state-centred Westphalian system to a post-Westphalian interdependence. The answer emerging from the Berlin workshop was that this would in fact be the case, since the least likely type of development is a linear one. The remaining question is 'different' in what sense? From a normative perspective, there are aspects of globalization which are positive and also aspects of regionalization that are negative. To come closer to their real meaning we need to specify the objects of analysis in both space and time.

THE JERUSALEM AGENDA: THE DYNAMICS OF REGIONALIZATION

Having realized the potential importance of regionalism in influencing the future world order, the next question was the 'whys' and 'hows' of its evolution. The second stage of the project thus dealt with the dynamics of contemporary regionalism, which had to be analysed in a comparative perspective. Regional integration is traditionally seen as a harmonization of trade policies leading to deeper economic integration and with political integration as a possible future result (perhaps as a 'spill-over' effect). As stated above, the concept 'new regionalism' refers to a more comprehensive process, implying a change of a particular region from relative heterogeneity to increased homogeneity with regard to a number of dimensions, the most important being culture, security, economic policies, and political regimes. The convergence along these dimensions may be a natural process or politically steered or, most likely, a mixture of the two. Culture takes a long time to change. Of importance here is rather the inherently shared culture which more often than not is transnational, national borders in many cases being artificial divisions of a larger cultural area. A transformation of the security regime (from security complex towards security community) is the most crucial factor. Changes in political regimes typically mean democratization. Democracy is a necessary but not sufficient condition, since it is a form which does not tell anything about political content. Changes in economic policies normally go in the direction of more openness, not only within the regional grouping, but, in the present context, also *vis-à-vis* the rest of the world. A more introverted collective self-reliance could, of course, also be the result of convergence among neighbours, but such a policy is, first of all, not on the agenda today, and, second, has been shown to be more difficult to co-ordinate among several states than economic liberalization encouraged by globalization.

As mentioned above, the search for the dynamics of regionalization can be carried out at different levels of world society.

- On the global level, the structure of the world system provides room-for-manoeuvre for the regional actors, at the same time as the process of regionalization in itself constitutes structural change towards multipolarity.
- On the level of interregional relations, the emergence and subsequent behaviour of one region affects the behaviour of others. European regionalism is, for instance, the trigger of global regionalization, at least in two different ways: one positive (promoting regionalism), the other negative (provoking regionalism).
- Regions constitute arenas for sometimes competing, sometimes converging national interests with respect to the dimensions mentioned above. If the overall trend within a particular geographical area is convergence of national interests, we can speak of an emerging regional actor. The importance of overarching systemic factors does not rule out the crucial role of domestic forces. Typically, regional politics is an aggregation and 'concertation' of national interests.
- The actual process of regionalization is triggered by events on the intrastate subnational level as well. One example is the 'black hole' syndrome or the disintegration of nation-states due to *ethnonational mobilization*. Another less violent form of disintegration is the strengthening of *microregions*, as the geopolitical environment creates a more direct approach to the macro economy for dynamic subnational regions.

The dynamics of regionalization were analysed through exploring changes of the different dimensions on various levels of the world society, and how these changes impinge on the process. Questions about national options can only be answered if we have a rather detailed knowledge of the internal debates in the respective states and communities, since the 'country positions' are nothing but the predominant point of view existing at any particular point in time. Although the region is slowly becoming an actor in its own terms, the nation-states typically conceive it as an arena where national interests could be promoted, and the latter are, of course, differently conceived by different social groups in society. Regionalization creates its own counterforces. Whereas certain groups may find it rewarding to move into the supranational space, others cling to the national space where they have their vested interests to protect. All this does not make the dynamics of regionalism easier to understand. But neither does it make regionalism simply an epiphenomenon of more basic systemic forces. Even if the European case could be seen as a paradigm, there was a strong consensus about the need to analyse the specific conditions for various kinds of regionalisms.

Regionalization does not come about unless the states in a particular region want it. It may come about through a more or less spontaneous or unintended convergence in terms of political regime, economic policy or security, but often one can identify a triggering political event, which sets the process in motion. Naturally, this political event is related to the main players in the region, the policy-makers, or regional great powers. The rise of regional powers is the other side of decline of hegemony. The defining criterion of a hegemonic structure is the non-existence of autonomous middle powers, and hegemonic decline thus implies multipolarity. Multipolarity, in turn, is what makes a regionalized world order possible.

In order to understand the regionalization in various areas it is thus wise to observe the behaviour of the policy-makers. We can divide them in two categories: those whose influence goes beyond a particular region, the *world powers*, and those whose influence is confined to a particular region, the *regional powers*. World powers may not be able to achieve hegemony on the world level, which, since the range of their influence is undefined and changing, means that there will be a certain competition among them.

The regional powers may be hegemonic, which implies a general acceptance or at least tolerance of their leadership throughout the region, or simply dominant, which means that they are looked upon with suspicion and fear among the minor players, the policy-takers. This latter category can be further subdivided into those who are *supportive* of the regionalization process (sometimes the smaller players are the main proponents), those who try to find their own path or maybe several paths, *the multitrackers,* and those who are left in the cold, *the isolated.*

This categorization assumes that there is a process of regionalization to which the countries can relate. It does not make much sense in a classical Westphalian system, where the actors are supposed to play purely from 'the national interest'. Of course what is conceived as 'national interest' does not disappear, but due to the imperative of global interdependence, it becomes inseparable from various shared transnational interests and concerns, which are manifesting themselves in the regionalization process. This is the meaning of a change from a Westphalian to a post-Westphalian logic.

In some cases regionalism grows from extended bilateral relations, for instance in the Americas where both NAFTA and Mercosur resulted from a situation where third parties (Canada and Uruguay), became anxious not to be left out from bilateralism, thus creating what might be called 'incipient regionalism'. The regional powers (in these cases USA and Brazil) usually prefer bilateralism to regionalism. This is very much the case in South Asia, where the small players softly imposed regionalism on the regional power, which then preferred (and still prefers) bilateral relations. The change from bilateralism to regionalism is thus one crucial indicator of increasing regionness of a region but, as here defined, increasing regionness can also result from overlapping bilateral agreements within a region, since such agreements imply policy convergencies in various fields. This more informal regionalization is nevertheless a regionalization in reality, and to realize this it is of importance to take the point of departure in the geographical area, and not from the formal regional agreements as such. On higher levels of regionness, however, more formal agreements and institution-building will be needed.

THE KATHMANDU AGENDA: PREFERRED OUTCOMES

Since the New Regionalism was conceived as a political and therefore also normative project it involves 'world order values', expressed in three preferred outcomes: peace, development, and ecological sustainability. The need to achieve these values by attacking the corresponding problems – war, starvation and environmental degradation – constitutes what we see as imperatives for regionalism. The third stage of the project thus focused on the consequences of regionalization in terms of these three values. The consequences of regionalism can of course be related to other, no less important, normative concerns, such as democracy and human rights, but these latter values are here treated rather as preconditions for regionalization. Furthermore, the outcome is discussed with reference to the region itself, not in terms of the expected 'global welfare', as is the case in most of the literature hostile to regionalism.

National disintegration, or the eruption of 'black holes', seems to reinforce the process of regionalization via threats to *regional security*. It may even form part of the process of regionalization, since the enlargement of economic and political space provides opportunities for different subnational and microregional forces to reassert themselves.

The collapse of political authority at one level opens up a previously latent power struggle at lower levels, and the process may in a complex multiethnic polity go on almost indefinitely. However, sooner or later there will be a reorganization of social power and political authority on a higher level of societal organization, most probably the region.

To the extent that there is a regional institutional framework which can be used for purposes of conflict resolution, there is a tendency for the region to intervene in situations of national disintegration.

The regional security complex has already become an important object of analysis, but it is important to consider the potential of regional conflict resolution as well. The regional level opens up previously untapped possibilities for solving conflicts built into the state formation. The larger region can absorb tensions that have become institutionalized. If violence breaks out, the regional actor can intervene in intrastate conflicts with lesser risk of provoking bilateral hostilities. A distinction can be made between five different modes of external intervention: unilateral, bilateral, plurilateral, regional and multilateral. The first can either be carried out by a concerned neighbour, or by a regional/superpower. In the bilateral case there is some kind of (more or less voluntary) agreement between the intervenor and the country in which the intervention is made. The plurilateral variety can be an *ad hoc* group of countries or some more permanent form of alliance. The regional intervention is carried out by a regional organization and thus has a territorial orientation. The multilateral, finally, usually means a UN-led or UN-sanctioned operation.

These distinctions are not very clear-cut, and in real-world situations several actors at different levels may be involved, the number increasing with the complexity of the conflict itself. Few conflicts are resolved in a more definite way, since there is rarely a solution without its new set of problems. Also for this reason – the need for continuous surveillance – the regional organization appears as the most relevant actor in the future.

The record of regional intervention in domestic conflicts and regional conflict resolution is a recent one and therefore the empirical base for making an assessment is weak. Incidents of national disintegration can make or break regional organizations depending on the nature of the already existing regional arrangements. In almost all world regions there have been attempts at conflict resolution with a more or less significant element of regional intervention, often in combination with multilateralism (UN involvement). Perhaps the future world order can be characterized as regional multilateralism or multilateral regionalism?

Developmental regionalism may provide solutions to many development problems for the South. There are seven possible advantages with different force in different contexts and situations:

- although the question of size is of lesser importance in a highly interdependent world, regional co-operation is nevertheless imperative, particularly in the case of micro states who either have to co-operate to solve common problems or become client states of the 'core countries' (the *sufficient size argument*);
- self-reliance, rarely viable on the national level, may yet be a feasible development strategy at the regional, if defined as co-ordination of production, improvement of infrastructure, and making use of complementarities (the *viable economy argument*);
- economic policies may be more stable and consistent if underpinned by regional arrangements which cannot be broken by a participant country without some kind of sanctions from the others (the *credibility argument*);
- collective bargaining on the level of the region could improve the economic position of marginalized countries in the world system, or protect the structural position and market access of successful export countries (the *effective articulation argument*);
- regionalism can reinforce societal viability by including social security issues and an element of redistribution (by regional funds or specialized banks) in the regionalist project (the *social stability argument*);

- regional management of environmental problems has become a motive force in regional integration in the North, while in the South the issue is how to exploit natural resources in a way that is sustainable (the *resource management argument*); and
- regional conflict resolution, if successful and durable, eliminates distorted investment patterns if the 'security fund' (military expenditures) were to be tapped for more productive use (the *peace dividend argument*).

The issue of resource management links the issue of development to the larger issue of *ecological sustainability*. It is well known that natural and political borders rarely coincide. It is, furthermore, increasingly realized that few serious environmental problems can be solved within the framework of the nation-state. Some problems are bilateral, some are global, quite a few are regional. Regional ecological issues are often related to water: coastal waters, rivers, and ground water. Three billion people (60 per cent of humanity) live within 100 km of a sea coast and put an enormous pressure on the marine and coastal resources as well as sensitive ecosystems (coral reefs and mangrove forests), both in terms of output (fish) and input (pollution). The fact that regional management programmes exist, in spite of nationalist rivalries, shows the imperative need for regional co-operation. Coastal areas are of course heavily influenced by larger river systems, which provide excellent focuses for the study of sustainable regional development. Cases investigated in this project are the Zambezi and the Mekong River systems, as well as the uneven exploitation of ground water resources in the areas around the River Jordan (see Chapters 7–9 in Vol. 4 in this series) Regional resource management is a way to tackle such ecological problems and prepare the ground for sustainable development.

The issues of security, development, and ecological sustainability form one integrated complex, at the same time as they constitute as many imperatives for deepening regional co-operation, if not regional integration. The levels of regionness of the regions in the process of being formed will continue to be uneven, but only the future will decide where the levels will be and where the balance between regionalization and globalization will be struck. However, political will and political action will certainly play their part.

POLICY RELEVANCE

In the new regionalism project there was also an attempt to enter into a dialogue with those who make and implement policy. At the Jerusalem meeting a policy-oriented conference devoted to the peace process in the region was thus organized. It was based on the idea that a meeting ground between the researchers, on the one hand, and, on the other, politicians practically involved in resolving the issues dealt with in the project could be fruitful both for policy-making and implementation and for further theoretical analysis. This experiment turned out to be a major event, as leading political figures in the negotiation process readily participated and took advantage of the opportunity to declare their solemn determination to continue the peace process in spite of recent disturbances. Thus, the idea of regionalism as a strategy of peace was confirmed, although it was made very clear that many more issues are involved. We learned that macro-processes are in reality the result of many competing and contradictory microprocesses.

Also at the Kathmandu meeting a more policy-orientated discussion was held in addition to the actual workshop, at the SAARC (South Asian Association for Regional Co-operation) headquarters, with the purpose of confronting the academic issues with the realities faced by practitioners who are dealing with regional co-operation in a rather difficult political context. Again it was made clear that the real world contains many more complicated issues than are usually accounted for in the somewhat abstract and reductionist academic discourses. On the other hand, the analytical approach provides comparative insights and serves the purpose of keeping the long-term strategy and the principal issues alive. A special session on regionalism and Nepali politics, including the democratization of the country, again confirmed the problem of regional co-operation in a highly uneven regional power structure.

Finally, the project in May 1996 was represented at a Belgrade conference, primarily dealing with 'Yugoslavia after the sanctions', but in reality initiating the painful but necessary debate on the need for all countries in the Balkans to get out of the Westphalian trap and co-operate in some kind of regionalist framework, or face further disintegration. 'Balkanization', in the constructive sense of increasing regionness, is a must in this most affected peripheral region.

Regionalism, then, is not a panacea, but nevertheless it remains an important phenomenon in the current global transformation. The new regionalism is a comprehensive process, not easy to grasp. The UNU/ WIDER project has come to its conclusion, but the theme is by no means exhausted, and the network it has established will certainly continue in one form or another into the new millennium, as reflected in this set of five interrelated collections of revised and edited project papers.

BJÖRN HETTNE
Project Director

Editors' Introduction

This book is a first in a series of five volumes reporting from a research project on the new regionalism sponsored by UNU/WIDER. In the prologue to this volume, which also appears in the four others, the overall framework, the main findings of the project, as well as questions for further research are summarized.

In trying to come to grips with the essence of regionalization, the three editors, at our first co-ordinators' meeting in Santiago, Chile (March 1994) soon realized that the processes of regionalization can only be understood within the context of globalization. To deal only with regionalization would be to miss the other side of the coin, which is globalization.

This particular volume thus deals with conceptions and meanings of the two processes which are bound to have a crucial influence on the shape of the 'new world order'. In this introduction, the editors spell out the issues referred to as 'the Berlin Agenda' in the prologue; that is, the question of how the phenomena of regionalism and globalism are interrelated. To the extent that theorizing about globalization takes into account the heterogeneity and contradictions of 'the global condition', the phenomenon of regionalism can be seen as an integral part of globalization, as one of its many manifestations. In this volume, however, we try to distinguish the two processes, although there are diverging views on their relationship and the degrees of compatibility or incompatibility between them. Basically, they relate to each other as challenge to response, globalization being the challenge of economic and cultural homogenization of the world, and regionalization being a social and political reaction; the 'return of the political'.

In Chapter 1, Björn Hettne develops a conceptual framework for analysing the process of regionalization in the context of globalization, which he claims is applicable to all regions (in various degrees of 'regionness') in spite of all historical, economic and cultural differences. The relationship between the two is dialectical, regionalization being the political corrective to globalized market-driven disorder and turbulence, not only on the level of the world but also in local systems. The chapter also discusses the dynamics contained in the regionalization process itself, both in terms of interrelated dimensions and in

terms of levels of the world system, which also interact in a complicated manner. Finally the consequences of regionalization are discussed in terms of world order values. The chapter originally served
as the project outline and therefore to some extent overlaps with the
prologue of this and the other four volumes.

James H. Mittelman, in Chapter 2, takes the view that the conflict
between regionalism and globalization is more theoretical than real.
The dynamics of regionalism is a chapter of globalization. Warning
against a Eurocentric bias in the New Regionalism Approach
(NRA), he also emphasizes the diverse regionalization paths, using
South East Asia and Southern Africa as the main empirical cases. In
discussing the various forms of regionalism, Mittelman develops the
strategy of transformative regionalism as a contrast to mainstream
neoliberal regionalism which primarily serves as a stepping-stone to
globalism. The strength of transformative regionalism ultimately rests
on its link to civil society, turning transnational and in the first
instance regional. The tendencies in this direction are certainly
embryonic, but they are no pipe dreams.

Samir Amin (Chapter 3) regards regionalism as a response, nay 'the
only efficient response', to the challenges of a continuously deepening
polarization, generated by the capitalist globalization process. Globalization is expressed (and thereby defined) through the five monopolies over (1) technology, (2) finance, (3) natural resources, (4) media,
and (5) weapons of mass destruction. These monopolies prevent
peripheries from achieving their development goals, which basically
means industrialization. Hence continued globalization means polarization. The appropriate level from which the five monopolies could
be effectively combated is the regional level.

Helge Hveem is concerned in Chapter 4 with the political economy
of regionalism and defines globalization as a basically economic process, whereas regionalization is seen as a political reaction, an attempt
to direct economic internationalization according to some political
goal. The actual causation is not well understood as we are in a very
early stage of theorizing. Hveem discusses three theoretical
approaches, namely realist/neorealist, institutionalist and cognitivist
(or constructivist). These three traditions have their distinctive perspectives on regionalization as well as on globalization. He places the
NRA in the third category.

In Chapter 5, Percy S. Mistry goes right into the 'stepping-stone or
stumbling block' debate, which he thinks has matured and become
more holistic after the conclusion of the Uruguay Round. In

particular, Mistry is keen to show that a new regionalism may support the emergence of a much needed new multilateralism. The old and by now eroded multilateralism, whose architecture was designed in 1945, is in crisis; it cannot deliver the goods, and may not survive for long. By strengthening plurilateral processes in a framework which gives the weaker nation-states some say in decision-making, the new regionalism may provide the necessary foundations for a better functioning multilateral system.

Bertil Odén, in Chapter 6, makes an inventory of different ways of conceptualizing and understanding 'the new regionalism' and discusses their relevance from the perspective of Southern Africa debates on regional co-operation. It is of course of importance to link the academic discourse to the debate on economic policies going on in various regions of the world. First, Odén outlines the very contrasting perspectives on the new regionalism which have appeared in the recent debate, from various conceptions of 'second-best' open regionalisms to the radical delinking perspective of Samir Amin, most participants in this project taking a middle of the road position. As far as the Southern African debate is concerned, the open regionalism concept constitutes the mainstream, although other perspectives are also represented. The question is which perspective will dominate. This situation reminds us about the importance of the regional power in a particular region, in this case South Africa. As Odén puts it: will South Africa play the role of the benevolent hegemon?

In Chapter 7, Ralph Pettman looks into 'regionalism' and 'globalism' with postmodernist glasses and finds limits and costs of conventional discussions, particularly in the choice of empirical referents. Globalism in particular is something that does not include but rather is supposed to transform non-Western cultures. Globalism and regionalism also entail an attempt to render women invisible as a global gender. From an Asian perspective ('Asia' being a reification of its own), Western modernity today looks as if it was in bad shape and in need of repair. The dichotomization of West and East also makes less and less sense in Pacific Europe. The postmodernist would be as concerned about what is not being said and what is excluded in reifications such as 'globalism' and 'regionalism'.

Kaisa Lähteenmäki and Jyrki Käkönen (Chapter 8) explore the impact of the new regionalism on the theory of international relations, in particular the mainstream realist tradition. It is obvious that it is this tradition which is hard to make compatible with the erosion of state sovereignty normally associated with the new regionalism. But the crucial point is whether future regions will serve similar purposes as the nation-states during the Westphalian era. The state can be replaced with another political subject without changing the essence of the approach. The challenge to realism is thus rather to develop it into a more generally applicable theory.

Richard Falk relates globalization and regionalization in an open way, exploring their relationship from a normative perspective. Thus, what he is concerned with in Chapter 9 is how 'positive' regionalism can support 'positive' globalism and vice versa. Regionalism is a welcome trend in so far as it contains negative globalism (the adverse impacts of global market forces) and mitigates pathological anarchism (the breakdown of order and decency in fragile nation-states).

The result of this study is, unsurprisingly, inconclusive. The question how the two processes really relate remains for others to explore. Are they distinct; are they mutually supporting and reinforcing each other; or are they contradictory? Or as James Mittelman puts it 'is regionalism a stepping stone or a stumbling block on the path toward globalization?' Let us also quote Richard Falk on this: 'How regionalism of varying attributes fits within globalization is a central world order concern for which evidence and interpretation is necessarily inconclusive'. We still have a major problem before us.

The problem (and challenge) is that the 'regions' which we try to theorize cannot be defined beforehand. They are emerging phenomena, defining themselves, but ambiguously forming part of the process of globalization, supporting it according to some, opposing it according to others. This ambivalent relationship is thus the particular concern of this book and we need some theoretical framework to handle it.

Since it probably is correct to say that regionalization relates to globalization as antithesis to thesis, we should first agree upon the meaning of globalization. Nobody denies its existence but one could read many things into it. How complex can we make it without losing the intellectual means to deal with it? Is it (or rather, should we conceive it) as primarily an economic process as Helge Hveem suggests? Hveem speaks about economic globalization and regionalization as the political response. This would be consistent with the view that regionalization constitutes Karl Polanyi's 'second movement' in contemporary form, even if the two movements imply a more comprehensive view of social change than 'economic' challenge and 'political' response. We face the usual dilemma of the trade off between analytical stringency and our ambition to grasp reality in all its complexity.

The issue is also fundamentally normative. As formulated by Amin, regionalization can either be seen as a subsystem submitted to the rationale of globalization, or as a substitutive to it, or as a building block for constructing a different global system. He takes the latter position. There may also be a softer position according to which the regional factor modifies the process of globalization away from the 'neoliberal triumphalism' towards a qualitatively different form of globalization, in which regional formations have an impact on the globalization pattern in the direction of universalism, meaning a more universal acceptability of the post-hegemonic world order. As pointed out by Pettman 'globalizing practices' may also move 'world affairs in more solidarist directions'.

What all this boils down to is what kind of globalism we will have. A 'different global system', referred to by Amin, is another word for the 'world order model project', with which Falk has been associated for a long time. This project has promoted a number of 'world order values', which turn up in the UNU/WIDER project's emphasis on development, peace and ecological sustainability (see, in particular, Vol. 4 in this subseries).

The MUNS (Multilateralism and the UN System) programme of the UNU, co-ordinated by Robert Cox, used the concept New Multilateralism as a normative concept, meaning 'a commitment to maximum participation in dialogue among political, social, economic, and cultural forces as a means of resolving conflicts and designing institutional processes'. The regionalization process contradicts basic multilateral principles as they are conventionally defined, but may be a step towards a 'new multilateralism'. This vision would seem to coincide largely with what Falk calls 'positive globalism'. In his assessment of contemporary regionalization tendencies not too many examples supporting 'positive globalism' can be found. Regionalism can thus be seen as an 'act of faith'.

Our use of the words new regionalism has thus both *positive* (here in the sense of factual: there are empirically documented new features in most of the current regionalization trends) and *normative* (these trends contain latent possibilities for a 'preferred' world order).

Those who see regionalism as some kind of remedy for problems created by globalization usually like to see popular forces from below in support of regionalization. There is, Odén exemplifies with the Southern Africa debate, certainly no strong manifestation of such forces. The current crisis within the EU is caused not only by diverging national interests (most important between 'federalists' and 'nationalists') but also to a cleavage between state and civil society (manifested in the debate on 'democratic deficit' and the constitutional tensions between the Council of Ministers and the European Parliament). The role of democratic forces is in most cases of regionalization rather feeble, which, as a matter of fact, is described as an advantage, an edge over the West, by leading politicians in East and South East Asia. However, as Mittelman points out: 'transformative regionalism rests on the strength of its links to civil society'.

One way to think of regionalism is to see it as a way of overcoming the contradiction between Westphalian and a post-Westphalian rationality. By the former is implied an interstate system with the following characteristics suggested by Robert Cox: the sovereign independence of states; each state motivated in its international behaviour by a consistent national interest; the interstate system regulated by a balance of power among the principal powers. Necessarily there is a rationality, underlying this behaviour, and socialized by citizens of a state – a Westphalian rationality – taking a particular state as the given guarantee for security as well as welfare. What is outside is conceived as chaos and anarchy. The disorder and turbulence people experience today comes with the realization that this guarantee can no longer be taken for granted, and the confusion is only increased when the two rationalities are mixed, a mixture typical for all periods of transition.

The post-Westphalian logic implies that the nation-state has lost its usefulness and that solutions must be found in transnational structures, global or regional. The confusion is sometimes increased even further by the presence of 'pre-Westphalian' attitudes and behaviour in areas where the nation-state always was weak and superficial from the beginning, and where it now irreversibly breaks down. But the main cause of conflict and turbulence is probably the antagonistic co-existence of Westphalian and post-Westphalian rationality, to which we consider the New Regionalism as a possible solution. It can be seen as the compromise between Westphalian and post-Westphalian rationality. This and the remaining four volumes will further elaborate on this.

1 Globalization and the New Regionalism: The Second Great Transformation
Björn Hettne

INTRODUCTION

In the debate on the still nebulous 'new world order', two
seemingly incompatible concepts have gained a certain pre-eminence:
globalization and _regionalization_. These two processes are going on
simultaneously, they deeply affect the stability of the Westphalian
state system, thus contributing to both disorder and (possibly)
a new global order. The question is how they actually relate. Are
they distinct and homogeneous; are they mutually supporting
and reinforcing each other; or are they incompatible and contradictory?

The answer to this question depends, of course, on how the two
processes of concern are defined, what empirical phenomena are
singled out for scrutiny, and what kind of theoretical framework we
use to interpret them. Thus, from the start, one has to clarify one's
ideas about each of them.

The relationship as such is perhaps not the most interesting issue,
since its nature logically follows from the inherent characteristics by
which we define globalization and regionalization. These characteristics cannot, however, depend merely on our theoretical inclinations,
but must also be derived from empirical observations of new economic and political processes actually going on in many parts of the
world and the emerging patterns which can be discerned. Many of
these geographical areas are increasingly acting as 'regions', a _region_
being defined here as a group of countries with a more or less
explicitly shared political project. Regions are emerging phenomena,
ambiguously forming part of the process of globalization, supporting it
according to some, contradicting it according to others. This ambivalent relationship is thus the particular concern of this chapter, as with

the whole volume, the first of five in a subseries dealing with the new regionalism.

This chapter tries to spell out the dynamics of the two processes and their relationship. The analysis departs from the hypothesis that

- *the two processes of globalization and regionalization are articulated within the same larger process of global structural change.*

The outcome in the form of a new world order depends on this dialectical rather than linear development and can therefore not be extrapolated or easily foreseen. It expresses the relative strength of contending social forces involved in the two processes. I shall first explore their possible meanings. The chapter then proceeds with the dynamics of regionalization, and finally discusses its consequences from a normative perspective.

THE CHALLENGE OF GLOBALISM

Since it probably is correct to say, or reasonable to assume, that regionalization in the current era relates to globalization as response to challenge, we should first agree upon the meaning of globalism and globalization. Compared to 'regional', with an impressive theoretical tradition behind it, 'global' is a more recent concept in social science, often used in a rather loose and ideological sense for which 'globalism' is the appropriate expression. Globalism (apart from indicating the general phenomenon, whatever that is) can thus be defined as programmatic globalization, the vision of a borderless world, in which territory has lost all importance and functionalism is predominant. More precisely, it indicates a qualitative change in the internationalization process, thus further strengthening the functional and weakening the territorial dimension. Whether this qualitative deepening in the process of internationalization is significant enough to deserve a new name, globalization, can always be debated (Hirst and Thompson, 1996).

In Chapter 1, as well as in the others in this volume, I see globalization as a qualitatively new phenomenon although there are different opinions as to its nature. Ralph Pettman (Chapter 7), however, is generally sceptical towards 'grand' concepts. Nobody denies the existence of globalization but one could read many things, good as well as bad, into it. 'Global' has been gradually replacing 'international', both for the reason of being more appropriate than the latter rather misleading concept and for indicating a deepening of the internationalization process. As suggested by James Mittelman (personal communication), globalization may be regarded as an integrative process, whereas internationalization is simply the spread of transnational activities. 'Global' refers to objective (compression of the world) as well as subjective (planetary consciousness) processes (Robertson, 1992). In spite of very concrete manifestations of globalization, the contemporary concern with phenomena such as 'interdependence', 'world order' or the 'global system' is to a large extent a cognitive phenomenon; that is, it is a matter of how the world is conceived.

If globalization implies an observed tendency towards a global social system, its origins may be traced far back in history. However, one could argue that the process reached a qualitatively new stage in the post-Second World War era, when many forms of human interconnectedness across state boundaries were doubling every 10 years, a tendency later reinforced through the revolution in information technology. This made the global system 'compressed'. The subjective sense of geographical distance is dramatically changed, some even speak of 'the end of geography'. Also in ecological terms the world is commonly experienced as one. In this context we are primarily interested in the economic dimension. Economic globalization would not have been possible, were it not for the relative political stability of the American world order, which lasted from the end of the Second World War and until the late 1960s. Since then, however, the world has, if not lacked a world order, at least tried to get along with a defective one. Globalization is increasingly contradictory and turbulent (Rosenau, 1990). The old is dying but the new is not yet born. A world order hardly completely disappears, only to be replaced by a newborn. Rather, what happens are significant (sometimes dramatic) adjustments, modifying the way it operates, until a qualitative change is ultimately established.

Thus, in spite of its obvious importance for understanding the emerging world order, we lack a theoretical framework explaining what globalization is all about. The reason for this state of affairs is that a complex and multidimensional phenomenon is approached from the point of view of many different disciplines which illuminate different dimensions and sometimes contradict each other (Fawcett and Hurrell, 1995). Thus a consistent framework is needed.

One obvious candidate for such a framework, with the advantage of not making the concept overly abstract, is the tradition of materialist theories concerned with the changing international division of labour. James Mittelman (1994) identifies three consecutive modes:

- the old division of labour, as analysed by classical political economy;
- the new international division of labour, concerned with the spatial reorganization of production starting in the 1960s; and finally,
- the global division of labour, where domestic economies are penetrated by global phenomena to such an extent as to signify a qualitative deepening of the process of internationalization, which Mittelman describes as primarily a phenomenon of diffusion.

The internationalization of production implies a strategy of international firms where resources of the earth are considered as a whole waiting to be exploited. Thus globalization can also be understood in terms of microeconomics (Oman, 1994). The globalist strategy of the firm, which became more widespread and evident during the 1970s, implied that different parts of the production process were located at points of greatest cost advantage. The transnational corporations (TNCs) thus combined the new technology, the emerging market in industrial sites and the worldwide industrial reserve army to their advantage, creating what came to be known as the 'new international division of labour' (Fröbel, Heinrichs and Kreye, 1980). The pattern of international investment thus changed, in a first phase, from the traditional industrial centres in Europe to the European periphery (in the USA the corresponding shift was from the East to the South – and then 'south of the border'), and, in a second phase, to any country in the Third World with a good supply of labour, political stability and other incentives, usually described as 'an appropriate investment climate'. This reallocation of industrial investment was made possible by a number of technological developments:

- improvements in communication and information, facilitating quick decision-making on how to take advantage of the changing global structure of comparative advantages;
- improvements in transport technology, reducing the importance of geographical distances in the overall economic calculus;
- improvements in production technology and labour organization, making it possible to decompose complex production processes.

Thus, skilled labour in the traditional centres was replaced by unskilled labour in former peripheries, for example in the export processing zones which increased dramatically during the 1970s and later were established even in mainland China. This is not to say that all Third World industrialization was of this dependent nature, but that the cases of indigenous, autocentric industrialization are still rare.

If one economic dimension of globalization has to do with the organization of production (the real economy), another equally important and increasingly autonomous one is the financial system. The recycling of petrodollars through commercial banks fuelled the economic transformation by providing the financial basis for Third World industrialization. At the same time, this flow of money paved the way for the debt crisis in countries where the industrialization strategy failed to catch on, or where investment was simply unproductive due to lack of competence (market realism) in economic planning. In the so-called 'most affected countries' the easy credit was used up in paying the oil bill, resulting in an intensified differentiation of the Third World, in development theory often referred to as 'the end of the Third World'. The centre–periphery model became irrelevant as the periphery entered the core, thus making the 'new' division of labour increasingly dated.

A handful of states emerged strong enough to out-compete the old economic cores as far as the classical industries and technologies are concerned. However, the overwhelming majority of Third World countries remained vulnerable, particularly in view of the rise of global corporate power. As economic units the TNCs, a striking new phenomenon in the post-war world economy, dwarfed most developing and even many developed countries. This implies a dramatically changing pattern of international economic relations, not adequately accounted for in conventional theories of trade.

Trade is of course the classical form of internationalization. The stable growth in world trade during the post-war decades was unique and will not be repeated. It can be explained by unprecedented economic growth in the OECD area, and a significant reduction in trade barriers, two conditions which underwent changes as the 1970s wore on (Kaplinsky, 1984, p. 77). The 1980s were marked by the 'new protectionism', which avoided open violation of GATT rules, but nevertheless found other ways to create 'non-tariff barriers', something which in the globalist camp was referred to as 'new protectionism' or 'new regionalism'. The very drawn-out Uruguay Round showed that the forces against free trade carry considerable weight, something which is conveniently neglected or explained in terms of irrationalism or 'rent-seeking' in economic theory.

Societies are, however, not only economic systems but also communities containing people who for good reasons refuse to disappear when they become superfluous, either as producers or 'consumers' (normally defined as those who can afford to buy the goods they need). The possible reactions to being unneeded and unwanted are according to a classical study: loyalty, protest and exit (Hirschman, 1970). There is, however, in the modern state little left to which to be loyal. Successful protests presuppose an accountable counterpart, something that is very hard to find in a globalized capitalism. This leaves exit as the only rational option. What this concretely means is migration: within the country, into neighbouring countries within the region, or internationally. This will further change the global division of labour in significant ways (Mittelman, Chapter 2 in this volume), but is also increasingly seen as having severe security implications (Hamilton, 1994) and, as now is particularly evident in Europe, will have a deep impact on the nature of the regional integration itself ('Fortress Europe' or a 'European House', that is the question).

It must be emphasized that the changes pointing towards a global division of labour are intertwined and reinforce each other in a most complicated fashion, at the same time as the globalization process itself contains its own contradictions. It also follows that many of these changes are subject to different interpretations depending on theoretical assumptions and ideological preferences.

THE NEW REGIONALISM: A RESPONSE

The global awareness resulting from globalization processes may certainly include negative expectations and a wish to halt or reverse the process of globalization, thus initiating a counter-process of 'deglobalization' (Robertson, 1992). One way of achieving this can be through a regionalist 'second movement' (Polanyi, 1957); that is, an attempt to bring the globalization processes and the transnational transactions under some political-territorial control. The new regionalism can also, intentionally or unintentionally, be a road to globalism of some sort. If so, the question arises whether this would imply a different globalism than the 'direct route' from the state-centred Westphalian system. The argument of this chapter is that this is indeed the case. There are in reality no linear developments. To the process of globalization there are counter-processes, leading to mixed outcomes in terms of levels of governance. Regionalism is one.

If we look back a decade or so, regional integration was not a very fashionable subject, having declined from a rather prominent position in the 1950s and 1960s (Haas, 1970; Østergaard, 1993). Why is it that regionalism is again attracting the curiosity and interest of the social science community? Either the content or the context of regionalization must have changed. My argument is that both have changed, and that argument is further pursued below.

Regionalization is, for obvious reasons, a more varied phenomenon than globalization, which implies a homogenization of the global space. As a response regionalization takes different forms both over time and between different cultural areas of the world. However it homogenizes regional space and reduces the sovereignty and changes the role of nation-states. The crucial issue in relating the two processes, I submit, is the development logic, which in the current regionalization process is captured and subsumed under a territorial as distinct from a functional interest. Regionalism implies a return of 'the political' in one form or the other.

The *new regionalism differs from the 'old' regionalism* in the following respects:

(1)   Whereas the old regionalism was formed in and shaped by a bipolar cold-war context, the new is taking shape in a multipolar world order. Regionalism and multipolarism are in fact two sides of the same coin. In spite of their military superiority and of course in varying degrees, the former superpowers are being downgraded to regional powers, competing with other emerging regional powers. The superpower organization of the world can be seen as a premature globalization and therefore the decline of superpowers implies a certain 'deglobalization'.

(2)   Whereas the old regionalism was created 'from above' (by the superpowers), the new is a more spontaneous process from within the region and also 'from below' in the sense that the constituent states themselves, but increasingly also other actors, are the main proponents for regional integration.

(3)   Whereas the old regionalism, as far as economic integration is concerned, was inward-oriented and protectionist, the new is often described as 'open', and thus compatible with an interdependent world economy. However, the idea of a certain degree of preferential treatment with the region is indicated or implied. How this somewhat contradictory balance between universal WTO regulations and specific regional concerns shall be kept is

left open. In the definition of new regionalism proposed here, I rather stress the ambiguity between 'opened' and 'closed' regionalism.

(4) Whereas the old regionalism was specific with regard to object-ives, some organizations being security-oriented and others being economically-oriented, the new is a more comprehensive, multidimensional process. This includes trade and economic integration, but also environment, social policy, security and democracy, including the whole issue of accountability and legit-imacy.

(5) Whereas the old regionalism only concerned relations between formally sovereign states, the new forms part of a global struc-tural transformation in which non-state actors are active and manifest themselves at several levels of the global system. It can therefore not be understood only from the point of view of the single region. It should rather be defined as a world order con-cept, since any particular regionalization process has systemic repercussions within and between single regions throughout the world, thus shaping the way in which the world is organized, most likely towards a power structure made up of core regions and peripheral regions. Even the core regions contain their own centre–periphery or North–South cleavages.

The new regionalism has been differently defined by different authors, but the concept usually refers to a 'second wave' of regional co-operation and integration that had started already by the mid-1980s but took off only after 1989 when the cold war came to an end. The decline of the earlier interest in regionalism was due both to the previous slow-down in West European integration, leading to the Euro-pessimism of the 1970s, and the almost universal failure of Third World free trade areas. Rather than leading to development, these free trade areas reproduced the global centre–periphery structure, polarizing the partners within the regions. This led to interstate conflicts and, of course, disillusions as far as regional co-operation as development strategy was concerned. Today there are again optimistic expectations about the usefulness of regionalism in different respects. However, since old and new forms of regionalism co-exist in time, I find the identification of new patterns of re-gionalization (co-existing with older forms) more relevant than identifying a new era of regionalization (Palmer, 1991). Relatively few new organizations are formed. In some cases the existing regions just continue as before, in others they widen the scope of action from security to development and vice versa.

We are dealing with an emerging phenomenon and it is therefore not useful to work with very precise definitions. Regions cannot be defined a priori, because they define themselves by evolving from an objective, but dormant, to a subjective, active existence. By 'region' in this context, I refer to 'macroregions', or sometimes to 'world regions', which can be used in a rather general and descriptive way. The former concept forms part of a theoretical framework in which the emergence of smaller (subnational or transnational) regions is causally linked to a macroprocess of regionalization. A 'world region' can be described in terms of different levels of complexity, the most comprehensive being to see it as a political subject with its own identity. This can be seen as an ideal model, which different geographical areas approach to various degrees. As will be further elaborated below, we could speak of degrees of regionness in analogy with concepts such as 'stateness' and 'nationness'. Regionalization is the process of increasing 'regionness', and this concept can refer to a single region as well as to the world system.

The process of regionalization from within can be compared with the historical formation of nation-states, with the important difference that a coercive centre, or at least the open use of force, is lacking in processes of regionalization. This presupposes a shared, non-coercive project among the potential members of the region in the process of formation. But this is not a sufficiently clear criterion. The difference between regionalism and the infinite process of economic integration is that there is a politically defined limit to the former process. This is a historical outcome of attempts to find a transnational level of governance which reinforces certain shared values and minimizes certain shared perceptions of danger. Like the formation of ethnic and national identities, the regional identity is dependent on historical context and often shaped by conflicts. And like nations and ethnies, regional formations, as here defined, also possess a subjective quality, and can consequently be seen as 'imagined communities' (Anderson, 1983).

The assumption is thus that despite structural and contextual differences, there is an underlying logic behind contemporary processes of regionalization. This logic does not refer to a single dimension. Some key dimensions are cultural identity, degree of economic and political homogeneity, and security order, in particular the relative

capability of conflict resolution; that is, handling and resolving regional conflicts without extraterritorial intervention.

The new regionalism also presupposes the growth of a regional civil
society, opting for regional solutions to some local, national and
global problems. The implication of this is that not only economic,
but also social and cultural networks are developing more quickly
than the formal political co-operation at the regional level. One rather
clear example of a regional civil society is the Nordic subregion, where
security policies during the cold war differed to a high degree among
themselves, while the respective national societies over a long period
converged towards a Nordic community. Europe is of course more
diverse, but there is, nevertheless, a unity in the diversity. The same
can to a larger or lesser extent be said about other world regions.
There are five degrees of 'regionness'.

(1) *Region as a geographical unit, delimited by more or less natural
    physical barriers and marked by ecological characteristics:* 'Europe
    from the Atlantic to the Ural', 'Africa south of Sahara', or 'the
    Indian subcontinent'. In order to regionalize further, this particu-
    lar territory must, necessarily, be inhabited by human beings; this
    brings us to the social dimension, which is essential for the way
    the concept of region is used here. Therefore, the first degree can
    be referred to as a *'proto-region'*, or a 'pre-regional zone'.

(2) *Region as social system, which implies translocal relations of varying
    nature between human groups.* These relations constitute a secur-
    ity complex, in which the constituent units are dependent on each
    other as well as the overall political stability of the regional
    system, as far as their own security is concerned (Buzan, 1991).
    The region, just like the international system of which it forms
    part, is anarchic. The classic case is nineteenth-century Europe.
    At this low level of organization, power balance or some kind of
    'concert' is the sole security guarantee. This is a rather primitive
    security mechanism. We could in this case therefore talk of
    a *'primitive'* region.

(3) *Region as organized co-operation in any of the cultural, economic,
    political or military fields.* In this case, region is defined by the
    membership of the regional organization in question. In the
    absence of organized co-operation, the concept of regionalism
    does not make much sense. This could be called the *'formal'* region.
    It should be possible to relate the 'formal region' (defined by
    organizational membership) to the 'real region' (which has to be

defined through less precise criteria) in order to assess the relevance and future potential of a particular regional organization.

(4) *Region as civil society, which takes shape when the organizational framework promotes social communication and convergence of values throughout the region.* Of course the pre-existence of a shared cultural tradition throughout the region is of crucial importance here, but culture is not only a given, but continuously created and recreated. However, the defining element here is the multidimensional quality of regional co-operation and the emerging societal characteristics indicating a *'regional anarchical society'.*

(5) *Region as acting subject with a distinct identity, actor capability, legitimacy, and structure of decision-making.* Crucial areas for regional intervention are conflict resolution (between and within former 'states') and welfare (in terms of social security and regional balance). The ultimate outcome of this could be a *'region-state'*, which in terms of scope can be compared to the classical empires, but in terms of political order constitutes a voluntary evolution of sovereign national, political units into a supranational security community. The higher degrees of regionness, and the explicit political ambitions to achieve that aim, define what I mean by the 'new regionalism'. The levels may express a certain evolutionary logic, but the idea is not to suggest a stage theory but a framework for comparative analysis. Since regionalism is a political project it may, just like a nation-state project fail. This, similarly, means peripheralization for the region concerned.

THE DYNAMICS OF REGIONALIZATION

The dynamics of regionalization must be understood in the context of globalization and can be analysed as processes going on:

- between various dimensions inherent in the process, and
- between levels of the world-system.

Dimensions

The process of regionalization implies a change from relative heterogeneity to increased homogeneity with regard to different dimensions, the most important being culture, security, economic policies, and political regime.

Culture
Cultural homogeneity is formed very slowly and the question here is rather the degree of original cultural affinity among the states involved in regional co-operation. In traditional integration theory with its economistic bias this factor has been completely neglected. If we think of regionalization more in terms of a political project it becomes crucial. Normally, regionalization necessitates a certain degree of cultural homogeneity to start with, what we can call an 'inherent regional civil society'. It is a necessary but not sufficient condition, since cultural similarity does not prevent states and social groups from fighting each other. The Nordic countries, for instance, are and have always been culturally very similar, which during the Westphalian phase did not prevent them from making war among themselves. In more recent times this cultural similarity made it easier for them to adopt very different solutions to their respective security problems and yet constitute what has been called a security community. In contrast, the relative cultural similarity among South Asian states has not prevented inter-state hostilities which are due to differences in the other dimensions (security policies, economic policies, and so on).

Security
This is another crucial dimension. It has even been used for defining regional systems (Buzan, 1991). Security divisions therefore imply economic divisions, as shown in the pattern of regional economic co-operation in Europe during the cold war. Consequently, a fundamental change of the security order paves the way for a new pattern of regional economic co-operation as well, as was also the case in Europe (Hettne, 1991). It should therefore be expected that the dismantling of the cold-war system dramatically changes the preconditions for regional co-operation globally. A greater South East Asia (ASEAN plus the Indochina region) and a reunification of the two Koreas are cases in point. The Indo-Pakistan conflict, although largely indigenous to the region, also had its cold-war dimension, which further complicated the issue. Similarly, a post-apartheid Southern Africa will be a quite different political entity compared with the situation that prevailed under apartheid.

Economic Policies

A common security order is a necessary, albeit not sufficient, precondition for regional integration. Of equal importance is the compatibility of economic policies. An autarkic ambition of a certain state, particularly if it happens to be the regional power (as has been the case with India in South Asia) will (assuming that the rest of the states are outward-oriented) effectively prevent a process of regionalization from taking place. Regional integration based on a shared commitment to the market principle is the normal case, but history has shown that free trade areas, in which unequal countries participate, regularly generate tensions which ultimately erode the regional arrangement. On the global level, the IMF and the World Bank exercise a near-monopoly over credit, as far as weaker clients are concerned. The conditions of access to this credit system, the economic conditionalities, are such as to homogenize the rules of the economic game throughout the world. In the case of regionalization, these rules are modified to suit the interests of particular regions, but without violating the global free trade regime ('open regionalism')

The homogenization of economic policies may pave the way for further regionalization in a spontaneous way, as when similar regimes are voted to power simultaneously, but it may also be a conscious political decision, as when the economic and political union was decided in Maastricht. This decision was obviously premature in view of the real differences among the members. Nevertheless, the decision will lead to a further harmonization of economic policies (through achieving the convergence criteria) in order to avoid or not to prolong two or more camps of 'different speed' within the European Union.

Political Regime

As far as political regimes are concerned, there are strong global forces favouring democratization of national political regimes. In principle, homogenization can of course be achieved through some other political principle, but we shall leave out that option as less likely. In 1991 the number of democratic states for the first time in world history exceeded the number of non-democratic states (Holm and Sørensen, 1992). To some extent this is the result of new political conditionalities in development aid. To the extent that important powers are transferred to supranational authority, a completely new problem of transnational democracy emerges (Archibugu and Held, 1995).

Levels

Let us now turn to the inter-level dynamics of regionalization. Region-alization is a complex process of change taking place simultaneously at many levels: the structure of the world system as a whole, the level of interregional relations, as well as the internal pattern of the single region: the region, the nations, the subnational and transnational microregions.

The Structure of the World System
The structure of the world system must permit a room-for-manoeuvre for the regional actors, at the same time as the increase in regionalism in itself constitutes global structural change towards multipolarity. Regionalization was made possible through hegemonic decline. The new regionalism was thus not consistent with the bipolar Cold War system, since the 'quasi-regions' in this system tended to reproduce the global division within their own respective regions. This pattern of hegemonic regionalism was evident in Europe, but it appeared in all world regions during the cold war. The neoliberal regionalism prac-tised by the USA (NAFTA, APEC, Atlanticism) serves the purpose of restoring hegemony (Mittelman and Falk, in Vol. 2 of this subseries). This is hegemonic regionalism in a different form from the earlier compromise of 'embedded liberalism'.

Interregional Relations
On the level of interregional relations, the behaviour of one region has an impact on the behaviour of others. European regionalism is the trigger of global regionalization, at least in two different ways: one positive (in promoting regionalism by providing a model), the other negative (in provoking regionalism by constituting a protectionist threat). NAFTA was partly a response to 'Fortress Europe'; and the idea of East Asian regionalism emerged as a defence against further fragmentation of the world economy, but would, of course, also con-tribute to its further fragmentation.

The Region
On the level of the region, or rather 'the region in the process of taking shape', the basic dimension is homogenization, the elimination of extremes, in terms of culture, security, economic policies and political system, as was discussed above. With the current level of 'regionness', it is hard to argue that a distinct regional interest is

being articulated. Rather the regions constitute arenas for sometimes competing, sometimes converging national interests which increase their control over global forces. To the extent that the overall trend is convergence of national interests, one can speak of an emerging regional actor. More commonly, one must understand regional politics as an aggregation of and 'concertation' of national interests. For this reason the best approach to grasp the ongoing and still shady process of regionalization is probably to identify, compare and analyse individual national options.

The Subnational Level
The process of regionalization is also triggered by different forms of disintegration arising from on the subnational level. Earlier examples of break-down of states are few, and tended rather to confirm the basic persistence of the interstate system. Today, the situation is different, and the reason is that the structure of the world order is changing, thus lifting the 'overlay' of stabilizing controls which formed part of the old order, the cold war. The growth of *ethnonational* movements (of which some will result in microstates) will increase the role of the region. Regionalization also reinforces the strengthening of *microregions*, as the geopolitical environment becomes transformed and creates new possible alignments and a direct approach to the world economy for the subnational regions. Again it is the national level that suffers, albeit in a less destructive way than in the case of ethnonationalism. Ohmae (1994, p. 80) rightly sees the microregions as the natural economic zones in a borderless world, but gives them the rather misleading name of 'region-states', misleading since they rather express the logic of a post-Westphalian world. In Europe the microregions clearly relate to the macroregional process (providing them with a stable transnational framework), in East Asia they operate in a global space. We could therefore make a distinction between 'open microregionalism' with a global orientation and a more 'secluded microregionalism' responding to the macroregion.

The domestic and the external processes are thus interrelated in complex ways, and there is a strong need for innovative and constructive leadership in countries which disintegrate, either due to ethnonationalism or microregionalism. The resort to parochial solidarities speeds up the process of national disintegration. The collapse of political authority at one level opens up a previously latent power struggle at a lower level, and the process may go on almost indefinitely in a complex multi-ethnic polity. However, sooner or later there will be a reorganization of social power and political authority on a higher level of societal organization.

To the extent that there is a regional institutional framework which can be used for purposes of conflict resolution, the tendency is for the region to intervene. Thus, the eruption of 'black holes' promotes the process of regionalization. It may even form part of the process of regionalization, since the changing regional configuration provides opportunities for different subnational and microregional interests to reassert themselves.

ALTERNATIVE WORLD ORDERS

The argument of this chapter is that the new regionalism is a reaction to and a modifier of globalization, which would seem to imply that global somehow is 'bad' whereas, by contrast, regional is 'good'. Such a position of course needs some nuancing. If regionalism, which is the argument here, means a return of the 'political' in a globalized world context, it is relevant to ask about political content. It is, furthermore, important to keep in mind that 'global' is different from 'universal'. Universal implies values shared by all people. Globalization implies a not necessarily wanted homogenization of the world. Global interests do not express universally shared concerns, but rather interests which happen to be strong enough to penetrate (and transform) all or most parts of the globe. This may ultimately lead to a universalization of values in a more or less linear fashion, but more likely to countermovements and more dialectical type of processes. It is here that regionalization enters the scene.

The crucial issue in relating the two processes, I repeat, is the development logic, territorial as distinct from a functional interest. The former is defensive and conservative, the latter offensive and revolutionary. As has been noted before, capitalism is more revolutionary than socialism, if the capacity to promote social transformation is the criterion. The question is, as always, what social transformation we want, and why – that is, *in terms of what values?*

Values of Globalism and Regionalism

Globalism (as ideology) was earlier defined as programmatic globalization, the vision of a borderless world in which territory has lost importance. It represents the ultimate manifestation of a post-

Westphalian logic. Typically, globalism coincides with the neo-liberal doctrine and is usually articulating the interests of strong economic actors, the big players on the global market but asserting, in a universalized language, the values of efficiency and competitiveness against corruption and mismanagement, described as 'rent-seeking behaviour' in neoclassical economistic terminology. A very different use of the term can be found among environmentalists, to whom the concept suggests a common planetary predicament of too many people (driving too many cars, and so on) on a small planet, which constitutes one single ecosystem. All other ecosystems form part of the planetary system, and this inescapable fact tends to be expressed in the term 'global', a concept which is part of incompatible value-systems.

The new regionalism can be defined as a multidimensional process of regional integration which includes economic, political, social and cultural aspects. It is a package rather than a single policy and goes beyond the free trade market idea; that is, the interlinkage of previously more or less secluded national markets into one functional economic unit. Rather, the political ambition of establishing territorial control and regional coherence *cum* identity (in Polanyi's terms: protecting regional civil society) is the primary regionalist goal. In this observation other differences between 'old' and 'new' regionalism referred to earlier are implied. The new regionalism belongs to a new global situation characterized by multipolarity.

For other than committed neomercantilists the question whether a regionalist world order is a positive or a negative development can, however, only be answered in relation to alternative world orders and with reference to specific values (Falk and Mendlovitz, 1973). In a review of the first wave of regionalism and regionalist theorizing, Richard Falk and Saul Mendlovitz made an assessment of the implications of the regional phenomenon in terms of five world order values: peace and security, development, human rights, ecological balance and democracy. In this section (to be further developed in Vol. 4 in this subseries), I focus on three 'world order values':

- security
- development
- ecological sustainability.

Can regionalism promote these values better than globalism?

Security

In the case of intra-state security problems, the predominance of the nation-state and a Westphalian political rationality prevents rational solutions, whereas the regional level opens up previously untapped possibilities for solving conflicts built into the state formation. These conflicts are only further stimulated in a process of globalization, implying marginalization of peripheral regions and weak social groups. The UN system, as we so far have known it, is operating in an international context which is becoming ever more different from the world in which the UN was born. The current world system permits and even enforces a process of regionalization in different parts of the world, at the same time as the increase in regional activity in itself constitutes structural change towards a regionalized world order.

The emerging regions can absorb tensions that have become institutionalized in the historical and now increasingly dysfunctional state formations. The regional actor can, with less risk of provoking bilateral hostilities, intervene in intra-state conflicts which threaten to become destructive and a threat to regional security. The outcome is by no means uniform. As noted before, incidents of national disintegration can make or break regional organizations. It must also be acknowledged, however, that regionalization may stimulate interregional conflicts, whereas this Orwellian scenario would be less likely in a globalized world.

Development

If by development we mean long-term development beyond macro-economic stabilization, what is the difference between globalization and regionalization, and the 'old' and the 'new' regionalism from a developmental perspective? Globalism is undoubtedly a condition encouraging economic efficiency, but the game is confined to players on the market. What about those parts of the world for which 'the market' shows no interest? Regionalism can counter problems of marginalization under certain conditions. First, the old regionalism was often imposed from outside for geopolitical reasons, and in such cases there were few incentives for economic co-operation, particularly if the 'natural' economic region was divided in accordance with the cold-war pattern. Secondly, the attempts at regional co-operation/integration that actually took place were often inherited from colonial times and did not go far beyond the signing of free trade treaties in a post-colonial situation that was inherently asymmetric. The outcome of these regional trade arrangements was rarely encouraging, as the global pattern of uneven development more often than not was reproduced within the region, and with political tension as a result.

In contrast, the new regionalism is more political than economic, and the economic approach is much broader than exchange of goods. Its approach to free trade is cautious, far from autarkic but more selective in its external relations and careful to see to the interests of the region as a whole. Such interests include wider economic issues such as infrastructural development, industrial policy, sustainable resource management and so on.

Ecological Sustainability
Sustainability links the issue of development to the larger issue of ecological management. In the industrialized world, the 'national economies' were built with little regard to the pollution problem in the larger region, and the big players repeated this pattern in a 'global reach'. Regional management of the problem of pollution has now become a strong motive force in regional integration. In developing areas the issue is rather how to exploit natural resources in a way that is not only sustainable over time but also fair with regard to various conflicting interests on the national level.

Few serious ecological problems can be solved within the framework of the nation-state. Some of the most threatening ecological problems are global, but quite a few are regional. The most important problems should be solved on a global level, but there are few operative global institutions for resource management and for the handling of ecological crises. Globalization is rarely defined as to include the creation of global institutions to solve global problems, ecological or other. Regional ecological problems are often related to water: coastal waters, rivers, and ground water. Examples are the South China Sea, Barents Sea, the South Asian river systems, the Mekong River system, the Nile, Euphrates–Tigris, and the uneven exploitation of ground water resources in the areas around Jordan. As is evident, these issues cannot be studied in separation from the issues of development and regional security (see Vol. 4 in this subseries).

Globalism and Regionalism as World Orders

Do globalism and regionalism provide possible world orders? Again, it is important how we define the concepts. In international political economy theory, 'world order' is usually referred to as an arrangement which provides the necessary framework for sustained transactions in the world economy. It is important to distinguish the theoretical meaning of the concept from its historically varying real life content – that is, specific solutions to the problem of world order at a particular point in time. Thus world orders are historical, and there are presumably alternative future world orders, more or less attractive or repulsive, depending on our perspectives and values.

A regionalized world order implies that the territorial logic of the old nation-state (mercantilism) is applied to the emerging regional systems (neomercantilism), albeit in a post-Westphalian context. Real developments depend on the dialectical relationship between the two logics, the forces of market expansion and the need for political control. The one constitutes a reaction to the other, but neither of them can be seen as a 'final' solution or 'the end of history'.

In order to function, a market, any market and particularly a global market, presupposes some kind of social order. It was the historical function of mercantilism to create 'national economies' out of localized 'natural economies'. The crucial issue is how global economic exchange can take place under the conditions of anarchy supposedly characterizing the international system. This constitutes a world order problem, a problem that can be solved in more than one way. One debate has focused on the importance of hegemonic stability, the regional implications of hegemonic decline. These are, on the economic level, a fragmentation of the world economy, and, on the political level, an increased rivalry between great powers.

Hegemony implies a set of rules backed by the authority (and credibility) of the hegemon. Hegemony is thus a special kind of power, based on different but mutually supportive dimensions, fulfilling certain functions (providing public goods) in a larger system which lacks a formal authority structure, and, consequently, is more or less voluntarily accepted by other actors. Thus, coercion implies dominance rather than hegemony.

The same distinction between hegemony and dominance can of course be applied to regional systems, but here the compatibility of regional hegemonies and a particular world order becomes an issue. The Cold War order was in fact dualistic, in the sense that a socialist subsystem existed as a challenge to the capitalist world order, providing rebellious states with a safe haven. In 1989 this subsystem broke down under the pressure of military burden, lagging technological capability, and exhaustion of the various dimensions of hegemonic power. In this bipolar system regionalism had been subsumed under the Cold War logic, which implied a linkage also between regional organizations and the fundamental cleavage of the system (hegemonic regionalism). A new world order thus also implies a new type of regionalism, the new regionalism, rather than hegemonic regionalism. Regional powers are no longer 'subimperialist' but driven by their own ambitions which very well could be hegemonic, if not on the global level so on the regional. 'Regional hegemonism', which is coercive and therefore rather should be called dominance, is a 'malign' form of neomercantilism, the new regionalism, which is non-coercive, a 'benign' form (see the discussion on Southern Africa in Chapter 6). The great task in creating a post-hegemonic future is thus to promote 'benign' rather than 'malign' neomercantilism, and make various regional hegemonies compatible with a peaceful world-order.

Towards Regional Multilateralism?

What can we expect from a post-Westphalian era, if by Westphalian we imply an interstate system with the following characteristics: the sovereign independence of states; each state motivated in its international behaviour by a consistent national interest; the interstate system regulated by a balance of power among the principal powers? Necessarily there was a Westphalian rationality underlying this behaviour, taking a particular state as the given guarantee for security as well as welfare. What is outside the state borders according to this rationality is chaos and anarchy. The disorder and turbulence people experience today comes with the realization that this guarantee can no longer be taken for granted, because the state, if it does not simply disappear, tends to represent external interests rather than defending 'its own' people. This confusion is only increased when the two rationalities of Westphalianism and post-Westphalianism are mixed, a mixture of rationalities that is typical for all periods of transition.

The post-Westphalian logic consequently implies that the nation-state has lost its usefulness and that solutions must be found in transnational structures, global (functional) or regional (territorial). At the same time solutions are looked for in subnational identities, territorial or ethnic. The confusion is sometimes increased even further by the presence of 'pre-Westphalian' attitudes and behaviour in areas where the nation-state always was weak and superficial, and where it therefore breaks down completely under the pressures of globalization. But a major cause of conflict and turbulence is probably the antagonistic co-existence of Westphalian and post-Westphalian rationality, to which I consider the new regionalism as a possible solution.

This use of the term 'new regionalism' has both a positive meaning (there are empirically documented new features in most of the current regionalization trends) and a normative (these trends contain latent possibilities for a 'preferred' world order). The argument can be summarized as follows. The dialectics of market expansion and attempts at political intervention in defence of civil society constitute the basic forces in societal change (Polanyi, 1957). In the future post-Westphalian world this takes place in a transnational space, in which the new regionalism represents the return of 'the political'; that is, interventions in favour of crucial values, among which development, security and peace, and ecological sustainability are the most fundamental.

In fact these three issues form one integrated complex, at the same time as they constitute as many imperatives for deepening regional co-operation, if not regional integration. Totally incompatible visions turn up, particularly with regard to the regional factor in the formation of the world order. In the language of classical realism a regionalized world order would be a conflictual structure of hostile 'civilizations', namely the West, Islam and the Confucian cultural area (Huntington, 1993). This dark vision is strikingly similar to the scenario in George Orwell's *1984*. It even contains the classical type of 'unholy' alliances (the Islamic–Confucian connection). My objection to Orwell is more or less the same as my objection to Huntington. They both seem to apply a Westphalian logic to a post-Westphalian context. The future regional actors will to my mind rather bear more similarity to traditional empires, albeit in a new world context, than to nation-states. This would imply, for instance, governance on a higher level but without cultural standardization and ethnic cleansing.

Against the 'realist' nightmares mentioned above, more positive visions are thus also posited. From the perspective of a rational global economic organization, Percy Mistry (in Chapter 5) argues that a new regionalism may support a new multilateralism. Similarly, in the MUNS (Multilateralism and the UN System) programme of the UNU, co-ordinated by Robert Cox, the concept 'New Multilateralism' was used as a normative concept, meaning 'a commitment to maximum participation in dialogue among political, social, economic, and cultural forces as a means of resolving conflicts and designing institutional processes'. The critique of the 'old multilateralism' was based on the fact that it derived its universals from the dominant society, whereas 'a post-hegemonic order will have to derive its universals in a search for a common ground among constituent traditions of civilisation' (Cox, 1996, pp. 518–19; see also the MUNS subseries published by Macmillan in 1997–9). In my view, a regionalized world order rather than continued globalization would facilitate such global cultural pluralism.

According to its critics, the regionalization process contradicts basic multilateral principles as they are conventionally defined. However, I believe that it may nevertheless be a step towards a 'new multilateralism', avoiding 'war among civilizations'. This more symmetric order would necessarily mean a reduced role for the West, something which actually conforms with the new global power structure. The intercivilizational dialogue gives a new meaning to history, in contrast with the 'end of history thesis' of ultimate Western dominance, and this kind of dialogue on a global plane presupposes that the parties to it possess a material base, which only could be guaranteed within a regionalist protective framework. This implies a world order characterized by a pluralist normative content. The problem with Western civilization is that it was historically defined as a negation of Oriental civilization, and this negativist cultural tradition is still very much alive. The major task for the West, before a step towards a pluralistic world order can be taken, is therefore to reconsider its pretentious claim to centrality and universalism, typical for insulated cultures, and develop a genuine respect for other cultures. This is a fundamental precondition for cultural progress.

References

Anderson, B. (1983) *Imagined Communities* (London: Verso)

Archibugi, D. and D. Held (1995) *Cosmopolitan Democracy, An agenda for a New World Order (Cambridge: Polity Press)*.

Buzan, B. (1991) *People, States and Fear: An Agenda for International Security Studies in the Post-Cold War Era* (Hertfordshire: Harvester Wheatsheaf).

Cox, R.W. with T. J. Sinclair (1996) *Approaches to World Order* (Cambridge University Press).

Falk, R. and S. Mendlovitz (eds) (1973) *Regional Politics and World Order* (San Francisco: W. H. Freeman).

Fawcett, L. and A. Hurrell (eds) (1995) *Regionalism in World Politics. Regional Organization and International Order* (Oxford University Press).

Fröbel, F., J. Heinrichs and O. Kreye (1980) *The New International Division of Labour* (Cambridge University Press).

Haas, E. B. (1970) 'The Study of Regional Integration: Reflections on the Joy and Anguish of Pretheorizing', *International Organization*, no. 24 (Autumn).

Hamilton, K. A. (ed.) (1994) *Migration and the New Europe* (Washington: Centre for Strategic and International Studies).

Hettne, B. (1991) 'Security and Peace in Post-Cold War Europe', *Journal of Peace Research*, **28** (3): 279–94.

Hettne, B. (1993) 'The Concept of Neomercantilism', in L. Magnusson (ed.) *Mercantilist Economies* (Boston: Kluwer).

Hettne, B. (1995) *Development Theory and the Three Worlds. Towards an International Political Economy of Development* (London: Longman).

Hirschman, A. (1970) *Exit, Voice and Loyalty: Responses to Decline in Firms, Organizations and States* (Cambridge, Mass.: Harvard University Press).

Hirst, P. and G. Thompson (1996) *Globalization in Question. The International Economy and the Possibilities of Governance* (Cambridge: Polity Press).

Holm, H. H. and G. Sørensen (1992) 'A New World Order: the Withering away of Anarchy and the Triumph of Individualism? Consequences for IR Theory', IPRA General Conference, Kyoto 1992.

Huntington, S.P. (1993) 'The Clash of Civilizations?', *Foreign Affairs*, 3: 22–49.

Kaplinsky, R. (1984) *Third World Industrialization in the 1980s. Open Economies in a Closing World* (London: Frank Cass).

Mittelman, J. H. (1994) 'Global Restructuring of Production and Migration', in Y. Sakamoto, (ed.) (1994) *Global Transformation* (Tokyo: United Nations University Press).

Ohmae, K. (1995) *The End of the Nation State. The Rise of Regional Economies* (New York: Free Press).

Oman, C. (1994) *Globalization and Regionalization: The Challenge for Developing Countries* (Paris: Development Centre of the OECD).

Østergaard, T. (1993) 'Classical Models of Regional Integration – What Relevance for Southern Africa?' in Bertil Odén (ed.) *Southern Africa after Apartheid. Regional Integration and External Resources* (Uppsala: The Scandinavian Institute of African Studies).

Palmer, N. D. (1991) *The New Regionalism in Asia and the Pacific* (Lexington).

Polanyi, K. (1957) *The Great Transformation* (Boston: Beacon Press).

Robertson, R. (1992) *Globalization. Social Theory and Global Culture* (London: Sage).

Rosenau, J. N. (1990) *Turbulence in World Politics. A Theory of Change and Continuity* (Princeton, NJ: Princeton University Press).

Sakamoto, Y. (1992) *Changing World Order: A Conceptual Prelude to the UNU Project on Global Structural Change* (Tokyo: United Nations University Press).

2 Rethinking the 'New Regionalism' in the Context of Globalization[*]

James H. Mittelman

Following its decline in theory and practice in the 1970s, regionalism both revived and changed dramatically in the 1980s, and has gained strength in the 1990s. Regionalism today is emerging as a potent force in the global restructuring of power and production.

In public discourse and among scholars, attention appears to be riveted on the questions: Is regionalism a stepping stone or a stumbling block on the path toward globalization? Are regionalism, often identified with the major trading blocs, and globalization complementary or competitive processes (for example, Emmerij, 1992; Griffin, 1992; and Young, 1993)?

The argument advanced here is that any imputed conflict between regionalism and globalization is more theoretical than real, for political and economic units are fully capable of walking on two legs. If globalization is understood to mean the compression of the time and space aspects of social relations (Mittelman, 1996a), then regionalism is but one component of globalization. Properly understood, the dynamics of regionalism are a chapter of globalization. But what is the key to understanding the evolving linkages between these multi-faceted processes?

'The new regionalism' approach (NRA) is an important advance over the different versions of integration theory (trade or market

* Some of the ideas in this chapter were developed under the auspices of the 'Programme on Multilateralism and the United Nations System', a project sponsored by the United Nations University, and through discussions with the program co-ordinator, Robert W. Cox. I am indebted to Mustapha Pasha, who generously shared documentary material; Meliton Salazar, whose research assistance was invaluable; and Linda Yarr for criticism of an earlier draft of this manuscript. For supporting my field work for this research, I am grateful to the World Society Foundation and the Professional Staff Congress of the City University of New York.

integration, functionalism and neofunctionalism, institutionalism and neoinstitutionalism, and so on). While this is not the place to rehearse a critique of each variant, all of them are deficient inasmuch as they understate power relations and fail to offer an explanation of structural transformation. In some ways a break with this tradition, the NRA explores contemporary forms of transnational co-operation and cross-border flows through comparative, historical, and multilevel perspectives.

Building on this foundation, I will try to provide the conceptual underpinnings for addressing the new regional realities in a coherent and analytical manner. This chapter stakes out the postulates that constitute the NRA, critically evaluates the literature, and extends the theoretical framework to include neglected dimensions. The architecture of the new regionalism is incomplete without analysis of the interactions among

(1)   ideas and their ties to institutions
(2)   systems of production
(3)   labour supply and
(4)   sociocultural institutions, all undergirded by
(5)   power relations.[1]

Although the discussion here will primarily be at a conceptual level, it will be supported by illustrations from my field work in South East Asia and Southern Africa in 1991 and 1993. These subregions provide a sound basis for comparison, for one is a key node in the world's most dynamic regional economy (the Asia–Pacific sphere), the other in an increasingly marginalized zone (sub-Saharan Africa). By drawing on the experiences of South East Asia and Southern Africa, this chapter will suggest some of the interactions among different levels of regionalism – macroregionalism, subregionalism, and microregionalism, to be defined below – and with the Westphalian state system.

I will first examine the concept of the new regionalism and, subsequently, challenge the Eurocentric scenario. The third section of this chapter identifies key actors and patterns of institutionalization under divergent conditions. Next is a discussion of relationships among the aforementioned elements missing from the extant theoretical framework. Although this chapter cannot provide a fully elaborated alternative conceptualization, it will point toward a reformulation of the new regionalism thesis.

'THE NEW REGIONALISM' APPROACH

Regionalism in the 1990s is not to be considered as a movement toward territorially-based autarkies as it was during the 1930s. Rather, it represents concentrations of political and economic power competing in the global economy, with multiple inter-regional and intra-regional flows.[2] During the 1930s, a period marked by autocentric regionalism, world trade dropped dramatically and protectionism was widely practised. Moreover, regions of trade and regions of currency were identical. Trading blocs were in fact named after major currencies – the sterling bloc, the yen bloc and so on. Today, in comparison to the 1930s, there are more currency blocs, and some of them do not correspond to the zone of trade – for example, the German mark in Eastern Europe, the US dollar in China and increasingly in the Baltics and other parts of the former Soviet Union. In the Third World, autocentric regionalism has involved calls for delinking and collective self-reliance, the goal of the 1980 Lagos Plan of Action, inscribed in the Final Act of Lagos' proposed African Economic Community (AEC). Today, the prospect of an inward-looking regionalism – the spectre of a 'Fortress Europe' – involves establishing a self-contained entity and closing the door to outside suppliers.

With the spread of deregulation and privatization, however, the outward orientation of neoliberal regionalism has meant the diminution of both states' and interstate organizations' ability to control aspects of trade and monetary relations (Hessler, 1994). Unlike autocentric regionalism, the neoliberal variety is extroverted; it entails liberalization, an opening to external market forces. In the neoliberal perspective, regional groupings need not be either building blocks or stumbling blocks to world order. Rather, they envelop large regions, their subsets, and smaller economies in a variety of institutional configurations that range from *de jure* pacts such as the European Union (EU) to a *de facto*, firm-driven, flying geese formation in the Asia–Pacific zone The current trend is to establish wider regionalism.

Within this compass are three levels of neoliberal regionalism, all of which interact with other elements of a globalized political economy, including states, which are partly permeable and partly able to regulate transborder flows. First, macroregions co-ordinate capital flows within a spatial unit but also provide access to the globalization process. The formation of macroregions involves a vast enlargement in the size of the market, a weakening of extant political units, and a reduction in the full meaning of citizenship. Citizenship is less meaningful because of the separation of citizenship and work – a growing trend with border-crossers and home-workers linked to transnational production processes through electronic means. Macroregions may thus be regarded as loose geographical units larger than the state with some political and cultural bonds, however varied and sometimes contentious.

Second, subregional patterns enlarge the concept of proximity to encompass factors other than geographical distance. Indeed, historical legacies and economic forces can provide the propellants for the migration of industries, employment creation, and spillovers to other areas as well as demonstration effects. Hence, within the Asia–Pacific region, there are attempts now under way to form nodes of states in growth triangles. Subregional economic zones, known as SREZs, transcend political boundaries but need not involve entire national economies. Rather, they intersect only the border areas of the national economies (Chia and Yuan, 1993, p. 226).

The best-established SREZ is the Greater South China Economic Zone, also known as the Southern China Economic Community, linking Hong Kong, Macau, Taiwan, and southern Guangdong and Fujian provinces of China in an informal grouping. Within the Association of South East Asian Nations (ASEAN), the Johor–Singapore–Riau Growth Triangle seeks to take advantage of Singapore's highly skilled, human capital, and well-developed infrastructure, Johor's land and semi-skilled labour, and Riau's land and low-cost labour. Drawing together a city state, peninsular Malaysia, and islands in Indonesia, this triangle constitutes a subregion lodged under a larger subregional rubric. Other SREZs, or growth triangles, are on the drawing board.

Finally, microregional patterns develop within the boundedness of sovereign states. For example, Catalonia, Lombardy, and Quebec are relatively autonomous entities within the political jurisdiction of states. In addition, industrial districts form a mosaic of highly interdependent economic and technological forces, themselves embedded in a more encompassing network of transactions. The State Council of China, for example, has decided that microregions (export processing zones) will be national pace-setters for reform and thus serve as locomotives to power economic growth.

Subject to globalizing tendencies, these processes intersect in a variety of ways, constituting 'the new regionalism'. Despite their diverse emphases, scholars generally agree that it differs from the earlier wave of regional co-operation in several respects. A growth area of scholarship (for example, Marchand, 1994; Morales and

Quandt, 1992; Robson, 1993), its essential features are encapsulated in the following composite.

The most important characteristics of the new regionalism are its truly worldwide reach, extending to more regions, with greater external linkages (de Melo and Panagariya 1992, p. 37; Palmer, 1991, p. 2). In comparison to the specific objectives of classical regionalism, the new regionalism is multifaceted, more comprehensive than the older paradigm. Unlike the pattern in the cold-war era, the new regionalism is developing in a multipolar context. Superpowers are not driving this movement from outside and above (as with the Central Treaty Organization or the Southeast Asia Treaty Organization, for example), but it is more spontaneous, springing from within and below (Hettne, 1994, p. 2). In this formulation, 'constituent states' are deemed the main actors, though the growth of a regional civil society, including social and cultural networks, provides impetus. Unlike Palmer (1991, p. 185), who maintains that significant breakthroughs, at least in Asia–Pacific regionalism, are primarily in the economic domain, Hettne (1994, p. 2) argues that the political dimensions of the new regionalism warrant stronger emphasis.

Elaborating on these points, Hettne advances a framework for comparing regions as a geographical and ecological units circumscribed by natural and physical barriers; social systems, which implies translocal relations, in some cases including a security complex; members in organisations; civil societies with shared cultural traditions; and acting subjects with their own identities, capacities, legitimacy, and apparatuses for making policy. Movement toward the higher levels of 'regionness' – that is, the latter criteria – in this multilayered conceptualization are said to delimit 'the new regionalism' (Hettne, 1994, pp. 7–8).

The exact form the new regional project might take is unclear. The growth of protectionist pressures and trade conflicts has led to the possibility that industrial production and trade will increasingly be organized in regional blocs. On this issue, one school of thought stems from the neoliberal notion and holds that by helping national economies to become competitive in the world market, regional integration will lead to multilateral co-operation on a global scale and thus reduce conflict. Another school regards the new regionalism as disintegrative, dividing the world economy into trade blocs, and ultimately promoting conflicts among exclusionary groups centred on the leading economies. Perhaps more theoretical than real, this debate has captured public attention, but tension among the macroregions is not the most interesting or potentially consequential aspect of conflict prompted by regionalizing tendencies, a theme to which we will return. Nonetheless, it does identify the contradictory nature of regionalism, which is both an integrative and disintegrative process, partly the result of the interplay among variants of this phenomenon in different zones of the global political economy.

The European Model versus African and Asian Models

The new regionalism is described as the model for a new type of political and economic organization. In what is perhaps the most elegant elaboration of this prototype, Hettne indicates:

> The comparative framework has ... been derived from studying the process of Europeanization, the development of a regional identity in Europe ... and applied to the case of other regions ... under the assumption that despite enormous historical, structural, and contextual differences, there is an underlying logic behind contemporary processes of regionalization.   (Hettne, 1994, p. 2)

Claiming that Europe is a 'more advanced' regional grouping relative to the arrangements on other continents, he uses this case as a 'paradigm for the new regionalism in the sense that its conceptualization eagerly draws on observations of the European process' (Ibid., p. 12).

As is well known, the 1958 Treaty of Rome established what is now called the EU. With six founding members, this unit has undergone three enlargements, and there are a number of applications pending. The Treaty of Rome set up an institutionalized system enabling the European Economic Community (EEC) to enact legislation equally binding on all of its members.

Hence, the paradigmatic case developed in an institutionalized setting, with declaratory purposes. Its mandate is state-centred, and has expanded according to a legally fixed framework and a series of deadlines.

African and Asian countries do not share the stated aspirations found in the Treaty of Rome and that inspired the EU. Legally binding instruments are not characteristic of the Southern African Development Co-ordination Conference, SADCC (known as the Southern African Development Community, SADC, since 1992) or ASEAN, and are unlikely to propel their experience. In fact, European-style integration has never been the objective in Asia–Pacific development and Africa, for – rhetorical flourishes aside – both regions lack political commitment to deeper integration.

The only initiative to institutionalize political co-operation in the Asia–Pacific region was Malaysian prime minister Mahathir bin Mohamad's idea, put forward in 1990, to form an East Asian Economic Grouping, which would bind Japan, China, South Korea, Taiwan, Hong Kong, and the ASEAN members. Unacceptable to the USA and meeting with reservations from the Japanese, it was transformed into a modest East Asian Economic Caucus (EAEC), or forum for discussion, and in 1993, incorporated within the Asia–Pacific Economic Co-operation (APEC) group (Mahathir, 1989; Stubbs 1994: p. 374), which had been established at the ministerial level in 1989. Containing the world's three largest economies – the USA with 22 per cent of world gross domestic product (GDP), Japan with 7.6 per cent, and China with 6 per cent (International Monetary Fund [IMF], 1993: Annex IV, pp. 116–19), APEC today clearly carries more economic weight than do the other macro regions. Also, the size of the Chinese economy is projected to surpass that of Japan and the USA early in the twenty-first century, becoming the biggest in the world.

Another difference is that unlike the EU, safeguarded since its precursors' inception by the North Atlantic Treaty Organization, security was a major reason for the formation of SADC and ASEAN, one seeking disengagement from *apartheid* South Africa and protection against Pretoria's destabilization campaigns, the other against any designs from revolutionary movements in China and Indochina. Further, in terms of economics, Europeans are joined by a high degree of trade among themselves, whereas intra-regional trade within SADC and ASEAN is slight. Intra-APEC trade grew from about 56 per cent of the Asia–Pacific total in 1970 to 65 per cent in 1990 (Drysdale and Garnaut, 1993, pp. 183–6). By 1992, APEC economies accounted for 75 per cent of each other's trade and 44 per cent of world trade (Garnaut, 1993, p. 17). In comparison, intra-SADC (and before 1992, intra-SADCC) trade never exceeded 5 per cent of the total international trade of its members, and intra-ASEAN trade is less than 20 per cent of its member states' world trade.

Owing to their dissimilar contexts, the Eurocentric model differs in essential respects from Asian and African regionalism. SADC and ASEAN have rejected a secretariat-led approach, opting instead for lean bureaucratic mechanisms. More importantly, SADC and ASEAN eschew emphasis on trade and, rather, aim for production-driven and

infrastructure-orientated arrangements. Whereas both bodies have
had measured success in improving infrastructure (especially trans-
portation in southern Africa), by all accounts industrial expansion
projects in the two subregions have not taken off and have not
generated substantial capital formation (Curry, 1991; Østergaard,
1993, p. 44).

Clearly, ASEAN and the macroregion within which it is embedded
are market-induced and private-sector-driven constellations. In fact,
Drysdale and Garnaut (1993, pp. 186–8, 212) suggest that 'the Asia–
Pacific model', also termed 'the Pacific model of integration', com-
prises a combination of three elements:

- trade liberalization augments economic performance and plays
  down political perceptions of any disadvantages in income distribution;
- trade expands without official barriers that discriminate between
  intraregional and extraregional transactions; and
- the reduction of non-official discrimination (for example, cultural
  barriers) to trade contributes powerfully to economic development.

One could refine this model by engaging in a discussion of the range
of its subsets in the subregions of the Asia–Pacific zone, but that
would take us too far afield. Apropos of South East Asia, what
bears emphasis is that ASEAN's engines of growth have been fuelled
by Japanese, and increasingly Korean and Taiwanese, private sector
investments. More important, however, is that unlike the portrait of
neoliberal regionalism vividly painted by Drysdale and Garnaut, the
11 members of SADC (which post-*apartheid* South Africa joined in
1994) have sought to respond to the shortcomings of market integration theory, especially its silence about equity and calls for redistribution.

The *development integration* model was introduced as an alternative
to a one-sided emphasis on efficiency maximization of existing capacity – not surprisingly, in the context of a low level of productive
capacity. This approach stresses the need for close political co-operation at the outset of the integration process. Not only does it assign
priority to the co-ordination of production and the improvement of
infrastructure, but it also calls for a higher degree of state intervention
than does the market model as well as redistributive measures such as
transfer taxes or compensatory schemes administered by regional
funds or specialized banks. Trade integration is to be accompanied

by attempts to promote co-ordinated regional industrial development. A counter-weight to economic liberalism, it seeks to redress external dependence, especially through the regulation of foreign investment. Hence, development integration is a multilevel approach engulfing production, infrastructure, finance, and trade.

In practice, the development integration model has fallen short of the professed aims of its architects in Southern Africa. In SADCC's first decade, its professional staff and representatives of member states infrequently consulted the private sector and failed to involve capital in planning regional industrial development. Partly as a result, its regional industrial strategy, while ambitious, is vague and largely unimplemented. Moreover, a distributional crisis besets intra-regional trade, with Zimbabwe accounting for large surpluses with all of its SADC partners save South Africa – the type of imbalance that Pretoria's membership will surely magnify. The more vexing issue, however, is the conflict between the fledgling model of development integration, weakly embraced by social forces in the subcontinent, and the institutionalization of the neoliberal concept, ascendant in the post-cold war world.

ACTORS, INSTITUTIONS, AND GLOBAL GOVERNANCE

The new regionalism conceptualization distinguishes between the 'formal' region and the 'real' region (Hettne, 1994, p. 7). This point deserves special mention because increasingly membership in international institutions imperfectly corresponds to transnational processes, many of them subsurface movements. As indicated, zones of production may arise spontaneously with little government or no government intervention, and bridge territorial boundaries. Furthermore, culture is constructed and reconstructed at speeds that differ from those of the workings of international institutions, usually at a much slower pace and occasionally forming a regionalized civil society, the Nordic community perhaps being the foremost example.

Clearly, with a multiplicity of interstate and non-state actors, there is a tendency toward fragmentation of institutions. The Asia–Pacific landscape is marked by a labyrinth of international institutions: APEC, ASEAN Free Trade Area, EAEC, Pacific Trade and Development Conference, Pacific Basin Economic Community, Pacific Economic Co-operation Council, South Asian Association for Regional Co-operation, and so on. So, too, is resource-poor Africa spawning these bureaucratically-laden entities, much too numerous to enumerate here but including the Development Bank of Southern Africa, Economic Commission of Africa (a United Nations body), East African Co-operation, Economic Community of West African States, Maghreb Union, Organization of African Unity, Common Market of Eastern and Southern Africa, and Southern African Customs Union. The list goes on. Not only is there a lack of coherence among these intergovernmental institutions, but they also articulate only sporadically with the bearers of change within civil society – women's movements, peasant organizations, environmental groups, pro-democracy advocates, and so on.

Globalization is not flattening civil societies around the world but, rather, combining with local conditions in distinctive ways, accentuating differences, and spurring a variety of social movements seeking protection from the disruptive and polarising effects of economic liberalism. Evidently, the state is caught in a dialectic of supranationalism and subnationalism. The nation-state reflects a seventeenth-century Westphalian concept, a territorial mode of political organization, which, according to democratic theory, is supposed to provide accountability to the governed. Yet, by condensing the time-space aspects of social relations, economic globalization transcends territorial states and is unaccountable to elected political officials or, rather, is accountable to unelected market forces. The tension between the territorially-based system of political organization and economic globalization embodying the market principle creates a disjuncture in governance at both the regional and world levels. Notwithstanding great expectations about a supposed revival of the United Nations, mainly its peacekeeping role, in the post-Cold War era, the existing set of international institutions risks becoming increasingly ineffective and obsolete, only partly because of resource shortages. In the emerging international division of power, the United Nations system attends to political crises, serving as an arena for contestation but, in the main, seeking to harmonize, rationalize, and stabilize patterns of hegemony. Meanwhile, the Group of Seven democracies (all Western capitalist countries plus Japan) attempts to co-ordinate the international economy, but it is a tall order for state officials to try to harness unaccountable global market forces. In light of the challenge that economic globalization poses for governance, a restructuring of international institutions will inevitably be inscribed on the policy agenda. It is an elusive task, not least because some regional or subregional movements (such as the Southern China

Economic Community, with over 200 million people), are without an institutional base and disavow institutional trappings (Stewart, Cheung, and Yeung, 1992).

What is to be institutionalized? In so far as international organizations are products of change within the global political economy, their task is to project a picture of a globally conceived society, a universal vision, and maintain the dominant world order. If so, they typically set general rules of behaviour as well as facilitate regional and global hegemony (Cox, 1982, 1987). Yet, international institutions are double-edged swords. In some instances – for example, decolonization and the anti-*apartheid* movement – they may promote counter-hegemony (Mittelman, 1976). They are agents of change and do have potential for innovation, especially in the realm of ideas, although the present tendency is to institutionalize neoliberal concepts and practices.

THE IDEA OF NEOLIBERALISM

The predominant set of ideas about world order in the 1980s and thus far in the 1990s is neoliberal thinking, partially a reaction to the influence of structuralism in the 1960s and 1970s, and now widely translated into policy prescriptions. By ideas, I mean the shared meanings embodied in culture. When transmitted transnationally, they help to maintain and reproduce a social order, specifically by eliciting consent from both dominant and subordinate groups. Not only may shared meanings entrench the continuity of a given order, but inasmuch as they contain the capacity to create and to invent new ways of life, universalizing values bear potential to serve as transforming agents.

On the policy side of the equation, there appears to be a resurgence of integration projects in the South. Perplexed about how to keep up with the enormous concentrations of power and wealth in the three macroregions, the dominant strata in Third World countries are attempting to establish new economies of scale. Although economic integration fell into disfavour as a development strategy in the 1970s and early 1980s, international agencies are now pumping money into regional projects. The bandwagon effect has brought aboard bilateral agencies as well as the World Bank (Mandaza, 1990; Thompson, 1991; Davies, 1992; Seidman and Anang, 1992). In this guise, neoregionalism can become a lookalike for neoliberalism.

.

Unlike strategies of collective self-reliance, the idea of neoliberalism centres on integration in the global economy. Whereas self-reliance typically leads to policies of import substitution industrialization, with goods formerly imported being produced locally, engaging the world economy implies an emphasis on export-orientated industrialization. Neoliberals claim that exports can only compete with international market prices if production is unfettered by price controls such as tariffs. The premise is that left to its own devices, the market is a far more efficient arbiter of economic growth and development than is the state. In a globalizing world, primacy is given to extra-regional markets rather than to intra-regional linkages.

Of course, there are tradeoffs in the neoliberal project. Deregulation, devaluation, and denationalization – a single package, all ingredients of structural adjustment programmes – entail welfare losses and distributional effects, for they spread the pain unevenly. In the absence of co-ordination of the elements of market reforms, neoliberalism may fragment into *degenerate regionalism*. There is degeneration from a more highly organized into a simpler type. Like the neoliberal project, this form of regionalism seeks to optimize a collectivity's position in the globalization matrix. Yet, degenerate regionalism is a defensive measure against further social disintegration, the symptoms of which include widespread corruption, pervasive crime, and gangsterism, often in collusion with the upper echelons of the state bureaucracy.

Hence, the 12 members of the Commonwealth of Independent States (CIS), a loose confederation established without the three Baltic nations in 1991 to harmonize interrepublican policies after the fall of the Soviet Union, have adopted diverse reform strategies and proceed at different speeds. In market restructuring, Russia has moved rapidly; Ukraine, Belarus, Kazakhstan, Turkmenistan, and Uzbekistan have avoided shock liberalization and have maintained a high degree of state control over production and prices; and Azerbaijan, Armenia, Georgia, Moldova, and Tajikistan have deferred the question of economic reforms until ethnic rivalries and armed conflicts are settled (Grinberg, Shmelev and Vardomsky, 1994).

Moreover, the spread of the market has fostered two poles, one European and the other Central Asian, in the CIS. Russia is so big and powerful relative to the other members that some of these newly independent states fear Moscow's influence and control over their energy and mineral resources. Except for gas-rich Turkmenistan, the CIS republics are economically dependent on Russia. They seek to maintain sovereignty and achieve collective security, heretofore highly problematic.

The outbreak of civil wars (Georgia, Moldova, and Tajikistan), international clashes (Azerbaijan and Armenia), Russia's military operation in the breakaway region of Chechnya, 25 million ethnic Russians dispersed precariously in several republics, and the widespread abuse of minorities, in some cases triggering an outflow of population, belie the link between a neoliberal regional economy and liberal politics. Post-Soviet Eurasia is marked not only by chronic violence but also by continuity in political leadership from the Soviet era, with an entrenched officialdom, or *nomenklatura*, aided by security police who have infrequently been demobilized, as well as a retreat from democratic values.

Under more auspicious political conditions, however, neoliberalism still promises economic growth, and offers flexibility in terms of policy initiatives in a dynamic and increasingly integrated world economy. The neoliberal vision rests on flexible responses to price signals and a high degree of division of labour adapted to new methods of production.

NEOLIBERALISM AND FLEXIBLE PRODUCTION

If the NRA neglects the question of production of what and for whom, it cannot explain changes in the geography of world capitalism. If so, it would fail to constitute more than a partial and limited view of the mosaic of regional development. Coincident with the ascendance of neoliberalism is the emergence of specialized regional production systems, with their own intra-regional divisions of labour both among countries and cross- cutting them within industries.

Within the ambit of globalization, there is a co-existence of two logics of production. Fordism is characterized by assembly line production which assigns workers to routine tasks requiring minimal skill or training. The speed of work is regulated by hierarchical control and scientific management techniques executed through the line and is not determined by workers. The Fordist method requires large-scale runs of standardized products to justify substantial investment in specific machinery and inventories of parts stockpiled on a 'just-in-case' basis, which can tie up working capital and augment costs.

By the late 1970s, Fordist mass production encountered increasing difficulty in achieving high levels of productivity gains, and in some locales labour succeeded in pushing up wages. The spatial reorganization of production entailed the spread of manufacturing from a handful of industrial countries to different regions, the fragmentation of the production process, and the introduction of new technologies. This restructuring raised nettlesome questions for the core–periphery concept of regional development, for some peripheral areas outstripped the core in such core-like activities as manufacturing as a major driving force of GDP (Scott and Storper, 1992, pp. 12–13).

Among other technological developments, the introduction and diffusion of microelectronic systems in production in the 1980s and 1990s have greatly increased flexibility in a wide range of industries. At the same time, there have been dramatic changes in the organization of industrial production. In the post-Fordist model, workers are multiskilled, trained for varied tasks, and operate in a decentralized framework subject to a relatively flat or informal hierarchy. Targeting customized goods in batch production, a Japanese 'just-in-time' system is adopted, whereby inventories are kept to a minimum. Competitiveness is translated into fast adaptation to change, or flexible specialization.

The introduction of flexible specialization systems makes regional production networks ever more important, for a premium is placed on spatial clustering of suppliers around plants, partly to ensure delivery times. Propinquity means lower costs and greater opportunities for matching needs and capabilities. Proximity to nearby suppliers and workers, installed within a production culture that encourages innovations from the shop floor, allows for fluctuations in market demand.

In the new flexible production subregions and microregions, there are several variations. Centres of flexible production are burgeoning in many Asian, Latin American NICs (newly industrializing countries), and near-NICs. In these economies, production activities are climbing the value-added ladder from labour-intensive to capital-intensive toward technology-intensive industries. The goal is to create competitive advantage and to achieve industrial upgrading; yet, the elusive last hurdle is technological innovation.

In Asia–Pacific regionalism, Japanese multinationals have expanded and have relied on the flexibility offered by a multiplicity of small and medium-size contracting firms. Regional complexes of industries are developing in such activities as electronics and computers. Many of the firms are owned by Chinese families and form networks of businesses. What is emerging is a regionally integrated production zone based on Chinese enterprises often fuelled by

Japanese capital (Stubbs, 1994, pp. 372–3). As the Japanese economy has become deeply embedded in the economy of the Asia–Pacific region, it has utilized a web of sociocultural structures as a conduit for flows of capital. Strong bonds of kinship and culture in geographically proximate areas can reduce transaction costs and provide a level of interpersonal trust that facilitates regional business.

FLEXIBILITY THROUGH SOCIOCULTURAL NETWORKS

The implementation of flexible specialization turns on not only a techno-economic structure rooted in a territorially concentrated system of production but also the qualitative aspects of a social milieu. Most important are cultural factors grounded in civil society, including the degree of trust and consensus underpinning the market and the industrial climate for generating skills for the work place. In other words, informal communication of ideas about building regionalism at different levels takes place within social institutions such as ethnic groups, families, clubs, and so on, some of them originating in pre-capitalist society (Goodman and Bamford, 1989; Asheim, 1992). In so far as the flexible specialization model as a productive system requires strong relations with civil society, sociocultural institutions may represent either a constraining or a potentially enabling factor in regional development.

Elsewhere I have explored the role of Chinese families as transnational linkages in Asia–Pacific's explosive economic growth (Mittelman, 1996b). What needs to be added to that analysis is the way that Japanese investment and aid set off the explosion, particularly in the South East Asian subregion. In fact, the expansion of the ASEAN economies cannot be understood without taking into account the geopolitics of South East Asia and the conjunction of the hegemonic interests of the two economic superpowers – the USA and, more recently, Japan.

After the USA pumped capital into South East and East Asia during the Korean and Vietnam wars, Japan gradually expanded its flows of capital throughout the region, but it is to the USA and not Japan that South East Asian countries export the largest portion of their manufactured goods. In the evolving triangular division of labour in Asia–Pacific regionalism, Japan and to a lesser extent the USA furnish investment capital, and South East Asia provides raw materials for Japan as well as cheap labour for the production of manufactured goods largely for the US market. Japanese capital has had an uneven impact on the economies of South East Asia, with Singapore attracting the biggest share of direct investment on a per-capita basis. Quite clearly, Singapore has been the chief beneficiary of capital flows and the geopolitics of the subregion (Stubbs, 1989, 1991).

With Japan's trade patterns shifting toward a regionally-based economy, Tokyo has helped ASEAN economies enlarge their export manufacturing sectors and augment the efficiency of Japanese manufacturers relocating in South East Asia. The regionalization of Japanese industry has created a little noticed incongruity in the economy of Singapore and perhaps those of other countries. One of the few countries to identify the extent of GDP generated by foreign or foreign-controlled factors of production, Singapore releases data which show that an increasing share of its output is foreign produced. From 1980 to 1991, foreign-produced GDP grew at a rate of 250 per cent compared to 147.5 per cent for indigenous GDP. Paradoxically, the foreign-controlled sector is able to find an array of profitable opportunities for expansion and investment in Singapore, while national capital is now lending abroad a greater part of its portfolio. Doubtless, the explanation partly lies in the locally controlled sector's competitive disadvantage in technology, showing just how hard it is even for a burgeoning economy in the Third World to jump the elusive last hurdle to advanced economy status (Kant, 1992; Bernard and Ravenhill, 1995).

The explanation also rests on the complex divisions of labour and power in the region. While Japanese direct foreign investment in Asia soared from $2 billion in 1987 to $8 billion in 1990 (two to three times as great as the US total), the telling point is that the bulk of value added stays with the Japanese; smaller shares accrue to junior partners in a flexible but structured manufacturing bloc. Retaining a clear-cut technological edge, Tokyo co-ordinates locational decisions in a regionally articulated division of labour, offering investment, aid, and know-how. Although there are still stand-alone Chinese conglomerates, ethnic Chinese throughout South East Asia are often partners linked to the Japanese in joint ventures. In a regional system which widely adopts Japanese methods of flexible production, big Chinese firms – the Liem group and Astra, for example – are vehicles for Japanese capital, sometimes as assembly plants or as distributors for corporations such as Fuji or Komatsu (Tabb, 1994).

Going beyond the interplay of Chinese family holdings and Japanese enterprises, it would be shortsighted merely to say that in regional development, culture facilitates flows of capital. The emphasis on powerful structures should not deflect attention from cultural discontinuities and the ways that these discontinuities are created. In the second phase of a Polanyian double movement (see previous chapter), a reaction to changing material conditions on a global and regional scale, individuals are not passive occupants but active agents who negotiate socially prescribed roles. They enter and shape decision-making in national and multilateral arenas by reconstituting culture beginning with micropractices. Strategies of countering social control in the work place or of reorganizing the production process involve renegotiating meanings, redefining customs, and pushing up against the boundaries of old social structures in more enabling ways (Kabeer, 1991). While other authors have provided graphic studies of the production–culture link at a local level, my interest here centres on regional interactions, with sociocultural institutions mediating the production process and labour supply.

FLEXIBLE PRODUCTION AND FLEXIBLE LABOUR MARKETS

As noted, the Fordist system of mass production and mass consumption has tended to give way to another structure. Post-Fordism entails a more flexible, fragmented and decentralized system of production making use of a segmented, in good part female, and often geographically dispersed labour force. Fordism is not defunct but based in different sectors of production, namely in low-skill services such as fast food and in various types of labour-intensive processes, sometimes in the peripheral (or export) zones of industrial systems. In these labour markets, culture plays a major role in segmentation, for current regulatory regimes are conceived in terms of exclusivity: employment is restricted to persons of indigenous culture or receiving countries insist on assimilation to local culture. Thus, culture is one of the instruments in the regulation of international migration, perforce an encounter of people who speak different languages, practice different religions, and have very different habits (Mittelman, 1994).

An integral part of the globalization process, large-scale transfers of population are requisite for the operations of many small-and medium-sized firms. Migrants are unevenly spread across the globe, the largest numbers, some 35 million, in sub-Saharan Africa, and another 15 million in Asia and the Middle East. The magnitude of remittances reached $66 billion in 1989, second only to oil as a share of international trade, and more than all international development assistance – $46 billion (United Nations Population Fund, 1993, p. 8).

Rooted in world inequality, migratory flows have expanded rapidly in recent years. From 50 million immigrants in 1989, the world total doubled to 100 million in 1992, the latter figure comprising 2 per cent of the world's population. Strikingly, a large portion of these people remain within their region of origin. An estimated 23 million represent 'internally displaced' persons, and the bulk of the world's 17 million officially registered refugees and asylum seekers stay in the region where they were born (United Nations Population Fund 1993, pp. 7, 8, 15). Taking into account other migration streams, most international migration today is within – not between – regions (Keely, 1992).

With the emergence of macroregions, the new regionalism internalizes the North–South problem. In vastly different ways, APEC, the EU, and the North American Free Trade Agreement (NAFTA) facilitate the mobility of capital and, also, labour. To enhance the competitiveness of open economies, and to provide labour market flexibility, countries at myriad levels of economic development have joined together, a process that will be taken one step further if Eastern European countries are admitted to the EU (Yamamoto, 1993).

In South East Asia's 'newly industrializing economies' (NIEs), high rates of economic growth coupled with a rapid demographic transition have resulted in elevated wages and labour shortages. Singapore, for example, has relied on foreign labour to mitigate problems in labour supply. Malaysia, which sends skilled workers to Japan, hosts about one million illegal migrants from Indonesia and others from Thailand. Unlike receiving countries in the subregion, the Philippines is a large supplier of contract labour and, also, a major exporter of skilled workers and human services. It is likely that migrants from Indochina will put further pressure on other parts of South East Asia.

The historical pattern of subregionalism in Southern Africa was shaped by South Africa's need for cheap migrant labour and services from neighbouring countries, which became parties to a highly unequal relationship.[3] In fact, dating back to the discovery of gold in the Transvaal, migrant labour has powered the engines of the South African mining industry. For South Africa's capitalists, a migratory labour system offered several advantages. So long as South Africa paid higher wages than the hinterland territories, it was sure to have a labour reserve. By recruiting workers from beyond its borders,

South Africa could keep wages in the mines depressed, ensuring that local labourers would not be diverted from home industries and farm enterprises.

South Africa's wealth in gold is largely attributable to an abundance of cheap labour rather than to massive deposits or to a superior grade of ore. Mines had to be abandoned when it was no longer profitable to sink deeper shafts. Meanwhile, the South African mining industry, taking advantage of low labour costs, has prolonged its life by breaking off ore at unprecedented depths before bringing it to the surface.

To understand present interactions in the subregion, it is important to indicate how the system of migrant labour developed during the *apartheid* period. The Transvaal mines recruited mineworkers from Mozambique and elsewhere to contracts of 12–18 months. During the first 6 months of employment, the workers received their full wages; thereafter, only 40 per cent, as the employer withdrew 60 per cent for remittance to Mozambique. The mines deposited this sum monthly in the South African Reserve Bank. Every quarter the Reserve Bank informed the Mozambique Banco Nacional Ultramarino (BNU) and asked if it preferred payment in gold or rand. The BNU always answered 'in gold', whereupon the Reserve Bank forwarded the appropriate amount directly to Portugal.

With the introduction of the two-tier gold price in 1968, the official rate was $42 per ounce and the free-market rate was $162 per ounce. Receiving gold at the official price and selling it at the unofficial price, the treasury in Portugal retained the difference between the two, sending payment for the miners' wages in escudos to Mozambique. In other words, Lisbon sold black labour to South Africa for gold, convertible at the free-market price.

In the period since 1975, when Mozambique graduated to political independence, South Africa sought to diversify its sources of migrant labour and to reduce the magnitude, part of its destabilization campaign against hinterland countries. Thus, the number of foreign mineworkers dropped from 237 832 in 1975 to 159 253 in 1991 (Davies, 1992, p. 13).

Nonetheless, migrant labour remains a crucial component of the post-*apartheid* and subregional economies. Large-scale rural–urban migration provides a labour pool for industries. Moreover, brain drain from other parts of the region benefits South Africa. Semi-skilled, skilled, and professional people are sapping the sending countries of human resources and are contributing importantly to

South Africa's economy. Just as South Africa attempts to convert its
economy from the old industries based on a racial monopoly of the
means of production – a plethora of laws designed by the
white redoubt to regulate labour supply – so, too, is the new power
structure trying to create competitive advantage, which entails flexible
specialization and a reconstituted labour market.

POWER RELATIONS

Looking at regionalism from the standpoint of power relations, it is
clear that the neoliberal agenda holds sway. In fact, there is little
evidence that other approaches, while important theoretical contributions, have been implemented with any degree of adherence. Autocentric regionalism and development integration schemes in the
ASEAN and SADC countries have not achieved co-ordination of
production on a subregional basis; they rarely articulate with either
the industrial bourgeoisie or grass roots movements. A number of
national projects promoted by subregional organizations could actually have been instituted without international intervention. Hence,
analysis of extant forms of regionalism necessarily focuses on the
neoliberal variant and the interests it serves.

Concerned as it is with purportedly universal laws of development,
neoliberal theory posits that, in principle, the same rules of economic
development can be applied across the board from the most developed to the least developed countries. As such, the theory is overly
mechanical and represents a slot machine approach to regionalism.
Taking an individualist approach, it is silent about deep structural
inequalities, especially the qualitative aspects of underdevelopment
lodged in the blockage of highly inegalitarian social systems. In addition, largely unnoticed is the contradiction between the openness of
neoliberal regionalism and its potential anti-regional thrust. In so far
as open regionalism strives for a worldwide market and hooks directly
into the global economy, it can skip over regional integration. The
rationale sometimes heard in business circles is that gains from trade
will be maximized through an efficient international division of
labour, not a regional one.

What is more, neoliberals' vision of market relations as a friction-
less world of shared meanings, the uncontested adoption of the
ideology of capitalism, is structurally blind to patterns of domination
and hegemony. Guided by a highly developed neoliberal agenda,

regional hegemony is a recurrent feature of the new regionalism, conspicuously so in the macroregions: Germany in the EU, the USA in NAFTA, and the sometimes strained 'bigemony' of the USA and Japan in the Asia–Pacific cluster.

The linkages in Japan–ASEAN relations aptly illustrate this pattern of asymmetry. If all imports and exports are included, Japan is ASEAN's largest trading partner, its major direct investor, and the chief source of official development assistance (Naya and Plummer, 1991, pp. 266–7). Although the USA has become the leading recipient of ASEAN exports, accounting for 21 per cent in 1988, the ASEAN countries are highly enmeshed in the Japanese vector of the globalization process: ASEAN is the base for production, and Japan is its core. As part of the 'JapaNIEs' integration scheme, many Japanese industries have relocated in South East Asia, with greater co-ordination of home-based enterprises and their overseas firms. ASEAN has become transformed into a production site for exports to the USA, Europe, and its own subregional market. The regional division of labour in such industries as automobiles involves the co-production of parts: within Toyota, for example, Indonesia and Thailand concentrate on diesel engines, stamped parts, and electrical equipment; the Philippines, transmissions; Malaysia, steering links and electrical equipment; and the Singapore office co-ordinates and manages various transactions. While both ASEAN countries and Japan can gain from such linkages, the ASEAN economies become marginalized from decision-making and more vulnerable to political and economic manipulation from Tokyo (Hamzah, 1991).

In other regions, too, the spectre of regional hegemony rears its head. To wit, the size of South Africa's GDP, $80.4 billion in 1989, is almost three times that of the total of the other 10 SADC members, $27.2 billion in the same year (Stoneman and Thompson, 1991, pp. 3, 11), and, by any measure, the military imbalance dwarfs such economic disparities, woven as they are in a complex web of historical interconnections.

Neoliberal theory has of course been put into practice in the form of adjustment policies drawn up by the World Bank and the IMF. The main beneficiaries of such neoliberal projects are internationally mobile capital, exporters who balk at restrictive trade policies, local industrialists to the extent that they are competitive with overseas enterprises, and domestic financial capital positioned to gain from liberalization and increased access to foreign markets (Hewitt, Johnson and Wield, 1992, p. 195). Not covered by the neoliberal umbrella are the interests of other social forces, which must seek an alternative venue.

THE ARCHITECTURE OF THE NRA

Having identified four responses to the pressures of global restructuring – autocentric regionalism, development integration, neoliberal regionalism, and degenerate regionalism (tendencies which can co-exist), it is important to search for signs of another conceptualization, a supplement to the NRA. The beginnings of a design for an alternative architecture may be found in the contradictory nature of globalization. Its integrative and disintegrative aspects establish a new polarity, which allows space for experimentation on a regional level.

On the one hand, a centralizing trend under globalization may provide either hegemony led by the USA or, more likely, co-hegemony, a form of multilateral governance directed by the triad of Europe, the United States, and Japan, perhaps with Japan serving as a junior constable for the USA (Mushakoji, 1994, p. 25). Centralizing globalization seeks to justify itself through universalizing values. It helps shape a hierarchical regional order, and transnational capital incorporates the regional project. However, the global restructuring of power regionalizes conflict. The post-cold war security situation is fragile because in the absence of countervailing power, vacuums are created. Hence, Sadaam Hussein believed that Iraq could invade Kuwait with impunity. Flash points now appear with great frequency. The on-going arms race and weapons sales in the Asia–Pacific and sub-Saharan Africa regions reflect the growing sense of insecurity in the wake of the cold war.

Another globalizing tendency is thus toward heightened competition and conflicts. The trend toward diversification takes two forms, one a structure of overlapping subregions and microregions, the other being more chaotic, involving myriad networks. In both cases, conflict arises because the present regional divisions of labour cannot be sustained. There are limits to the relocation of 'sunset' and 'residual' industries, for cheap-labour areas are pressing for additional foreign direct investment, higher value added, skills, and technology. In addition, the initial SREZs are spilling over into contiguous locales – for example, the Johor–Singapore–Riau Growth Triangle now extends north to Malacca and is spreading from Batam to other Riau islands. Growth triangles in the Asia–Pacific region overlap, and more are forming. In fact, competition among SREZs may eventually outstrip rivalry among countries, and each zone will seek its own niche in the regional and international divisions of labour (Chia and Lee, 1993, pp. 267–8).

New regional clusters of conflict may be detected on levels other than among subregional zones. China's microregions (export-processing zones) compete with a subregional body, ASEAN, for investment. In turn, ASEAN is losing investment to a national unit, Vietnam, with its low-cost manufacturing base. In a contradictory relationship propelled by neoliberalism, a number of investors from ASEAN have turned to Vietnam, contributing to its infrastructural, manufacturing and service sectors (Kumar, 1993, pp. 36–7).

Without attempting to provide a complete inventory of such regional clusters, it is clear that focusing too heavily on the macro level underestimates the importance of the micro issues. The micro-dimensions are especially important precisely because new production methods and technological conditions encourage specialization and diversification. The introduction of frontier technologies calls for small capital initiatives, not gigantic multinational R&D ventures (Mushakoji, 1994, p. 21). Moreover, there is opposition to the emergence of growth triangles. Opponents raise the question of distribution of benefits not only in terms of the nation but also in light of ethnic and racial access. Hence, the growth triangle among Johor, Singapore, and Riau has heightened tension between communal groups in that the Chinese Malaysians appear to benefit disproportionately from their relationships with Chinese Singaporeans (Akrasanee, 1993, p. 14).

While hegemony contains social conflict, it does not eliminate it altogether. The dominant culture sets limits to opposition, but in transitional conjunctures created by structural transformations, fundamental challenges may be mounted. In other words, hegemony is not a stable condition; it is always being created and undermined.

At present, a counter-thrust to neoliberal restructuring is emerging in what might be called the stirrings of *transformative regionalism*. While only embryonic, it is partly a defensive reaction mounted by those left out of the mosaic of globalization, particularly in zones outside the macroregions. The political and economic programme is not unlike that of the development integration model: close political co-operation at the beginning, not the end, of the project; equity and balance in relations among member states, including redistribution and increased trade based on regional industrial planning. Though a weakened actor, the state must be an active agent in transforming integration; its main roles are to rationalize production, build infrastructure, and promote exchange. Stressing self-organizing, the alternative formulation calls for regionalism that flows from the bottom upwards and is linked to new forms of cultural identity – the women's movement, environmentalists, pro-democracy forces, and so on. At the end of the day, the possibilities and limitations of transformative regionalism rest on the strength of its links to civil society. Creative potential for bringing about sustainable growth and democracy lies in popular support and a sense of involvement of multiple strata of the population.

Is this a pipe dream or a process given concrete expression? In 1989 in Japan, and in 1992 in Thailand, various movements and networks issued a call for a People's Plan for the Twenty-First Century (PP21). The PP21 process is an effort to promote a popular and democratic movement for social transformation. Trans-border concerns – the role of migrant women in Asia's growing sex industry, the struggle against environmental degradation wrought by the construction of golf courses and other resort facilities on agricultural lands, the role of Korean workers in Japanese-owned firms operating in Korea, and so on – are central to the agenda. There is recognition that the new vision can best be put into practice through co-ordinated regional action (Hart-Landsberg, 1994).

Similarly, the São Paolo Forum, founded in 1990, meets annually and brings together parties and social movements from around the Americas to discuss ways to build an egalitarian form of regional unity. What animates the forum is the magnitude and consequences of late twentieth-century neoliberal restructuring in Latin America. Neoliberal globalization – *cum* macroregionalism in Mexico – has displaced vast numbers of workers and peasants, pushing them into the informal sector, where they adopt survival strategies in a range of legal and illegal activities. Restructuring is depriving the state of its ability to regulate economic life, furthering the outflow and internal concentration of wealth. The social consequences are severe, with a teeming underclass barred from meaningful or productive participation in society. Although the forum has not fully detailed an alternative project, it stresses redirecting hemispheric integration away from US hegemony and toward Latin American integration 'with a nationalist focus and a continental perspective that addresses North–South inequalities'. With the restructuring of world capitalism, the solution is not seen as withdrawal from the global economy or exclusive interaction among Latin Americans themselves. Rather, emphasis is placed on regional co-operation and collective action (Robinson, 1992).

Although the Latin American experience differs in many ways from the integration process in Southern Africa, a common item on the agenda in both regions is the inclusion of social charters in integration agreements. One issue inscribed in these charters is enabling integration to serve as a mechanism for enhancing workers' rights and standards across a region. Other elements are corrective measures so that the pain of adjustment in integration does not fall heavily on the poor, the establishment of funds to invest in depressed areas, a resolution of debt, reform of immigration laws, environmental protection, some management of trade, the deepening of democratic practices and the creation of democratic regional institutions. In the Southern African Trade Union Co-ordinating Conference/Congress of South African Trade Unions/National Council of Trade Unions 'Draft Social Charter', the South African trade union movement has addressed some of these points (Davies, 1992). If they have to be prioritized, the last of the aforementioned challenges is the one that is likely to be the most telling: how to promote a strong regional civil society so as to involve people in decision-making at every level in a democratic way?

Notes

1. Some of these elements are integral to a Coxian framework for explaining the dynamics of the global political economy. See Robert W. Cox, *Production, Power and World Order: Social Forces in the Making of History* (New York: Columbia University Press, 1987).
2. Paragraphs in this section have been adapted from James H. Mittelman, 'Global Restructuring of Production and Migration', in Yoshikazu Sakamoto, (ed.) *Global Transformation: Challenges to the State System* (Tokyo: United Nations University Press, 1994) pp. 276–98.
3. The following discussion on the mining industry in Southern Africa is derived from James H. Mittelman, *Underdevelopment and the Transition to Socialism: Mozambique and Tanzania* (New York: Academic Press, 1981) pp. 59–61.

50   *Rethinking New Regionalism*

References

Akrasanee, N. (1993) 'Economic Regionalism: Which Way Now?' Presented to the international conference on *Southeast Asia: Challenges of the 21st Century*, Aug.–Sep. Institute of Southeast Asian Studies, Singapore.

Asheim, B. (1992) 'Flexible Specialization, Industrial Districts and Small Firms: A Critical Appraisal', in H. Ernste and V. Meier (eds) *Regional Development and Contemporary Industrial Response: Extending Flexible Specialization*, pp. 45–63 (London: Belhaven).

Bernard, M. and J. Ravenhill, (1995) 'Beyond Product Cycles and Flying Geese: Regionalization, Hierarchy, and the Industrialization of East Asia', *World Politics*, 47 (2): 171–209.

Chia S. Y. and L. T. Yuan (1993) 'Subregional Economic Zones: A New Motive Force in Asia–Pacific Development', in C. F. Bergsten and M. Noland, (eds) *Pacific Dynamism and the International Economic System*, pp. 225–69 (Washington, DC: Institute for International Economics).

Cox, R. W. (1982) 'Production and Hegemony: Toward a Political Economy of World Order', in H. K. Jacobson and D. Sidjanski (eds) *The Emerging International Economic Order: Dynamic Processes, Constraints and Opportunities*, pp. 37–58 (Beverly Hills: Sage).

Cox, R. W. (1987) *Production, Power and World Order: Social Forces in the Making of History* (New York: Columbia University Press).

Curry, R. L. (1991) 'Regional Economic Co-operation in Southern Africa and Southeast Asia', *ASEAN Economic Bulletin*, 8 (1): 15–28.

Davies, R. (1992) 'Integration or Co-operation in a Post-Apartheid South Africa: Some Reflections on an Emerging Debate', Bellville, South Africa: Centre for Southern African Studies Working Paper Series, University of the Western Cape (Oct.)

Drysdale, P., and R. Garnaut (1993) 'The Pacific: An Application of a General Theory of Economic Integration', in C. Fred Bergsten and Marcus Noland (eds) *Pacific Dynamism and the International Economic System* (Washington, DC: Institute for International Economics) pp. 183–223.

Emmerij, L. (1992) 'Globalization, Regionalization and World Trade', *Columbia Journal of World Business*, 27 (2): 6–13.

Garnaut, R. (1993) 'The Changing International Environment and Its Challenges for the Asian Market Economies', presented to the international conference on *Southeast Asia: Challenges of the 21st Century*, Institute of Southeast Asian Studies, Singapore (Aug.–Sep.).

Goodman, E. and J. Bamford, (eds) (1989) *Small Firms and Industrial Districts in Italy* (London: Routledge).

Griffin, K. (1992) 'Globalization and Regionalization: An Exploration of Issues', In U. Kirdar (ed.) *Change: Threat or Opportunity for Human Progress?*, vol. 1: *Political Change* (New York: United Nations) pp. 105–20.

Grinberg, R., B. Shmelev and L. Vardomsky (1994) 'New Regionalism in the Post-Soviet Space', presented to the workshop on *Regionalism and Globalism*, United Nations University/World Institute for Development Economics Research, Berlin.

Hamzah, B. A. (1991) 'ASEAN and the Remilitarisation of Japan: Challenges or Opportunities?' *Indonesian Quarterly*, **19** (2): 141–67.

Hart–Landsberg, M. (1994) 'Post-NAFTA Politics: Learning from Asia', *Monthly Review*, **46** (2): 12–21.

Hessler, S. (1994). 'Regionalization of the World Economy: Fact or Fiction?', presented to the International Studies Association Annual Meeting, Washington, DC.

Hettne, B. (1994) 'The New Regionalism: Implications for Development and Peace', in B. Hettne and A. Inotai, (eds) *The New Regionalism: Implications for Global Development and International Security* (Helsinki: United Nations University World Institute for Development Economics Research) pp. 1–49.

Hewitt, T., H. Johnson and D. Wield (1992) *Industrialization and Development* (London: Oxford University Press).

International Monetary Fund (1993) *World Economic Outlook* (Washington, D.C.: IMF) cited by W. Dobson, 'APEC: Redefining the Region?' Presented to the international conference on *Southeast Asia: Challenges of the 21st Century*, Institute of Southeast Asian Studies, Singapore (Aug.–Sep.).

Kabeer, N. (1991). 'Cultural Dopes or Rational Fools? Women and Labour Supply in the Bangladesh Garment Industry', *European Journal of Development Research*, **3** (1): 133–60.

Kant, C. (1992) 'Foreign Sector in Singapore's Economic Development, 1980–91', presented to the Institute of Southeast Asian Studies, Singapore.

Keely, C. (1992) 'Economic Integration and International Migration, Presented to the conference on *Social and Economic Aspects of International Migration*, Institute of European and American Studies, Academia Sinica, Taipei (Jun.)

Kumar, S. (1993) 'New Directions for Economic Growth in Southeast Asia', *Southeast Asian Affairs 1993*, editorial committee, pp. 22–39 (Singapore: Institute of Southeast Asian Studies).

Mahathir, Mohamad bin. (1989) 'Regionalism, Globalism and Spheres of Influence: ASEAN and the Challenge of Change in the 21st Century' (Singapore: Institute of Southeast Asian Studies).

Mandaza, I. (1990) 'SADCC: Problems of Regional Political and Economic Cooperation in Southern Africa: An Overview', in A. Nyong'o, (ed.) *Regional Integration in Africa: Unfinished Agenda* (Nairobi: African Academy of Sciences) pp. 141–55.

Marchand, M. H. (1994) 'Gender and New Regionalism in Latin America: Inclusion/Exclusion', *Third World Quarterly*, **15** (1): 63–76.

Melo, J. de and A. Panagariya (1992) 'The New Regionalism', *Finance and Development*, **29** (4): 37–40.

Mittelman, J. H. (1976) 'Collective Decolonisation and the U.N. Committee of 24', *Journal of Modern African Studies*, **14** (1): 41–64.

Mittelman, J. H. (1981) *Underdevelopment and the Transition to Socialism: Mozambique and Tanzania* (New York: Academic Press).

Mittelman, J. H. (1994) 'Global Restructuring of Production and Migration', in Y. Sakamoto (ed.) *Global Transformation: Challenges to the State System* (Tokyo: United Nations University Press) pp. 276–98.

Mittelman, J. H. (1996a) 'The Dynamics of Globalization', in J. H. Mittelman, H. J. (ed.) *Globalization Critical Reflections*, vol. 9: *International Political Economy Yearbook* (Boulder, Co.: Lynne Rienner).

Mittelman, J. H. (1996b) 'Rethinking the International Division of Labour in the Context of Globalization', *Third World Quarterly*, **16** (2): 273–95.

Morales, R. and C. Quandt (1992) 'The New Regionalism in Developing Countries and Regional Collaborative Competition', *International Journal of Urban and Regional Research*, **16** (3): 463–75.

Mushakoji, K. (1994) 'Japan, the JapaNIEs, and the Japanese in the Post-Cold War Asia–Pacific Region', *PRIME*, 1: 13–31.

Naya, S. and M. G. Plummer (1991) 'ASEAN Economic Co-operation in the New International Economic Environment', *ASEAN Economic Bulletin*, **7** (3): 261–76.

Østergaard, T. (1993) 'Classical Models of Regional Integration – What Relevance for Southern Africa?' in Bertil Odén (ed.) *Southern Africa after Apartheid* (Uppsala: Scandinavian Institute of African Studies) pp. 27–47.

Palmer, N. D. (1991) *The New Regionalism in Asia and the Pacific* (Lexington, Mass.: Lexington).

Robinson, W. T. (1992) 'The São Paulo Forum: Is There a New Latin American Left?', *Monthly Review*, **44** (7): 1–12.

Robson, P. (1993) 'The New Regionalism and Developing Countries', *Journal of Common Market Studies*, **31** (3): 329–48.

Scott, A. J. and M. Storper, (1992) 'Regional Development Reconsidered', in H. Ernste and V. Meier (eds) *Regional Development and Contemporary Industrial Response: Extending Flexible Specialization* (London: Belhaven) pp. 3–24.

Seidman, A. and F. Anang, (eds) (1992) *Twenty-First-Century Africa: Towards a New Vision of Self-Sustainable Development* (Trenton: Africa World Press).

Stewart, S. M. T. Cheung, and D. W. K. Yeung, (1992) 'The Latest Asian Newly Industrialized Economy Emerges: The South China Economic Community', *Columbia Journal of World Business*, **27** (2): 30–7.

Stoneman, C. and C. B. Thompson (1991) 'Southern Africa after Apartheid: Economic Repercussions of a Free South Africa', *Africa Recovery*, **4**: 1–12.

Stubbs, R. (1989) 'Geopolitics and the Political Economy of Southeast Asia', *International Journal*, **44**: 517–40.

Stubbs, R. (1991) 'The ASEAN Dimension in US–Japan Trade Relations', presented to the Canadian Council on Southeast Asian Studies Meeting at York University, Toronto (Oct.).

Stubbs, R. (1994). 'The Political Economy of the Asia–Pacific Region', in R. Stubbs and G. R. D. Underhill (eds) *Political Economy and the Changing Global Order* (New York: St Martin's) pp. 366–77.

Tabb, W. K. (1994) *The Post War Japanese System* (New York: Oxford University Press).

Thompson, C. B. (1991) *Harvests under Fire: Regional Co-operation for Food Security in Southern Africa* (London: Zed Books).

United Nations Population Fund (UNPF) (1993) *The State of World Population* (New York: UNPF).

Yamamoto, Y. (1993) 'Regionalization in Contemporary International Relations', presented to the conference on *Regionalization in the World Economy*, Tokyo (July).

Young, S. 'Globalism and Regionalism: Complements or Competitors?', in C. F. Bergsten and M. Noland (eds) *Pacific Dynamism and the International Economic System* (Washington, DC: Institute for International Economics) pp. 111–31.

3 Regionalization in Response to Polarizing Globalization
Samir Amin

Regionalization is an ambiguous concept. It may be designed as a subsystem submitted to the rationale of globalization, or as a substitute to it, or as a building block for a reconstruction of a different global system. This last view is the one which I shall defend here. This chapter develops the thesis that the building of large integrated regions in the Third World – particularly in Africa and the Arab world, but also in Latin America and South East Asia – is the only efficient response to the challenges of a continuously deepening polarization generated by the capitalist globalization processes. This response commands in its turn the type of regionalization needed, as well as the patterns through which the relationship between the regions and the global system are to be organized, with a view to curving the evolution of that system towards reducing polarization. It encompasses simultaneously the designing of correct economic strategies of delinking to be considered in the frame of those large regions and the responses to the political security problems, as well as to the challenges associated with ethnic and cultural diversities.

The World Expansion of Capitalism is Based on the Globalized Law of Value which Implies an Unavoidable Polarization

There are two ways of considering modern social reality. Either we put more emphasis on what we define as 'capitalism' at its highest level of abstraction, meaning the contradiction 'capital/labour', and we derive the historical limits of capitalist society from the contradictions particular to that economy. This option fatally inspires a gradualist perception of a required evolution through stages; retarded (or peripheral) capitalist societies have to catch up with the advanced model. Or we give more importance to the analysis of what I call 'really

54

existing capitalism', meaning by that a system which in its world expansion has generated a polarization between centres and peripheries which cannot be overcome in the context of capitalism. This vision of the modern world raises the unit of analysis to the world level. It is based on a theory of the global internationalization of the law of value in opposition to the prevailing liberal doctrine.

The liberal doctrine is based on the idea that the development process is simply synonymous with market expansion, and that, at the world level, it is just the product of a permanent adjustment process of national reality to world constraints. The naive version of the doctrine reduces the adjustment to the liberalization of trade and flows of capital. In its *realpolitik* version it considers the state policies as also basic parameters favouring or disfavouring this adjustment. This is therefore reached through the combined forces of state intervention and market dynamics. The theory pretends that the generalized market allows the maximization of growth and a balanced distribution. But the so-called generalized market is efficient, only provided it encompasses all the products and all the factors of production (capital and labour). The liberal doctrine pretends to have found its legitimacy in the fact that this type of complete integrated market has given the expected results. Yes... late and only in developed capitalist countries. The trickery is to extend this conclusion at the world-system level, even though the world market remains a truncated market, reduced to commodities and capital, excluding the free movement of labour and therefore a global labour market.

Keeping in mind that my analysis is situated at the world level, the various social forces which make up the world capitalist society find their place in this frame. By considering the world system as the central unit of analysis, we take the true measure of a social fact whose reach is decisive in the understanding of deciding stakes in social struggles, meaning that the labour reserve army of capital is geographically located in the peripheries of the system. The integration of fractions of this reserve army into the active labour army – always partial – is either done locally by the 'semi-industrialization' which characterizes the peripheries of today and tomorrow or migrations towards the centres. But this last option only concerns a small fraction of the world reserve army.

It is sometimes argued that migrations bringing labour to the work place are no longer needed, since informatization techniques of distance control have made possible the decentralization of production processes, the globalization of the production replacing therefore that of the labour market. The fact is true in itself, but the conclusions derived from it are certainly exaggerating considerably its impact. The manpower involved in such processes is and will remain in the foreseeable future negligible as compared to the hundreds of millions of people which constitute the reserve army in the peripheries.

Thus, we understand why history does not support the liberal hypothesis and that polarization is the unavoidable consequence of the truncated market on the basis of which really existing capitalism operates. In that way, the submission of national policies to the supreme criteria of universal 'competitivity' is a false response to the real challenges with which societies are faced.

I derive from this analysis a major conclusion: that polarization cannot be overcome as long the 'rules of the global game' are accepted, that is, the subordination to the so-called 'laws of the market', in fact the laws of a truncated global market excluding the formation of a global labour market. For those subunits in the global system – local communities, nations – which are the victims of capitalist globalization there is no alternative to 'delinking' from those rules. But the whole question remains: How? In which frame? To what extent? The radical wings of historical socialism and national liberation movements imagined delinking in the frame of the nation-state. Should we consider also large regions (such as Africa) as a necessary frame for that process? My concept of regionalization relates directly to this challenge.

The Forms of Polarization are in Permanent Evolution

The evolution from an international economy to the interpenetration of national economies in the world productive system, which characterizes the current era, does not open up itself to the homogenization of the planet, but to the reinforcement of the contrast centres versus peripheries.

(1) The modern economic system of developed capitalist countries has been built up progressively during several centuries, essentially on a national basis.
This means that this build-up was the product of a specific combination of social alliances particular to each country, which allowed a stable establishment of the bourgeoisie's hegemony,

through which a national state could be characterized by a particular political culture. The dominant social formations of the world system established in this way have shaped, in their turn, an international economy. We qualify it as an international economy because the behaviour of operators in this system is determined by the structures of the national social hegemonies in the central partners.

This edifice is now giving up to a new stage of capitalism. Progressively the elements of autonomy of national economies are fading to the benefit of a transgression of national production systems through the reduction of barriers to trade and movements of capital, shaping a global production system.

Is this evolution offering any chance to Third World countries? By integrating with this globalization process, can they overcome their historical under-development? Can they catch up with the developed countries?

I come to my conclusion: in fact the unequal development created and continuously reinforced by the capitalist expansion gives birth to a very diversified world. Consequently, no universal solution – 'the market' – can be effective and accepted. In this way, the significant difference between various world regions implies the adoption of specific policies which cannot be derived from the sole market rationality. The imperatives of our era imply the reformulation of the world system on the basis of polycentrism and regionalism.

It is vital that a true place be given to Third World countries and regions within that conception of world polycentrism. These countries and big regions which are able to co-ordinate their visions must submit their mutual relations to the requirements of their internal development and not the opposite, meaning not just adjusting themselves to the expansion of the world capitalism. This is the meaning of my concept of delinking, which implies a 'mutual adjustment' of both North and South, not a unilateral adjustment of the South.

(2) Capitalist polarization has appeared in successive forms during the evolution of the capitalist mode of production.

(i) The mercantilist form (1500–1800) before the industrial revolution as fashioned by the hegemony of merchant capital in the dominant Atlantic centres, and the creation of the peripheral zones (the

Americas) in function of their total compliance with the logic of accumulation of merchant capital.

(ii) The so-called classical model (1800-1945)   which grew out of the industrial revolution and henceforth defined the basic forms of capitalism, whereas the peripheries – progressively adding all of Asia (except for Japan) and Africa, to Latin America – remained rural, non-industrialized. Because of this their participation in the world division of labour was via agriculture and mineral production. This important characteristic of polarization was accompanied by a second equally important one: the crystallization of core industrial systems as national 'autocentred' systems which paralleled the construction of the national bourgeois states. Taken together, these two characteristics account for the dominant lines of the ideology of national liberation which was the response to the challenge of polarization:

• the goal of industrialization as synonym for liberating progress and a means of 'catching up',
• the goal of the construction of nation-states inspired by the models of those in the core.

Modernization ideology was thus defined. The world system from after the industrial revolution (after 1800) until after the Second World War was defined by this classical form of polarization.

(iii) The post-war period (1945–90) was one of the progressive erosion of the above two characteristics. It was a period of the industrialization of the peripheries – unequal to be sure, but it was the dominant factor in Asia and Latin America – which the national liberation movement did its best to accelerate within peripheral states having recently regained their political autonomy. This period was simultaneously one of the progressive dismantling of autocentric national production systems and their recomposition as constitutive elements of an integrated world production system. This double erosion was the new manifestation of the deepening of globalization.

(3) The accumulation of these transformations resulted in the collapse of the equilibria characteristic of the post-war world-system.
The post-war system rested on three pillars:

• the Welfare State and Fordism in the capitalist West

- Sovietism in the Eastern countries
- developmentalism in the Third World (the Bandung project, a national bourgeois perspective).

Each of these pillars defined a social and political order for each of the regions concerned, a certain balance in the relations between them as much on the economic as on the political and ideological level. It excluded in principle regionalization, each 'nation-state', whatever group it belonged to, being a basic unit in this tridimensional world system. Yet at the political level it implied three military groupings: NATO, the Warsaw Pact, the Non-Aligned Movement (NAM). Gradually these systems, at the same time competitive and complementary, have been eroded until, at the end of our cycle, they collapsed one after the other, thus bringing the cycle to an end. From that moment the world has entered a period of turbulence which accompanies the restructurations being made and their eventual articulation around qualitatively new principles.

The crisis began in the capitalist West and called into question the myth of unlimited growth. In turn a hardening of North–South relations accompanying the crisis of capitalist accumulation hastened the disillusionment with developmentalism in the Third World. Radical regimes collapsed one after the other and surrendered to reactionary structural adjustment policies imposed by the West during the 1980s. The collapse was the result not of external aggression but of a combination of the internal contradictions of the Bandung project and of the external crisis accompanying the overthrow of the existing world system. Sovietism, the third pillar of the post-war system, had the most shattering collapse. Here too, of course, collapse resulted from a dramatic acceleration in the Soviet Union's 'conventional' capitalism, as well as from external factors, namely, Washington's victory in the arms race.

History never stops. The completed post-war cycle can also be seen as a transition between what came before and what follows. At the end of the Second World War, existing capitalism still retained certain fundamental characteristics of its historical heritage.

The historically constructed national bourgeois states formed the political and social framework for national capitalist economies, with national productive systems, broadly controlled and directed by national capital; these states were in strong competition with each other and together constituted the centres of the world system. After the centres had their successive industrial revolutions during the nineteenth century, there was a near total distinction between industrialization at the centre and absence of industry at the periphery.

Since the Second World War both characteristics have gradually changed. After regaining their political independence, the peripheries embarked on industrialization, although on unequal terms, to the point that apparent homogeneity previously induced by a shared lack of industry gave way to increasing differentiation between a semi-industrialized Third World and a 'fourth world' that had not begun to industrialize. Capitalist globalization throughout the centres broke through the boundaries of national productive systems and began to reshape them as segments of a worldwide productive system.

The post-war cycle may now be regarded as a period of transition between the old system and the new. The essential characteristics of the new system need to be described, and its contradictions and trends identified. The uneven development at the periphery and the globalization of capital are the main challenges facing theoretical analysis and social and political practice.

Is Third World industrialization the start of a geographical spread of capitalism that will gradually obliterate the centre–periphery polarization? Or will the polarization be replicated in new forms? If so, what forms?

Is the lack of industrialization in the Fourth World a mere delay in the homogenizing expansion of capitalism on a world scale? Is the delay attributable to internal factors specific to the societies in question or to profound laws whereby polarization differentiates among the peripheral countries and marginalizes some of them? Does the decline of efficiency in the nation-states require an alternative system of political management of the capitalist system on national and world scales? Are we on the road to building such a system? If so, what will its characteristics be and what laws will operate?

To answer these questions we must take into account both the laws governing capital accumulation and the political and ideological responses of different social sectors to the expansion of capitalism. The future remains uncertain. Actually existing capitalism must adapt to the political solutions of the struggles occasioned by conflict of social interests.

I shall summarize the answer I have given in recent years. Third World industrialization will not end the polarization that I believe is inherent in world capitalism. It will shift the mechanisms and forms to other levels determined by the financial, technological, cultural and military monopolies enjoyed by the centres, but it will not replicate the developed countries' social evolution. Western society was first transformed by the industrial revolution and the ongoing agricultural revolution.

The vast lands of the Americas served as an escape valve for the pressure brought by European population growth, while colonial conquest assured an abundance of cheap raw materials. Fordism came along to alleviate the historic tension between capital and labour, facilitated by the reduction of the reserve army of labour in the centres. By contrast the industrializing Third World has none of these favourable factors to soften the savage effects of expanding capitalism. Here the co-existence of a rapidly increasing active labour army and an ever plentiful reserve labour army leads to acute and potentially revolutionary social conflict. This characteristic situation of modern peripheral capitalism creates political and ideological circumstances conducive to the formation of popular alliances between the active working class, the peasants, and the impoverished marginalized masses in the reserve army of labour.

In the Fourth World the social system becomes grotesque. The overwhelming majority are the marginalized poor and peasant masses excluded from any agricultural revolution. The minority ruling class can make no claim to historical legitimacy. Struggles in the work places are weak because of marginalization, so the conflict shifts to the cultural plane. This is symptomatic of the crisis but offers no genuine response to its challenge.

In the developed West the conflict between the globalization of capital penetration eroding the historic role of the nation-state as the management framework for historic social compromises and the permanence of political and ideological systems based on national realities will not be easily resolved. Neither US military hegemony nor a German-dominated European 'supermarket' can resolve the problem. Dividing responsibilities on a regional basis by linking various parts of the South and the East to one of the three centres in the developed North or West is no answer, either. In the short term the Soviet collapse is bound to bring a capitalist expansion similar to that of the periphery. Social democratic responses along Western models will not be allowed to develop here.

During the post-war cycle political and ideological conflicts and the expression of progressive alternative projects have been constrained by the historical shortcomings of the three prevailing ideologies: Western social democracy, Eastern Sovietism, and Southern national liberation ideology. The left on a world scale has shown some signs in the recent past of going beyond these visions.

In any case, the post-war period did not favour regionalizations, in principle at least (except for the political military isolation of the 'East', formerly 'socialist', and for the political bloc of the non-aligned 'South'). Strategies of capital expansion were designed in the perspective of a global open economy, while political systems would remain strictly national. Yet the period is also that of the process of European integration, starting in 1958 with the Treaty of Rome establishing the European Common Market, now, as of 1993, the European Union. Was this evolution an exception to the rule? We should qualify this judgement. The project started with a US initiative, that of the Marshall Plan in 1947 supporting the re-establishment of intra-European trade, as a subsystem of the global open system, not as an alternative to it. Even later, when Europe had 'caught up' and appeared as a competitor, it does not (or not yet?) see itself as a 'Fortress Europe' 'delinking' from the global system. On the other hand in the Third World, in spite of a large number of 'Regional organizations' established here and there (notably in Africa – ECOWAS for West Africa, PTA for East and Southern Africa – but also ASEAN in South East Asia, the Andean Pact in Latin America and so on), the Bandung project remained basically 'national'. Regional integration was thus systematically sacrificed when considered in conflict with 'national interest', that is, the building of a national autocentred modernized bourgeois state.

(4) The collapse of the post-war system is not leading by itself to a new world order characterized by new forms of polarization, but to 'global disorder'.

The chaos which confronts us today comes from a triple failure of the system, which has not developed:

- new forms of political and social organization going beyond the nation state – a new requirement of the globalized system of production;
- economic and political relationships capable of reconciling the rise of industrialization in the newly competitive peripheral zones of Asia and Latin America with the pursuit of global growth; and

- a rapport other than an exclusionary one with the African periphery which is not engaged in competitive industrialization.

This chaos is visible in all regions of the world and in all facets of the political, social, and ideological crisis. It is at the origin of the difficulties in the construction of Europe and its inability to pursue market integration and parallel integrative political structures. It is the cause of the convulsions in all the peripheries of Eastern Europe, of the old semi-industrialized Third World, of the new marginalized Fourth World. Far from sustaining the progression of globalization, the current chaos reveals its extreme vulnerability.

The predominance of this chaos should not keep us from thinking about alternative scenarios for a 'new world order' even if there are many different possible future 'world orders'. What I am trying to do here is to call attention to questions which have been glossed over by the triumphalism of inevitable globalization at the same time as its precariousness is revealed.

The reader will no doubt have discovered that this analysis of world capitalism is not centred on the question of hegemonies. I do not subscribe to the successive hegemonies school of historiography. The concept of hegemony is often sterile and not scientific because it has been so loosely defined. It does not seem to me that it should be the centre of the debate. I have, on the contrary, developed the idea that hegemony is far from the rule; it is the exception, the rule being conflict among partners which puts an end to the hegemony. The hegemony of the USA, seemingly in effect today – perhaps by default – is as fragile and precarious as the globalization of the structures through which it operates.

In my opinion the debate should start with an in-depth discussion of what is new in the world system produced by the erosion of the previous one. In my opinion there are two new elements:

- the erosion of the autocentred nation-state and the subsequent disappearance of the link between the arena of reproduction and accumulation and that of political and social control which up to now had been defined precisely by the frontiers of this autocentred nation-state.
- the erosion of the contrast: industrialized centres/non-industrialized peripheral regions, and the emergence of new dimensions of polarization.

(5) A country's position in the world pyramid is defined by its capacity to compete in the world market.

Recognizing this truism does not in any way imply sharing the bourgeois economist's view that this position is achieved as the result of 'rational' measures, the said rationality being measured by the standard of the so-called 'objective laws of the market'. On the contrary, I think that this competitivity is a complex product of many economic, political, and social factors. In this unequal fight the centres use what I call their 'five monopolies'. These monopolies challenge the totality of social theory.

(i) Technological monopoly This requires huge expenditures that only a large and wealthy state can envisage. Without the support of the state – something liberal discourse does not mention – most importantly for military spending, most of these monopolies would not last.

(ii) Financial control of worldwide financial markets These monopolies have an unprecedented efficacy thanks to the liberalization of rules governing their establishment. Not so long ago the greater part of a nation's savings could circulate only within the arena – largely national – of the financial institutions. Today these savings are handled centrally by institutions whose operations are worldwide. We are talking of finance capital, capital's most globalized component. The logic of this globalization of finance could be called into question by a simple political decision to delink, even if limited to the domain of financial transfers. Moreover, I think that the rules governing the free movement of finance capital have broken down.

This system had been based on the free floating of currencies on the market (according to the theory that money is a merchandise like any other) with the dollar serving *de facto* as a universal currency. The money as merchandise theory is unscientific and the position of the dollar is only *faute de mieux*. A national currency cannot fulfil the functions of an international currency unless there is a surplus of exports in the 'international currency' country, thus underwriting structural adjustment in the other countries. This was the case of the UK in the late nineteenth century. This is not the case of the USA today, which finances its deficit by imposed borrowings. Nor is this the case for the USA's competitors: Japan's surplus (that of Germany disappeared after reunification) is not sufficient to meet the financial needs occasioned by the structural adjustments of the others. Under these conditions financial globalization, far from being a 'natural' process, is an extremely fragile one. In the short run it leads only to permanent instability and not to the stability necessary for the efficient operation of the processes of adjustment.

(iii) Monopolies of access to the planet's natural resources The dangers of the reckless exploitation of these resources is now planet-wide. Capitalism, based on short-term rationality, cannot overcome these dangers posed by this reckless behaviour, and it therefore reinforces the monopolies of already developed countries. Their concern is simply not to let others be equally irresponsible.

(iv) Media and communication monopolies They not only lead to uniformity of culture but also open up new means of political manipulation. The expansion of the modern media market is already one of the major components of the erosion of democratic practices in the West itself.

(v) Monopolies of weapons of mass destruction Held in check by the post-war bipolarity, this monopoly is again the sole domain of the USA, as in 1945. If 'proliferation' risks getting out of control it is still the only way of fighting this unacceptable monopoly in the absence of democratic international control.

This five monopolies taken as a whole define the framework within which the law of globalized value operates. The law of value is the condensed expression of all these conditions, hardly the expression of objective 'pure' economic rationality. All of these processes, their conditioning, annuls the impact of industrialization in the peripheries, devalues their productive work, and overvalues the supposed value added to the activities of the new monopolies from which the centres profit. What results is a new hierarchy in the distribution of income on a world scale, more unequal than ever before, subordinating the industries of the peripheries, reducing them to subcontracting. This is the new foundation of polarization, presaging its future forms.

   I am using here purposively the concept of monopoly, not that of oligopoly. I submit that these five structural imbalances between the centres as a whole and the peripheries also as a whole operate as a monopoly of the first group is *vis-à-vis* the second. This does not mean at all that each of the five branches identified is operated within the centre by a single monopoly, or even by a national monopoly for each of the countries involved. In fact these branches are built up by a number of private (or public) oligopolistic firms, albeit supported by appropriate state policies.

It is now more than obvious that combating those five monopolies is impossible as long as the nation-state is considered the only basis for that struggle. Regionalization is the only alternative, not only for efficient autonomous efforts in the various fields of economic development, but no less in the domains of communications and security. In this respect, in the absence of strong regional security arrangements, the ugly present system will continue, the USA operating as a 'global policeman' to the exclusive benefit of the Western common 'interests' (as formulated by the G-7), re-establishing a US unilateral hegemonic political position in the global system.

In contrast to the dominant ideological discourse, I therefore maintain that 'globalization via the market' is a reactionary Utopia. We must counter it by developing an alternative project of globalization consistent with a humanistic perspective. Implied in the realization of such a project is the construction of a global political system which is not in the service of a global market but which defines its parameters, just as the nation-state historically represented the social framework of the national market and not its field of deployment. Regionalizations find their place and role in that frame.

Polarization in the global system has generated a contrast – and therefore a conflict – between societies: those of the centre (North) and those of the periphery (the South and probably the former East). This concept is wider than the concept of conflict of States. It takes into account the fact that globalization generates conflict between groups of firms, many of which being based in several countries of the centres and the peripheries. We have already noted that globalization has put an end to the concidence between the space of the autocentred economic productive system and that of its political and social management (the political state). This process has eroded the capacity of the state to run appropriate efficient policies and therefore reinforced the autonomy of groups of firms *vis-à-vis* any state. GATT is a good example of that evolution: it is an arena in which groups of firms rather than states operate, and the geometry of their alliances and conflicts change according to the specific issues at stake. But society in general, and capital in particular, still need political means to operate, and these continue to be provided by the state. Therefore capitalist competition and societal conflicts will continue to generate interstate conflict.

For Africa and the Arab World the Patterns of Development Pursued in the Frame of Post-War Globalization Processes Have Been Disastrous

These patterns of development have led the region to its current marginalization in the global system. That trend cannot be reversed without a reconstruction of these regions as integrated autonomous systems.

(1) The results of post-war development efforts in the Third World have been extremely unequal, measured in terms of conventional economic growth.
They would appear even more unequal if measured by the criterion of globalized capitalism, – that is, the capacity to operate in competitive open global markets.

The ideology of development has found its most radical expression in what I call the 'Bandung era' (1955–75). This ideology did not mark a divorce with the foundations of the world capitalist perspectives. Additionally it remained strictly national.

The tentatives of a radical 'national' reconstruction were included in what I call the spirit of Bandung. It meant to advance a national bourgeois modernization project, which was objectively part of the new dynamics of the world capitalist expansion (the industrialization of the peripheries), based on internal economic and social reforms (agrarian reform, nationalizations, populism, and so on). The conflicts with Western interests were limited; and 'non-aligned countries' could mobilize Soviet support to negotiate better terms. This strategy has collapsed as a result of its internal limitations (that of populism) revealing what I call the illusion of the impossible national bourgeoisie project today. The 'tentatives' of this radical nationalism have sometimes left behind them some achievements on which it is difficult to go back (initiation of industrialization and social changes). In other cases, mainly in sub-Saharan Africa the extreme fragility of the state structures through which they were carried out, have led to lesser results. Towards the end of this era the collective attempts to negotiate better international terms, known under the name of 'New International Economic Order' (1975) was met by a global refusal of Western countries, as a prelude to the 'counter-offensive' initiated from 1980. The alignment of Europe on the American strategy, pushed by the World Bank and the IMF, should be seen as part of that generalized offensive. But the collapse of the Bandung project has left more problems than it has solved.

The post-Second World War era had completely ended and the brutal acceleration of the collapse of the Soviet power is its most obvious manifestation. Are we heading under these conditions, toward the reformulation of the integrated world system and on these basis, toward a new more or less generalized expansion, even if it will be as always forcibly unbalanced? The discourse of powers and dominant ideology do not allow to see anything but this perspective, without even being able to assess obstacles other than purely 'temporary' whatever the exploding and growing internal contradictions which make this perspective less possible.

Restoration of the periphery to a *comprador* role is an accomplished fact. World Bank structural adjustment policy is its manifestation. But restoration to a *comprador* role does not end history. Bandung had many forms. According to circumstances and social and political conditions peculiar to each country and the play of world and regional forces, we have several families of transformations that have gradually occurred in the post-war cycle:

(i) above-board capitalist development accompanied by a so-called liberal ideology, although often characterized by state intervention, determinedly modernist and open to the world system (but seeking to control that opening) – South Korea, Taiwan, Mexico, Brazil, Turkey, Iran under the Shah, and some other Asian countries are typical of this model;

(ii) populist, strongly statist, and never democratic experiences, ambivalent about integration into globalization (with stronger emphasis on control of external relations than the preceding countries, or purporting to want this), usually self-styled as socialists and often supported by the USSR. Some of these experiences have gone further in industrialization, and others less so according to their historical legacy – Nasser's Egypt, Algeria and Iraq are examples of the first kind, and Tanzania and Ghana of the second;

(iii) experiences regarded as 'Marxist', as in China, North Korea, and Cuba. They begin, as in the Soviet experience, from a radical revolution inspired by the doctrine of the Third International. They are now aiming, in China openly, for a capitalism that purports to control its relations with the dominant world system;

(iv) Experiences that have never escaped from a commonplace neo-colonial framework, recording growth in some cases (Côte d'Ivoire and Kenya) or obstinate stagnation in others (the Sahel countries) in totally passive surrender to external stimulus.

There are many crosses between these theoretical families and sometimes a shift from one strategy to the other in the political phases of modern history. India, for example, is a mixture of the first two groups, but in whole regions of the subcontinent it remains a Fourth World country. Vietnam is formally in the third group but remains a Fourth World country.

These huge transformations have bequeathed us a different situation from that of 1945. Here one must take as key to the analysis the criterion of globalized capitalism – that is, the presence or absence of segments of the local productive system 'competitive' on a world scale or capable of becoming so without too much trouble. We therefore have distinct Third and Fourth Worlds.

The new Third World is made up of all the countries in groups (i) – (iii) that have achieved sufficient modernization according to the criterion of world competition. In this group come all the big countries of Latin America, East Asia (China, both Koreas, Taiwan), Eastern Europe, and the former USSR. This, I believe is, tomorrow's real periphery. It is obvious that their peoples may not necessarily accept the cruel fate capital has reserved for them.

The new Fourth World is made up of all other countries, in Africa and the Arab and Islamic world. They come in a variety of shapes and sizes. Some have taken steps to industrialization but have failed to become competitive (Egypt, Algeria, and South Africa, for example). Others have not entered the industrial revolution (sub-Saharan Africa, the West Indies, Central America, Pakistan, Bangladesh and Indonesia). Some are financially 'rich', such as the thinly populated oil producers (the Gulf states and Gabon). Others are to varying degrees 'poor' (from Côte d'Ivoire to Somalia). My criterion is not per capita income but the capacity for productive integration in the world system.

Some countries are a mixture of these characteristics. India is a classic example. Some are trickier to classify, as they are potentially or partially capable of moving from Fourth to Third World status: Zimbabwe, South Africa, Egypt, Algeria or Vietnam, for example.

These Third and Fourth World peoples all face the same challenge, but the circumstances of their fight are different. The challenge comes from peripheral capitalism that has nothing good to offer in social or political terms to the ordinary majority. The Third World peripheral social formations juxtapose a significant active army of labour and a reserve army that cannot be absorbed. This creates objective conditions for a strong popular social alliance capable of crystallizing through struggles over management of the productive system and democratization of politics and society. The barriers to this crystallizing are also real and diverse. The ideological obstacle in the legacy of Sovietism or the historical limitations of Maoism are not the least. Will the peoples manage to free themselves from the illusions of capitalism and avoid foundering in jingoistic nationalism? China is also in this group: can its avant-garde revive Maoism with a genuinely democratic component-autonomous organization of the ordinary people to counter concessions made to capitalism?

In the Fourth World social formations we are facing a situation in which the concept of 'people' remains ill-defined, in the absence of a viable productive system. These 'peoples' are in conflict with power systems which are themselves also not rooted in a solid productive system. These social formations may look 'rich' or 'poor'. They may be non-industrialized or so badly industrialized that the policy of return to a *comprador* role puts local industry at risk of being dismantled. I have explained how a disastrous but real aspect of the problem was a slide into conflict in imaginary realms. In the Middle East and Muslim world this factor is currently the main obstacle to crystallization of a democratic and popular alternative. The best guarantee for success in the imperialist agenda to restore the region to a *comprador* role is the alliance of oil wealth and the obsolete traditionalist discourse of Islam, notwithstanding its 'fundamentalist' aspirations. It is obviously under way. Anti-democratic handing of social conflicts becomes necessary because the agenda offers nothing to ordinary people and can be implemented under cover of religious traditionalism. In sub-Saharan Africa the flight into myth may take other forms, such as ethnicity, and can lead to a country's total disintegration, as happened in Ethiopia, to the detriment, of the future. The weaknesses of society find an echo likewise in the ambiguities of 'battles for democracy'. Without a crystallization of popular social forces capable of endowing democracy with a progressive content, what can be expected of multiparty politics and elections?

The picture described here considers societies, and beyond large regions of the world where these societies are located, therefore also groups of countries. But one may consider some countries and societies escaping the fate of the region to which they belong. It has often been argued, specifically with respect to small countries, that their integration in a larger developed region may offer them a chance of higher growth and even social progress. The Czech Republic, for instance, might be attracted by its integration in the German economic space. I remain sceptical *vis-à-vis* such popular views, typically those of a *comprador* attitude. Puerto Rico is fully integrated in the US system, and yet remains a colony.

(2) The strategic choices of the European Union has a direct responsibility in the failure of development in sub-Saharan Africa.
For the whole of sub-Saharan Africa, the reconstruction after independence based on the Balkanization of political map and neo-colonial alliance to the EU could not go very far. It has contributed in maintaining this region in an 'agro-mining' specialization which corresponded very well to the basic principle of centres – peripheries polarization of the past (from the industrial revolution to the Second World War). But it was not as such the axis of a new emerging polarization, based on the industrialization of peripheries. The Lomé Convention bears a heavy responsibility in this involution (the creation of 'Fourth World') of the most part of the continent.

● *What are the reasons justifying the negative choices of the European community?*

A study of the structural and conjunctural position of Europe within the international competition helps in answering this question. For a long time Europe covered the deficit of its trade with the USA and Japan by the surplus it obtained through trade with the Third World and the Eastern bloc. Thus, to be able to play the game of the world market, it needed to keep these unequal relations in its zones of influence. Simultaneously Europe has found a main outlet for its expansion in the modernization of its own peripheries (Southern Europe) and its proper internal modernization. On the other hand, the USA and Japan, by largely exporting their capital (mainly in Latin America and South East Asia), have dominated the process of delocation of industry in the Third World, while Europe has opened itself up to massive importation of labour from the Third World in order to sustain the rate of its internal expansion. It is not pure chance that this immigration was mainly from the European dependent zone (Arabs, Africans and Carribeans), which are more hit by the unbalanced global capitalist development. As Europe is relatively deprived of natural resources (as compared to the USA), it also attached a great importance to the security of its supplies from Africa and the Middle East.

(3) What are the medium-term prospects for Europe, the Arab world and sub-Saharan Africa?

Rather than begin our analysis by creating a picture of what the 'ideal' relations between the different parts of this region 'should' be like, it seems to me more worth while to look at what would be required for such an objective to be achieved. One will then see that developments in the recent past have made the future attainment of this ideal more rather than less problematic. One will also see that the convulsions which are already on the horizon can in no way be seen as being compatible with the ideal schema of development, but that they will on the contrary aggravate the contradictions in the system.

The 'ideal' model, of course, rests on a certain set of values, on certain criteria of assessment. I would define these criteria as follows:

- a closing of the gap (in terms of levels of development) between the different partners of the region – Western Europe, Eastern Europe, the countries of the former Soviet Union, the poor, semi-industrialized Arab countries, the populous and financially rich oil-producing countries, the countries of Southern Africa;
- an acceptable degree of national autonomy, enabling the elaboration of policies appropriate to the specific problems of these greatly differing countries, policies which provide progressive solutions to their essential social problems;
- a controlled opening-up of the countries of this region towards each other and towards other regions of the world.

It goes without saying that the realization of this 'ideal' would necessitate profound changes in the existing power structures, the substitution of new social hegemonies for those which currently define those power structures. To be more precise, such substitution would involve:

(1) the creation of a labour hegemony in the countries of Western Europe which could replace the hegemony of capital;
(2) the building of a popular social alliance to replace the hegemony of the State bureaucracy in the former USSR, tempered today by

the chaotic rise of the confused and ambiguous forces of nationalism and populism;

(3) the building of national popular alliances to displace the hegemony of the *comprador* classes in Africa and the Arab world.

Thus we can see the enormity of the tasks necessary for the attainment of the 'ideal' model for the region; for the social and political actors who might form the basis of such developments exist only as potential forces, while the political organizations and ideologies which currently occupy the stage are unable to come to grip with what is really at the heart of present-day conflicts.

If by an effort of the imagination we leave behind us the obstacles to the achievement of these transformations, one can see that the 'ideal' model in question would presuppose the consolidation of our three great regions (Europe, the Arab world and Africa) and the articulation of their interdependencies in such a way as to promote their development on the progressive and democratic social lines defined above. But we must also define the structure of the regional consolidations envisaged and the obstacles which will have to be overcome in the process. Some form of 'European integration' is to my mind not only desirable but necessary, though certainly not according to the current model (integration of the market according to liberal principles without any common, progressive political or social dimension), whether the latter remains limited to its present 12 members, or expands progressively eastwards. The concept of a 'common home', however vague, corresponds better to the requirements of our vision, because it presupposes a margin of relative autonomy which would make possible the specific application of appropriate policies in the less competitive partner states. Such a formula would not exclude a greater degree of integration within a smaller group of the more advanced countries, provided that any such integration fully maintained its progressive social dimension (the hegemony of the working classes), something which is absent from the European conception of integration. The building of 'African unity' and 'Arab unity' is the Southern corollary of this, and a precondition of progress towards the 'ideal' model if only for the obvious and oft-repeated reason that the states born of the Balkanization of the continent are incapable of taking up the challenges of modern development. In a progressive vision of a truly common future Europeans, Africans and Arabs must accept that they will be mutually strengthened by the consolidation of their respective regional unities and they must therefore cease to see the latter only as a danger.

Developments in recent years have certainly reinforced all the negative aspects of the polarization between the core countries and the peripheries which is inherent in 'actually existing capitalism': an increasing gap between the EU states and the countries of the Arab and African 'Fourth World'; the consolidation of the Balkanization of the continent and the increasing vulnerability of the countries of the region, an increase of internal social inequalities in almost all countries; limits placed on the cause of democracy and so on.

It appears to me even more serious that in Europe the dominant political and ideological forces on the left as on the right have been unable to conceive of Arab unity as something which might be desirable. Europe has still not rid itself of its traditional imperialist attitude which sees the 'other' – especially if this 'other' is culturally different – as an enemy who must be kept weak and divided. The world system of actually existing capitalism rests on this fundamental principle and there is no sign that Western opinion is about to renounce it. For the last 50 years in the Middle East that barbaric world order has had only one strategic aim: to maintain what is coyly described as access to oil – in plain English, the Western powers' domination over that resource in order to ensure that its exploitation be submitted solely to the demands of the economic expansion of the West (a situation which does not exclude conflict – albeit muted – between OPEC countries over how to exercise control over the oil). In pursuit of this aim, two complementary means are used:

(1) the divisions of the Arab world world have been perpetuated and the survival of the archaic Gulf regimes of Saudi Arabia, Kuwait, and the Emirates ensured in order to prevent any possibility of the oil revenues being used for the benefit of the Arab peoples;
(2) the absolute military supremacy of Israel has been guaranteed (notably by helping in its development of nuclear weapons). The Gulf War demonstrated that Europe had no specifically European conception of its relations with the Arab world independent of the American approach.

The different medium-term 'scenarios' proposed for North–South relations within this region can now be reconsidered in the light of what has been suggested above. The basic criterion by which the different scenarios can be distinguished is always in the final analysis the degree of independence of (Western) Europe *vis-à-vis* the USA, and the degree of regionalization within the world system which could accompany such independence.

The scenario of a collective European neo-imperialism dominating 'its' Arab and African South may have appealed to certain nostalgic minds, but the Gulf showed it to be impossible. If the oil is to be controlled by 'the West', the only way it can be done is directly by the US military, and the only alternative that Europe might be able to suggest would be friendship with the Arab peoples. This is no longer an option: since 1945, the UK has opted for absorption by the United States; Germany, preoccupied with the prospect of economic expansion eastwards, will keep a low profile in other areas; and France, having renounced the Gaullist principle of refusing to amalgamate its interests with those of the USA, has in the process marginalized itself. Even the hope of breaking up the Arab world by coupling the Maghreb to Europe did not last very long. As a result, 'regionalization' within the world system remains very relative. For if it is true that the USA and Japan have a greater and more direct presence in the Southern part of 'their' regions (Latin America and South East Asia respectively), the Arab world does not belong to the 'sphere of influence' of the EU but to that of the USA just as the whole of Southern Africa reorganized around South Africa probably will tomorrow. The 'European sphere' risks being reduced to the African Fourth World. Moreover Germany seems to be aware of this and is acting accordingly. As for the countries of the former USSR, they are far from having regained the capacity for having any kind of presence beyond their own borders. In the medium term, Europe does not exist, it is a political dwarf.

Should we then be talking about a restoration of US hegemony, laid to rest a little hastily? What is beginning to develop is, in my opinion, something quite different: a trio formed by the USA, Japan and Germany in which these countries have quite distinct roles and prospects. Japan and Germany will increase their advantage in the competition for economic markets, while the USA will play the role of the *gendarme* charged with maintaining this rather peculiar world order – a role which will be damaging to their economic competitiveness over the longer term. This order, which will probably be with us for the foreseeable future, I have called 'the Empire of Chaos'. It is not a question of a new world order a little less bad than the one we are leaving behind us (the post-Second World War era), but a kind of military world order as complement to the savage, neoliberal capitalist order. With this in mind, the Americans have already produced a theory of low-intensity conflict management. I am not sure whether the Gulf War has not in fact shown that the North–South conflicts inherent in this conception of the world order have already exceeded the intended 'ceiling' of intensity. I rather fear that the medium-term future will demonstrate only that actually existing capitalism is without a doubt barbaric, but that in its new, neoliberal clothing it is nothing more than barbarism unrestrained.

It is in this frame that I would classify what I call the neo-imperialist concept of regionalization, attaching different parts of the South to their North preferential partner: Africa behind Europe, Latin America behind the United States (the NAFTA scheme belongs to that neo-imperialist pattern), South East Asia behind Japan. The United States and the global institutions submitted to them (IMF, World Bank, GATT) which were fundamentally hostile to any type of regionalization in the post-war period, are now promoting these forms of neo-imperialist arrangement, consonant with the 'sharing the burden' strategy implied by the USA's relative economic decline. The regionalization that we need has nothing to do with those projects.

The neo-imperialist pattern of regionalization should not be reduced to three broad, large Northern-dominated regions (US–Latin America, European Union–Eastern Europe–Africa, Japan–East and South East Asia). A more realistic vision requires moving further down the scale, with a view to paying due attention to the unequal position of countries within these large subsystems (such as Brazil versus Paraguay, or South Africa in Southern Africa and so on). and all the historical, political and geostrategic dimensions of the problem. Some futurologists have drawn a picture of the twenty-first century world system as reorganized around some 15 regions coagulated around regional 'leaders' (such as Brazil, Israel, South Africa and so on). These plans are often produced by powerful agencies, influential in major governmental systems, particularly in the USA. They may give inspiration to actual political strategies of alliance between major centres and subregional privileged allies. Yet all these refinements do not change the fact that this vision of regionalization within the global system is based on a concept of global market logic.

Globalization, that is, the unilateral submission to the so-called rationality of the global market, is not really an alternative. It does not go beyond management of the crisis, and does not offer ways and means to overcome it. Therefore the only realistic alternative should proceed from combining:

(1) positive changes at the 'grass roots' (that is, the national levels), encompassing their ideological and political dimensions, opening the way to labour–popular social hegemonies;
(2) regionalization with a view to creating reasonable frames efficient for the political and social management of negotiated interdependencies, going beyond the strait-jacket which the nation-state represents today with respect to the challenge of the 'five monopolies' generating polarization; and
(3) the progressive building of a global political truly democratic system, far away from the concept of hegemony, offering a frame to the operation of interregional interdependencies.

Starting by the global end of the chain, I submit that a global political system would thus have major responsibilities in each of the following four domains:

(1) The organization of global disarmament at appropriate levels, liberating humanity from the menace of nuclear and other holocausts.
(2) The organization of access to the planet's resources in an equitable manner so that there would be less and less inequality. There should be a global decision-making process with a valuation (*tariffication*) of resources which would make obligatory waste reduction and the distribution of the value and income from these resources. This would also be the beginning of a globalized fiscal system.
(3) Negotiation of open, flexible economic relationship between the world's major regions which are unequally developed. This would reduce progressively the centres' technological and financial monopolies. This means of course the liquidation of the institutions presently running the global market (the so-called World Bank, the IMF, GATT and so on) and the creation of other systems for managing the global economy.
(4) Starting negotiation for the correct management of the global/national dialectic in the areas of communication, culture and political policy. This implies the creation of political institutions which would represent social interests operating on a global

scale, the beginning of a 'world parliament' going beyond inter-state mechanisms that exist now.

Elsewhere, I did consider in some detail a number of those proposals, particularly relating to a set of new global arrangements to replace the Bretton Woods institutions, now out of date in my opinion.

Bretton Woods institutions were conceived for the management of the global open system reconstructed gradually after the war, along with US hegemony. In that respect the monetary system was designed to ensure the working of the dollar standard. The World Bank was conceived as an instrument to control the flows of so-called 'aid' to developing countries and ensure that this aid perpetuate the dependent unequal participation of the South in the global open trade network, with GATT promoting the gradual opening of this trade. Later – as of the early 1970s – the global capitalist system moved into a long-wave down turn, as we have said. The roles and functions of these institutions were therefore revised in order to adjust to new targets, which are related to the 'management of the crisis' (and not at all conceived to move towards a solution to it). I stressed this point and tried to show how, in that frame, IMF and the World Bank have been turned strictly into managers of the Third World debt, nothing more. I also related this debt management function to the overall management of the enormous and growing liquid surplus capital which finds no outlet in productive investment and therefore has to be guided towards financial speculative investment. The US external debt, along with the Third World debt, floating rates of exchange, high rates of interest constitute together the rationale of that crisis management. Simultaneously GATT develops ways and means to protect – and reinforce – the monopolies of the developed centres (which are part of those five monopolies referred to above), not to promote free trade as it pretends.

I suggested another set of institutions and arrangements, in consonance with the needs of a polycentric world:

(1) replacing the IMF by a set of regional monetary funds and/or arrangements, the IMF co-ordinating their interactions; I consider the proposal of transforming the IMF into a Global Central Bank premature and dangerous;

(2) replacing the World Bank by an arrangement providing the transfer of capital from surplus countries to developing regions

(instead of their transfer to cover the US deficit as the global capital market operates currently);

(3) replacing GATT by a Multiregional Trade Organization in which collective negotiations on conditions of trade would be conducted.

All these proposals are in consonance with a strategy of regionalization aiming at the building of a polycentric world.

It is more than evident that current trends are not going in the direction described above and that the humanist objectives are not those being fought about today. I am not surprised. I would in fact be surprised were it otherwise. The erosion of the old system of globalization is not able to prepare its own succession and can lead only to chaos. Dominant forces are developing their activities in the framework of these constraints, trying to manoeuvre for short-term gain and thereby aggravating the chaos. Their attempt to legitimate their choices by the stale ideology of the 'self-regulating' market, by affirming that 'there is no alternative', or by pure and simple cynicism, is not the solution but is part of the problem. The people's spontaneous responses to the degradation are not necessarily more helpful. In a time of disarray illusory solutions, such as fundamentalism or chauvinism, can be very politically mobilizing. It is up to the left – that is its historic mission – to formulate, in theory and in practice, a humanistic response to the challenge. In its absence and until it is formulated, regressive and criminal scenarios will be the most likely order of the day.

The difficulties confronting the European project today are a good illustration of the impasse of 'globalization by market mechanism'. In the first blush of enthusiasm over the European project no one foresaw these difficulties. Yet they were perfectly predictable by people who never believed that the common market by itself could create Europe. We said that a project as ambitious as this one could not be accomplished without a left capable of making it socially and culturally progressive. If not, it would remain fragile and the least serious accident would be fatal. It was necessary therefore for the European lefts to make sure that each step of the integration of the markets was accompanied by a double series of measures – on the one hand ensuring that profits go to the working classes, thereby reinforcing their social power and their unity; and on the other, beginning the construction of a political system which supersedes the nation-state and which is the only unit that can effectively manage an enlarged market. This did not happen. The European project, in the hands of the right, was reduced to mercantilist proportions, and the left sooner or later offered its support without imposing any of their conditions. The result is what we see before us: the economic downturn has put the European partners in an adversarial position. They can only imagine solutions to their problems (notably unemployment) that are at the expense of others, and do not even have effective tools for doing that. They are increasingly tempted by involutive pullbacks. Even the sincere efforts to avoid such action on the part of French and German politicians on the right and on the left have resulted only in incantation.

Little Europe (the EU) is experiencing problems at the same time as big Europe is giving a new meaning to the challenge. This is an opportunity for the lefts to rethink the European project as a whole and to begin the construction of a confederal political and economic big Europe, that is anchored on the left by a reconstructed and united European labour force. They have missed this opportunity, and, on the contrary, have backed the forces of the right which were in a hurry to profit from the collapse of the Soviet Empire by substituting a wild capitalism. It is obvious that the 'Latin-Americanization' of Eastern Europe can only weaken the chances of success for a European project anchored on the left, and that it can only accentuate the disequilibrium among the Europe of the EU to the benefit of the only partner able to profit from this evolution: reunited Germany.

The crisis of the European project is one of the major challenges confronting the construction of the new globalization. But these involutive manifestations, these inadequate and tragic responses to the challenge of the construction of a renewed global system, are not found exclusively in Europe. They are seen throughout the former Third World, especially in regions marginalized by the collapse of the old world order (sub-Saharan Africa and Arab–Islamic areas), and also in the new Third World of the East (as in the former USSR and former Yugoslavia), where we see autodestructive involutions rather than responses equal to the challenge.

Given this background, there are a few scenarios which are proposed as realistic. I will show that they do not reply to the exigencies of the construction of an acceptable and stable world order. They therefore do not provide an exit from chaos.

The European question is at the centre of theorizing about the future of globalization. With the breakdown of the European project and the threat of disintegration, forces faithful to the European idea could believe it useful and possible to regroup to their 'second-best' position, that is, a German Europe. There is reason to believe that in this scenario the British ship would sail close to US shores, keeping its distance from 'continental Europe'. We have already started down this path and some have even legitimated this choice by giving priority to the 'neutral management of money' (a technocratic concept based on ignorance of the political meaning of money management), and conferring it (where else?) to the Bundesbank! I do not believe that this caricature of the original European project can be truly stable, for neither Russia nor France will accept the erosion of their positions which is implied by it.

To make matters worse, the preferential position of the USA is not challenged under the scenario of Germany's going it alone or of a German Europe. Nor is it clear that there is anything in this project that could challenge America in any of the areas of the five monopolies discussed above. A German Europe would remain within the US orbit.

There is a second scenario – for lack of an alternative – a second edition of 'American hegemony'. There are many variations. The most likely one is a 'sharing of the burden' associated with neo-imperialist regionalization, hitching Latin America to the US wagon and Africa to the German–European one (with crumbs for France), but not the Gulf oil region and the 'common market of the Middle East', which would remain the domain of the USA. The US presence is felt by the military occupation of the Gulf and indirectly by their alliance with Israel. And, one can say, by the symmetry of leaving Southern Asia to Japanese expansion. But there is no egality implied in this division among the three centres discussed above; the USA retains its privileged position. Here too I do not believe that neo-imperialist options of this type guarantee the stability of the system. They will be disputed here and there by revolts in Latin America, Asia, and Africa.

We should therefore focus our attention on Asia, which has been largely outside the Euro-American conflict. It has often been observed that Asia – from Japan to communist China, to Korea (Singapore, Thailand, Malaysia and even India) – has not been affected by the crisis and have registered successes in terms of growth and efficiency (measured by competitivity on the world market). One cannot quickly jump ahead and say that Asia will be the locus of the next hegemony. Asia, in this globalizing concept, is more than half the world's population! This population is divided among distinct states. In the place of vague concept of hegemony one could substitute one of Asia becoming the principal region of capitalist accumulation. It remains to describe in detail how this is occurring, the articulation between the different nations, and between them and the rest of the world. There are variants of the model. The easiest to imagine – the domination of Japanese imperialism in the region – is, in my opinion, the least plausible. Admirers of Japan's recent success too often underestimate Japan's vulnerability. It is because of this vulnerability that Japan remains tied to the USA. It is not seriously probable that China, or even Korea, would accept being subordinated to Japan. Under these conditions the maintenance of an inter-Asian equilibrium would depend on forces external to the region and here again only the USA is a candidate for this role, which would prolong its primacy on the world scene.

Nonetheless it is highly probable that the positions of these Asian countries in the world-system will be reinforced. In particular intra-East Asian integration may continue to progress and therefore simultaneously reinforce the relative autonomy of the region *vis-à-vis* the rest of the system and its competitive power at the global level. The success of the region in this respect is already acknowledged. That invites us to recall that the countries of the region have not first conquered a competitive position in the global market and then after moved towards their regional integration (whether remaining open or turning back to the regional market in a defensive posture). They have and continue to run along the two fronts: global competitivity and regional integration. How will the USA react to this? All strategies of alliances will, in my opinion, revolve around this question. It goes almost without saying that the development of China threatens all global equilibria. And that is why the USA will feel threatened by its development. In my opinion the USA and China will be the major antagonists in future conflict. What will Europe's attitude be? It is hard to tell today.

Current developments suggest different possible scenarios, none of which question the cause of 'North-South' polarization. The commanding logic of the capitalist system perpetuates the centre – periphery polarization. Its modes of operation are ever renewed and will in the future be founded on the five monopolies around which I constructed my argument.

One could say that there is nothing new in this view because polarization is almost part of the natural order of things. I do not conclude on this note precisely because this is what has changed over the last five centuries: peoples peripheralized by capitalist world expansion, who seemed for a long time to accept their fate, have over the past 50 years not been accepting it any longer and will accept it less and less in the future. The positive aspect of the universalization which capitalism inaugurated – and which cannot get beyond its present truncated version – is the worm in the fruit. The Russian and Chinese revolutions began the attempt to go beyond the system on the basis of the revolts of peripheral peoples – and this will be continued in new versions. The final explanation for the instability of the 'world-system' in progress is found here. Of course the conflicts that will occupy the forefront of the stage in the future will, as always, not all be of equal importance. I would intuitively give the determining role to future conflicts opposing the peoples of Asia and the dominant systems. This does not mean others will not participate in this generalized revolt against polarization, just as it does not mean that transformations and progress will not emanate from the very centres of the system. I have written elsewhere about this aspect of the problematic of the socialist transformation of the world and I will not go into it here. This does not exclude failures, dramatic ones when people resolutely refuse a universalist perspective. I have also written about this elsewhere.

A humanistic response to the challenge of globalization inaugurated by capitalist expansion may be idealistic but it is not Utopian. On the contrary, it is the only realistic project possible. Let it just begin to develop and powerful social forces will rally to it from all regions of the world.

This is the way to renew the perspective of global socialism. In preparation ideological and political forces must regroup in order to be capable of combating the five monopolies which reproduce capitalism. This combat will create conditions for 'mutual adjustment'.

In this struggle we have to reconsider fundamental questions on the ideological cultural front :

- the universal/particular dialectic;
- the relationship between political democracy and social progress;
- the dialectic of so-called economic efficiency (and the ways it is expressed: the 'market') and values of equality and fraternity;
- the definition of a global socialist objective in the light of all the above.

On the political front we have to develop world organizational forms which are more authentically democratic so as to be capable of reshaping economic relations on the basis of less and less inequality. In this perspective it seems to me a high priority to reorganize the global system on the basis of large regions which would group scattered parts of the peripheries. This would be the place for the constitution of Latin American, Arab, African, South East Asian regions, alongside China and India (the only continental countries on our planet). I propose that this objective receive priority treatment in the new agenda of the 'non-aligned movement'. The regional grouping do not exclude others such as Europe or the former USSR. The reason for this exigency is simple: it is only on this scale that one can effectively combat the five monopolies of our analysis. The construction in turn of a truly global economic and financial system becomes possible on this basis.

Of course the transformation of the world always begins by struggles at its base. For without the beginning of changes in ideological, political and social systems on the level of their national bases, any discussion about globalization, polarization and regionalization remains a dead letter.

4 Political Regionalism: Master or Servant of Economic Internationalization?
Helge Hveem

INTRODUCTION

Economic internationalization, mainly in the form of foreign direct investment (FDI), has been a characteristic of the world economy for many decades. It has, however, grown at an uneven pace during the last two decades. After a slump during the 'debt crisis' from 1982 to 1988, growth resumed and has become almost exponential in the 1990s. Growth, however, was faster in some sectors and macroregions of the world economy than in others.

Internationalization, by means of FDI and other economic mechanisms for exercising control across nations, affects the power base of political institutions at various levels. It also affects the efficiency of some of the instruments which these institutions have traditionally employed. This chapter discusses the implications of the internationalization process for shaping trade patterns and for the capacity of states to pursue industrial and trade policies. It discusses the hypothesis that regionalism is a political response to economic internationalization and its alternative: that the causal relationship is in fact the reverse.

Three theoretical perspectives on regionalism are discussed: *the realist, the institutionalist and the cognitivist*. Regionalism could reflect hierarchy and be motivated by domination strategies, but alternative interpretations do also apply. Parsimonious causal theory is not to be advocated at the present stage of research. Regionalism could thus open up an avenue that promises both sustainable development and other voluntarist options for particular regions to follow (AFTA, Mercosur, PTA, and so on). It could overlap with, but also

85

challenge unilateralist and bilateralist strategies in international relations as illustrated in the area of international trade. The question
whether regionalism is a stepping-stone to, or a stumbling-block for,
the renewed efforts to relaunch multilateralism in trade (the World
Trade Organization) is particularly crucial. But, above all, regional
strategies and processes should be related to the process of globalization as a particular aspect of economic internationalization and one
which affects the structure of international trade.

THE ARGUMENT

The present proliferation of research on 'regions', 'regionalism' and
'regionalization'[1] reflects several different and partly contradicting
methodological, theoretical and political ambitions. Public discourse
on regionalism and on cases such as NAFTA, the Maastricht Treaty
and the Internal Market, is often highly normative and conflictive.
The researcher should not entertain unrealistic ideas about the possibility of separating scholarly from public discourse. But the first part
of my argument is that we need less normative and more reflective
approaches to the research area. We are still not in an advanced stage
of scholarly reflection on the issue. Therefore we still need to develop
the epistemology and ontology of regionalism theory.

In this chapter the concept of 'region' will be reserved for international regions: that is, collectivities that reach beyond the borders and
political jurisdiction of nation-states. Regions internal to the nation-
state will not be considered. The concept 'region' normally has
a geographical connotation and refers, as in Buzan's definition of
a regional security system, to 'relations among a set of states whose
fate is that they have been locked into geographical proximity with
each other' (Buzan, 1991, p. 188). This definition is a useful starting
point. As we shall see later, however, behaviour directed at the region
in order to vest identity in or organize activity around it, should not be
confined to those states nor to other actors who are located in the
region concerned. The delimitation of a region is thus normally, but
not always determined by geography alone.

My focus will be on the political economy of regionalism, or the
relationship between political action and the provision of wealth, not
on the relationship of these factors to security, strictly speaking. I am,
in other words, preoccupied with such processes which are aimed at
creating, at maintaining, or at modifying the provision of wealth
within the organization of a region. That body of ideas, values and

concrete goals which direct such processes will be referred to as *regionalism*.

If scholarly reflection is to supersede the tendency for much of not only the public, but even scholarly, discourse to treat the phenomenon superficially and *à la mode*, it is important to start with a presentation and discussion of theorizing efforts. I shall identify three main approaches and then proceed to discuss their potential for understanding the phenomenon. Following Rosenau (1990) I assume that theory-building requires applying an open model by using the eclectic approach as a starting-point. This, however, does not mean that causation theory should not strive to develop a core, a limited set of assumptions and hypotheses. Parsimonious explanations are less costly than plural ones. The latter are, however, usually more realistic and hence to be preferred as a starting point. My second assumption is, thus, that we are still not at the point where strict causal links between regionalism as a body of ideas, values and goals and on the other hand concrete manifestations of intra-regional interaction can be established generally.

Another reason to avoid superficiality is the fact that not all intra-regional activity is caused by regionalism. Growth in intra-regional investment or trade flows are for example often used as indicators of regionness. This is not necessarily a valid indicator. Increased economic flows within a region may be caused by the decision of companies to expand their market in order to reap economies of scale, or invest abroad to circumvent national barriers to entry. In such cases a relative increase in intra-regional as compared to interregional flows does not necessarily reflect regionalism. Intra-industry trade is one phenomenon which may be related to company strategy as much as to regionalist motives and policy. The occurrence of increased economic (and social) interaction within a region should be referred to as *regionalization*. Regionalism may certainly cause regionalization, but not always. Regionalism should thus be analytically distinguished from regionalization.

For some observers regionalism appears to be simply either a threat to international liberalism or an effect, or instrument, of (imperial) hierarchy. Influential scholars who also play a political role, express hostility toward the phenomenon. Thus Bhagwati (1992) looks upon regionalism as a threat to multilateralism, whereas Nye (1992) contends that it represents a barrier to technological diffusion processes (which he sees as inherently global) and a source of vulnerability to smaller countries (which are in need of a global multilateral regime

for their protection). Others take a definitely positive view of regionalism and look upon it as a source of control, identity and wealth.
I shall review such views briefly when turning to the three theoretical
approaches to regionalism.

Bhagwati holds the view, also advocated by Hettne and Inotai
(1994), that contemporary regionalism is 'new regionalism', or in his
words *second regionalism* (as opposed to the one that was practised in
the 1960s). In Bhagwati's definition, regionalism is 'preferential trade
agreements between a subset of nations' (Ibid., p. 535). This is clearly
not an exhaustive definition of the phenomenon, but one which
reserves it for the arena of trade policy solely. Bhagwati's conception
is, however, appropriate in one particular sense: it indicates that
political action by (collective) state institutions is at the core of the
phenomenon. This is one of the main arguments in the present
chapter as well. The concept should definitely *not* be used to
denominate any kind of action and/or effect of economic transactions
or political action. In arguing thus the present chapter reflects as
much the 'old regionalism' as the 'new' that is highlighted in this
and the other four volumes in this series.

Many observers compare, and several of them indeed see a corre-
spondence of, the present trends towards regionalism with the experience of the inter-war period. Received wisdom is that the 1930s
represented a peak in the protectionist movement of the modern
trade system and that regionalization was one visible effect of that
movement at the time. I will not take issue with that literature in the
present context with the exception of one aspect: the assumption that
I may use the lessons of the 1930s to understand the 1990s. In
rejecting that assumption I agree with the conclusion drawn by Milner
(1988), but for partly different reasons than the ones she offers. In
what is referred to as a 'domestic political theory of regionalism',
contemporary regionalism is explained by three factors:

- the growing dependence of firms on exports;
- the greater degree of firm multinationality; and
- the shift in the composition of trade among the developed market
  economies from inter-industry to intra-industry trade (Milner, 1988;
  Busch and Milner, 1994).

First, and for reasons which were given above, it may be misleading to
use trade patterns, in particular growth rates, to indicate regionalism.
Doing that implies a too narrow conception of regionalism which is

indicated by more than a willingness to create and/or divert trade. Secondly and more important, the main explanatory factor offered to account for regionalization tendencies ought to be challenged. In Milner's own words, the three factors or trends referred to 'are motivating international firms to demand, and states to supply, regional trade arrangements' (Busch and Milner, 1994, p. 268). I do not believe that regionalization can be explained simply as a response to firm strategy, not even if one limits the discussion to international trade only.

Bhagwati also ought to be challenged when he concludes that regionalization – whether intended or not, but in his view mostly intended – is trade-diverting. In his view it creates negative outcomes for the global community with respect to the creation and distribution of wealth. But regional trade arrangements are not as a rule trade-diverting. They may be trade-creating[2] both for their members and for non-members (Fouquin, 1993). As Simai correctly points out, bilateral, regional and global multilateral co-operation need not be contradictory, but may be mutually supportive (Simai, 1994). Over this issue there is, however, a very heated debate which dates back to well before the classical article by Viner (1950). The debate reflects an issue that in the contemporary debate is coined in the question: is regionalism a stepping-stone or a stumbling-block to universalism? Also – and in a similar historical perspective – there is reason to doubt that contemporary regionalism is really very 'new' – that is different from the ones that we used to know in post-colonial, cold war times.

In what follows I shall focus on the link between political action and economic internationalization. Should in fact regionalism be seen as a political response to economic internationalization as suggested by Busch and Milner? Or: to what extent and under which conditions is public policy rather initiating and directing economic transactions? If my analysis departs from the assumption that the first question is to be answered in the affirmative, no unidirectional linkage (unilinearity) is assumed. On the contrary, by 'political response' it is not assumed that political institutions merely react passively and *post hoc* to the activities of economic agents. I shall therefore look at the second question for the potential of political processes directing economic, well aware that the analytical perspective should look at the relationship between the two as an interplay of forces where the two may mutually affect each other. As we shall see the direction of causation and the effects of that interplay are shaped by either bargaining among collectivities, by hierarchies or markets, or a combination of them with no fixed and stable ordering of their importance.

At the end I shall attempt to draw some conclusions with respect to the implications of the analysis for North–South relations and the development options of the South. As I pursue a political economy approach throughout, the very last part of the chapter is intended to open up a broader and more long-range historical systemic view.

THREE APPROACHES TO REGIONALISM

Regionalism is an aspect of the pursuit by social actors of strategies which are designed to affect one or several of the following important factors: the distribution of power, the pooling or splitting of identity, the flow of goods and services, and the (re)distribution of wealth.

Some institutions are by definition pursuing the regionalist option primarily or only; the Commission of the European Union being a case in point. The establishment of the European Coal and Steel Community was a distinctly political decision meant to avoid that capacity build-up, competition and subsequent over-capacity in these strategically important industrial sectors would become the source of inter-European (French–German) controversy. Those institutions could not generally speaking be said to be the result of a demand by private firms. They were set up by the nation-states to promote policy objectives that were common to national political institutions. As in the still rather unique case of West European integration, collective institutions represent some degree and form of co-ordination, conflict resolution or supranational decision-making. But most public institutions with some autonomous capacity to act pursue regionalism only as one out of several goals and hence regional co-operation as one among several strategic options. Nation-states pursue mixed motives because they represent complex political interest formations. This means that regional institutions may also be the target of state strategies to shape and change them, or even to weaken or destroy them. As an example both a former major economic power (UK) and a relatively small member state (Denmark) managed to obtain exemptions from the general obligation to join the unionizing project of the Maastricht treaty. A mixed-motive foreign policy (UK still being strongly linked to the USA) and domestic politics were both actively behind these outcomes.

Generally speaking, the more powerful the actor, the more autonomous it is and hence the more options it would be able to make use of. Thus the government of the USA may use a mixture of global multilateralism (as in the Uruguay Round), regionalism (NAFTA), bilateralism (as towards Japan) and unilateralism (as in the case of anti-dumping action not authorized by a GATT panel). Also the increasing regional character of European politics that is envisaged in the Unitary Act of 1985 is not only meant to enlarge the common market, but is as well meant to strengthen the position of the European Union (EU) in its conduct of bilateralist policy towards the USA and Japan. Developing countries, on the other hand, have often been simply adapting to the acts of more powerful agents, or maybe adopting them more or less directly. Several of the attempted regional institution-building projects in Africa and Latin America appear to have been modelled on the European Community (Chime, 1977). An example is the newly created Union of Central American States.

How may we account for the behaviour of an actor, more or less powerful, when choosing regionalism among several theoretically available options? Broadly speaking there are three theoretical perspectives or approaches to the issue: the realist or neorealist, the institutionalist, and the cognitivist or 'constructivist'.

The *realist* perspective sees the international system as basically anarchic, run by egoistic actors. As this perspective assumes that nation-states are the dominant actors, it assumes that states are unitary actors who, according to the principle of rational behaviour, promote their own interests as expressed in the ordering of their utility functions. The two other perspectives may also contain contributions assuming unitary actors, but they assign a different set of goals to the actors. Realists look upon actors as positional: they calculate their options according to their own relative gains and losses, and they are thus constantly engaged in a struggle for power to be able to secure for themselves maximum utility. In a typical realist perspective regionalism is the outcome of a situation where a major power acts out of one of the following three factors:

(1) the capacity offered by its own power position and a design to promote its own interests (imperial version);
(2) an attempt to counter the (threatening) power of another major nation (balance of power version); or

(3) an effort to build a system of collective goods, such as free trade, monetary stability, and so on (the liberal, hegemonic stability version).

In what is referred to as its *neo-realist* version, the realist perspective has adopted a structuralist view. In that revision a few elements of institutionalist thinking have entered, but two realist elements remain as constants:

- that the international system is anarchic rather than hierarchical; and
- that it is characterized by interaction among units with similar functions (Waltz, 1979; Keohane, 1989).

The main institutionalist element is an assumption that anarchy under certain conditions may be modified by inter-state co-operation and that institutions which are set up to organize such co-operation represent a 'glue', or a buffer. It regularizes interaction among the units which would otherwise, in the absence of these institutions, tend towards conflict. Institutionalist elements are, however, not considered by the neo-realists to be very important.

The *institutionalist* perspective is primarily associated with the view that action is the result of the application of rules and procedures of the actors' own choosing. Institutionalists are branching out into at least two broad schools: one which view the action as conditioned by international regimes or conventions, and another which explains action as a result of policy-making processes taking place within the actor. Institutionalists of the first type would be concerned with creating the institutional conditions for integration, conflict resolution in a context of conflict, and for implementing principles set down in international regimes. They would challenge the realist view by focusing on conditions for modifying anarchy and the (mis)use of power at the international level.

Some of the assumptions of realism is, however, taken into account by this first school of institutionalists. But some others look upon key realist assumptions as something of an exception, not the rule. Thus Hirschman's classical study of Nazi Germany's mix of bilateralist and regionalist policy (the Schachtian strategy) found the making of a region by linking Central European nations to Germany an abnormal strategy, a rather cynical imperialist design to make these nations totally dependent on German power and thus an instrument of its foreign policy (Hirschman, 1980).[3]

Institutionalists of the second category view policy as the outcome of domestic political processes and the functioning of state institutions and state–civil society relations. Some would, for instance, explain the achievements of Nordic regional integration when it comes to harmonizing social and economic policies by referring to the extensive co-ordination and consultation taking place between state and local bureaucracies. Or they would see the achievements of the EU in similar functions recently as the result of community institutions in Brussels.

While institutionalists tend to view broad institutional factors as having a stable role and a predictable influence on actors' behaviour, cognitivists view them as being subject to change. The cognitivist perspective presents actors as reflective, capable of adapting to challenges imposed by changes in their social and physical environment and to the behaviour of other actors. They act on feeling of identity, on a sense of community and mutual responsiveness. According to cognitivist theories actors learn through interacting with each other and adjust behaviour according to the insight they gain. The cognitivist approach opens up for a dynamic and voluntaristic view of policy-making and puts less or little emphasis on rationalistic assumptions or determinism. Regionalism would thus be explained not as a result of structural or institutional factors, but on the contrary as an instrument for changing existing international structures and institutions to create new identities, opportunities and alliances. Rather than believing in the determinacy of international structures and the stability of actor interests as is characteristic of rationalist theory, cognitivists emphasize that actors are capable of restructuring international society and reshaping interest formations. Cognitivism holds that actors attempt to pursue their own strategies based on their own particular ideas and goals. In another and overlapping representation of this perspective, referred to as the 'constructivist' approach to international political economy, a sociological approach takes precedence over the economic when explaining behaviour. Nation-states are not structurally or exogenously given entities; they are constructed by historically contingent interactions (Wendt, 1994). This means that regional entities can also be constructed through building new loyalties and identities 'above' the nation-state. The fact that there are different and competing national conceptions of the region explains why there is conflict over region-building and why it is thus problematic (Waever, 1990).

This perspective was laid out in a slightly different version and at an earlier stage by Seers (1983). His perspective on European regionalism as a process of creating an 'extended nationalism' is being adopted by Hettne to constitute the defining criterion for the 'new regionalism' (Hettne, 1994). If pooling of identities is a major factor in the regional project, it may be affecting international relations with benign or malign outcomes, depending on the circumstances, on the intentions behind the project, and on other parties' reaction to it (the play of friend and foe, or 'we–they' perceptions). Regionalism could be interpreted and understood within the context of the 'end of history' debate. The convening of an 'Asian Leaders' Forum' during the summer of 1994 is by some interpreted as a project for pooling of identities. It could be interpreted as a response to 'Westernization' (globalization as convergence by Asia to the West) and as a political process designed to define an 'Asian identity' (Funabashi, 1993). The 'Singapore School' (Jones, 1994) and prime minister Mahatir's preference for an Asian regionalism rather than that of the Asian–Pacific one (APEC) could possibly be interpreted in terms of such a project and analysed within a context of competing regionalist ambitions.

These three perspectives highlight particular interest and structural factors, institutional variables and common interest, and cognitive factors and voluntarist aspects, respectively. But all must face and cope with certain constants. It is for instance widely assumed that geography is such a constant factor. It is a widely held view that physical proximity is a defining criterion of a regionalism strategy. This, however, is not to be taken for granted.

First, the case for such a view is weakened, the larger, more geographically extended, is the region which participants define as the framework for 'their' particular regionalism project. There is no 'natural' region. Its delimitation – the drawing of its geographical domain – is always affected by politics. Everybody realizes why Cuba is not part of Caribbean integration schemes, but why is Myanmar not yet and Vietnam already a member of ASEAN? If Turkey is a 'natural' member of NATO, why not of the EU? Geography is thus far from the only, or maybe even not the most important factor in determining the composition and the viability of a regionalism project.

Secondly, and again assuming that actors have a choice among several options, it would seem that the logic of geography could be overruled by either a hegemonic power or the commonality of interest factor. The sterling area or the franc zone are examples of the first of these factors – that of hegemony as a source of non-contiguous regionalization. In other cases an additional condition for regionalism is that the potential advantages of geographical proximity must be supplemented by a commonality of interest among those who belong to the geographical region concerned. The Organization of Petroleum-Exporting Countries (OPEC) may have required cultural and political homogeneity of the Organization of Arab Petroleum Exporting Countries (OAPEC) in order to become effective. But OAPEC would probably not have become effective either without the community of pure economic self-interest among members of OPEC in high oil prices.

Also, and thirdly, the Uruguay Round represented a new experience in that new coalitions were developed across regions. Such coalition-building went far beyond the regionalism project and could, on certain conditions, be seen as an alternative to it. Such coalitions as the Cairns Group and other *ad hoc* sector-specific or issue-specific – alliances represented a new trend compared to the coalition-formation on the North versus South dimension, the UNCTAD caucusing or regional groupings that have been typical of global political bargaining in the past (Kahler and Odell, 1989). The new trend seen in the Uruguay Round, which by the way did not completely substitute these former patterns, cannot simply be referred to as a hegemonic project. The fact that major powers sometimes form part of such coalitions is no proof that they run it completely, or that other participants do not join for their own good reasons, for example, on the basis of community of interest. This again underlines the limited validity of the argument that regionalism is to be defined by geography. In addition it may as a matter of fact shed some doubt on the validity of the case for regionalism as a political strategy.

The appearance of cross-regional coalitions alongside with regional and traditional political groupings is another proof of the increased complexity of present international politics. As indicated in my opening questions this increased complexity may reflect a corresponding variety of responses to the process of globalization. But I also opened up for the alternative hypothesis: that the political precedes and directs the economic agent, including in choosing regionalism strategy. Turning to this issue, I first have to discuss what exactly is globalization.

REGIONALISM AND GLOBALIZATION

Globalization is, briefly stated, internationalization which operates at the global level. Definitions of 'globalization' abound; I shall make no attempt to cope with the variety in an exhaustive way. One good attempt identifies six aspects (RIPE, 1994) which largely overlap with my own proposal for definition criteria (Hveem, 1994):

(1) the emergence of a global financial market,
(2) transnationalization and the fact that technology is becoming redundant at an increasing rate,
(3) the organization of production at a global level,
(4) the rise of a transnational economic diplomacy whereby firms and nation-states bargain among each other on the world stage,
(5) rise of global cultural flows and associated universal identity, and
(6) the emergence of a global geographic space as relatively more and regions and nation-states as relatively less important (see Chapter 2).

Not all of these are equally important. Moreover, what is of considerable importance is how they interact or relate to each other. Some suggestions on this have already been made above. I shall not go much further into that question here. It is rather proposed that we should depart from the three theoretical approaches and then restrict the term to mean '*economic globalization*', relating production, technology flows and financial flows to each other as the most important indicators of globalization. Doing so I start by stating what globalization is not and then proceed to indicate, mostly by referring to suggestions made by others, some key elements which should be included in the concept. Having done that we may turn to the theoretical issue just referred to.

Realists would see globalization as a result of a changing world order in the strictly political and military security arenas. They emphasize factors such as the range of military weaponry, the spread of far-reaching and fast communication opportunities and the fact of global warming as making regionalized frameworks for action obsolete. Institutionalists would see globalization as an element of the implementation of universal principles of action such as collective security (under the UN), non-discriminatory (MFN) trade policies, national treatment of investments, or the spread of particular political (democracy) or economic institutions (private property rights, competitive market). Cognitivists finally should probably put their emphasis in defining globalization, on the spread and commonization of ideas, spread of information ('the Global Village'), or the penetration of one business culture (Fordism in the French regulation school tradition, the just-in-time practice in Japanese business culture, and so on).

One important task for further research is to investigate whether and how these various aspects overlap, link or interact in concrete processes of globalization. The present chapter can only give some hints for an answer of this question. It would seem most appropriate to restrict the term 'globalization' to represent the economic sphere, not security or culture, knowing how much these spheres may in fact be interacting.

'Economic globalization' is not increase of interregional as opposed to intra-regional trade. At best trade flows should be used as an indicator (if the ambition is empirical-positivist) of the phenomenon, not a definitional element. It is public policy on trade which is of interest to us. If one observes that a nation-state pursues a policy favouring interregional rather than intra-regional trade, that state not only is likely to favour GATT/WTO prescriptions for low or no trade barriers, but to actively discourage customs unions or FTAs. In this case we would witness a globalization project.

However, we probably come closer to a correct understanding of the meaning of the concept when we turn to flows and patterns of foreign direct investment (FDI). Transnational investment of this category seeks to control factors foreign to the home country of the investor. It is control mostly exercised by private agents, financial or industrial capital, but which has clear implications for the distribution of power in the interstate system. It is the capacity of FDI to affect the power core of the system which makes it more relevant than trade patterns for our subject.

Transnationalization transcends the domain of the public sector and undercuts the formal monopoly of the state on directing the foreign relations of nation-states. Depending on whether one pursues a Marxist or a non-Marxist line, theorizing links to this fact explicit or implicit assumptions about the resulting power relationship. I follow Stopford and Strange (1991) in arguing that it is fruitful not to assume that only one particular type of relationship is stable and generally applicable across the North–South dimension. I do not assume that there is an organic relationship between the state and capital (in the North) in their respective relations with the South. Rather one assumes a tripartite relationship where all three actors – home state government, host state government and corporate headquarters – pursue their own particular strategies, bargain among themselves and ally only on an *ad hoc* basis. The 'North' and 'South' categories, by the way, are by now, with the growing differentiation of the South and the economic rivalry in the North, mostly obsolete; they are used only as a matter of convenience. Rather there are relations among nation-states in the North–South system being shaped by bargaining over concrete issues which relate to the distribution of power and wealth. We witness shifting coalitions among actors across the North–South divide. The Cairns Group in the Uruguay Round negotiations on agriculture is but one example.

There are still elements of co-ordination and collusion which follow the Marxist or liberal economic assumptions about a community of interest, or common identity, ideas and institutions among, for example, capitalists. Theorizing on the issue a good while ago, I assumed the emergence of a 'global political economy' characterized, *inter alia*, by a close co-ordination among culturally assimilated decision-makers with common interests in profits or politics helped by the diffusion of modern communication technology (Hveem, 1973). This global 'technocapital structure' has come about in one sense: the communication revolution has offered opportunities to penetrate all parts the world system and laid the technological and partly organizational foundation for centralization of power. But other aspects of the evolution of the international system since the 1970s have contradicted the prediction then made. Among the most visible of those aspects is the conflicting character of the relationship among both nation-states and corporate leaders competing in stagnating or dwindling markets and under the impact of surplus capacity conditions. Strategic alliances and mergers abound, but we are at the same time reminded that an alliance usually becomes subject to external or internal pressure which may, sooner or later, undermine it. 'Strategic trade theory' is but one of the theoretical and empirical underpinnings of this proposition (Tyson, 1992).

The proposition that globalization largely if not totally directs the process of regionalization builds on a combination of structuralist and institutionalist theory. Whether cast in a neo-Marxist or non-Marxist version, it argues that the logic of the global corporation or the competitive market (representing in the extreme version 'the end of history') enforces a new global order to which the nation-states have but to adjust according to their respective capabilities. The proposition is, however, not totally tenable.

There is some prima-facie evidence for it. The patterns of foreign direct investment (FDI) over the last two decades are among other things one of increasing concentration in the Triad structure – agglomerations of investment around the United States, the EU and Japan (UNCTC, 1991). During the 1980s, and at the turn of the decade in particular, the pattern was that 'the foreign direct investment within the Triad has outpaced that in the rest of the world. The increasing share of intra-Triad stock reflects, in part, the growing strategic orientation of transnational corporations from the Triad towards other Triad members' (ibid., p. 84). But inter-regional FDI and trade still do not dominate over intra-regional. The report goes on to say that 'National economies are becoming increasingly linked in regional groupings, whether through initiatives at the political level, as in the case of the integration of the European Community, or through activities at the private-sector level, as in the case of regional networks of Japanese corporations in Asia' (ibid.). Several reports (UNCTAD, 1993 and 1994) sustain the general impression of an exponential rise in FDI (in the 1990s) in particular in the Triad. At the same time the reports see the emergence of regional clustering of FDI as something which is caused by different factors in the various regions. The organizational aspects of globalization are thus not universal, but differentiated across regions.

But is this a transitory phenomenon? If one assumes that globalization has primacy over regionalization, the question is: does continued globalization sooner or later lead to convergence of actors on the whole range of variables that affect economic performance, not the least political regulatory regimes upheld by national authorities? Corporate agents have already assumed co-ordinating roles at the regional level in several sectors. As an example, the Association of European Aluminium Producers organized an effective implementation of an export quota system to sustain higher prices, thus affecting price setting at the 'free' metal exchanges such as the London Metal Exchange. The governments of some home countries of the aluminium corporations are said to have been actively promoting a cartel arrangement, the main purpose of which is to limit the expansion of Russia's aluminium exports and allocate quotas among members.[4]

Support of the Commission of the European Union apparently was also vital to ensure the success of this project. There appears thus to be some pressure on regional authorities to take on a regulatory role that can no longer be assumed by individual national governments. But in the case of the aluminium cartel, intergovern-mental co-operation outside of Brussels appears to have been the key factor. The Busch–Milner hypothesis is apparently not validated by this particular case either.

The logic of transnational corporate capital does not represent a factor that accounts more than other factors for regionalization. The Unitary Act, the foundation of the process that led to *inter alia* the Internal Market, was not forced on political authorities by eco-nomic sectoral interests. While there was certainly some interest in creating a regional market which could support European firms in their competition with US and Japanese firms globally (Ohmae, 1985), the Act was first of all a result of the activity of political actors, that is interaction and a certain convergence of views among the governments of the Community (Moravcsik, 1991). It was also more the result of intergovernmental co-operation among autonomous national institutions than of the kind of role played by supranational institutions that is assumed by the neofunctionalist theory of integra-tion (Haas, 1964).

Another *force motrice* in promoting integration are social groups and their ideologies. The latter represent what may be referred to as civil society. Social groups which carry social rather than economic goals appear to be the typical carriers of the ideology of the 'new regionalism'. Their role cannot be fully nor correctly accounted for by, for example, functionalist theory which focuses on the role of societal actors as opposed to that of political institutions as agents of integra-tion (Mitrany, 1961). The communication theory of integration is probably more appropriate here (Deutsch, 1957). It sees the building of networks of communication and exchange of various sorts as a primary condition for integration to take place among nation-states. When communicative channels are multiple and well developed, views converge and building of a shared feeling of security result. Deutsch looked at the building of a North Atlantic community for empirical support of his theses. What is the role and importance of such processes in the present world and beyond the North? And besides: does the formation of the EC and NAFTA indicate a fragmentation of the North Atlantic community?

We need to know more about these questions. One final observa-tion would underline that point. It refers to what may be called the 'Chinese network' (see Chapter 2). This is a phenomenon, among similar phenomena, which reflects the non-contiguous character of nationality and the nation-state. We do not know whether the phenomenon of global ethnonational networks typically tends to promote global as opposed to regional identity and integration. For our purpose the 'Chinese network' represents the tendency, so obvious and very visible in the late 1980s and the 1990s, for Chinese residing outside of China to invest in the mainland as well as in other parts of Asia. Estimates are that at least half the FDI in China over the last few years – the single most dramatic boom in FDI world wide recently – have been made by expatriate Chinese, residing not only in Hong Kong and Asia, but even farther away. These investments stimulate production agreements and trade among countries in which investors reside. Most of these resulting flows of goods and services are taking place within Asia.

AN EVALUATION OF AND SOME FURTHER ISSUES FOR THEORY-BUILDING

These perspectives lead me to conclude with four general observations. First, political action is still making a difference, or more: it is vital for understanding why regionalism comes about and regional cooperation takes place. Research should therefore explore who are the actors and which are the motives behind regionalization in concrete historical cases. Secondly, and as a corollary to the first point, we anticipate more rivalry and bargaining in a multipolar system, less leadership by hegemony or hierarchy as in the unipolar system. This is a realist and structuralist point. It says that regionalization comes as a result of changes in the structure of the global system and the response of the main political entities to it. United States hegemony may not have declined as much as Paul Kennedy (1987) contends, but certainly enough in the economic system to make bargaining over issues possible. This line of strategic thinking was very much behind the Internal Market, and the outcome of the Uruguay Round appears to support this conclusion as well.

The third point is that the cognitivist perspective should supplement the combination of a realist and institutionalist perspective, a combination chosen by many colleagues. Doing that may lead us to recast or modify the importance normally attached to geography, transaction costs and the like in assessing the potential for regional strategies. It also supports the notion that regionalism has much, or primarily to do with identity. Emphasizing the cognitivist approach also puts us in a better position to understand the role played by communicative processes in creating the basis for co-operation at the international level.

The fourth and final point is potentially the most radical challenge to theorizing. It refers to the fact that political practice, as do economic processes under internationalization, to a large extent makes the distinction between international and domestic levels of political activity obsolete. The point is not necessarily that the nation-state is 'through as an entity'. Instead of sustaining the Sovereignty at Bay thesis of Vernon (1971) it is submitted that the 'second image reversed' assumption of Gourevitch (1978) and carried further by Putnam (1988) and others are promising ways to approach the issue of determining the relationship between political entities at various levels of social organization, that is the relationship between the nation-state and a regional entity in particular. Summarizing their points the relationship between entities at the international and national levels is one of a two-way influence where interstate bargaining is supplemented and supported (or hindered) by bargaining between the state and its domestic clients, such as business elites, organized interest groups, voting communities and so on. The authority of a regional body *vis-à-vis* that of state institutions may thus be a function of the ability of that body to bargain effectively with (member) states, or in many cases even particular interest formations within the nation-state. In political and realist-institutionalist terms, one may therefore say that a regionalist strategy is successful to the extent it manages to discipline members to make them abide by common rules, collective policy and refrain from free-riding on the collective good produced by the regional institution.

One of my assumptions has been that there is no general, unilinear relationship between globalization and regionalism. The process of globalization in the economic sphere appears to be spreading, but is still not dominant to the extent that national, regional or subregional levels of organization are becoming obsolete. Regionalism is sometimes a response to the globalization process, but it is quite often initiated with little or no relationship to it. Besides, the globalization process may create a counter-movement of the Polanyi type which halts or reverts it. Theorizing which overlooks these factors and holds economic and sociocultural globalization to be a one-way movement is certainly making a fatal error.

The implication of this observation is that Ohmae is not correct when he generalizes that 'on the global economic map the lines that now matter are not imposed by political fiat. They are drawn by the deft but invisible hand of the global market for goods and services' (Ohmae, 1993, p. 79). Processes are very much the result of a visible political hand, including that of regionalism as we have defined it. But it is not always easy to say what the hand is doing and why.

Another assumption is that the 'new regionalism' may be partly reflected in the role of societal actors, but that their actual role needs to be more researched. Extending the Chinese network – the effect of which is to contribute to internationalization, but above all probably to a regionalism in Asia that is integrating mainland China with Hong Kong and Taiwan plus some other pockets of Chinese capitalism in Asia – could, by a stretch of our imagination perhaps, be said to represent a 'region state' in Ohmae's words. But it comes about through political action, in particular the change to an open door economic policy in China after the late 1970s, and as a result of the manifestation of ethnonational identity. It is not primarily a result of discreet market forces. The creation of the European Economic Area (EEA) and NAFTA is the result of both market forces and company strategy (interpenetration of manufacturing industries and services in particular requiring co-ordination of national policies) and of political action. The latter is not only quite important, but in fact decisive at times. And the problems facing the prospect of an Asian grouping which includes both Japan and the Asian NICs, one of Ohmae's favoured projects, are more political or sociopolitical than economic. In some other contexts it is private agents, or a bottom-up process, who appear to drive the regionalism project ahead despite the reluctance or non-action of public, state agents. One example of such bottom-up regionalism efforts is probably the proposed Barents Sea Region.

Three Propositions

These general observations and the illustrations that followed, lead to three hypotheses which reflect some of the questions which I asked in the introductory part.

(1) *Regionalism is not simply a response to globalization, but is more often a matter of identity.* It is often reflecting a voluntarist tendency – a design to organize spheres of interest (realism), organize co-operative or conflict-resolving procedures and processes (institutionalist) or pool identity and/or knowledge in order to strengthen a community of interest (cognitivist). Or regionalism

may be a response to some other idea or community of interest, in particular to internationalizing or globalizing forces. I have argued that the former are more important than the latter.

(2) *Regionalism is often but not always initiated by state institutions, whereas it is usually organized and managed by them.* Other actors, societal groups as well as economic interests, may occasionally assume a leading role in initiating, but not in managing regional institutions. It is in how these various actors, at various levels of social organization, interact that we may trace the answer.

(3) *Regionalism is not as a rule a stumbling-block to globalism, but could act as a stepping-stone.* Which tendency prevails depends on the historical circumstances and the effects of the processes to which it leads.

Globalization is normally caused by economic actors who perceive their interests as being less tied to the economic spheres of nation-states or international regions, more tied to global markets and in particular to global production and technology networks. Regionalism may be motivated by a desire to modify or counteract globalization, in the name of regional identity (thus the EC's response to *le defi americain* and its attempt to counteract the image of Eurosclerosis). In so doing political actors may of course be lobbied by economic agents, such as labour unions or more importantly less competitive manufacturing firms or their organizations. If globalization were the driving-force in the whole of the international system – that is, had a strong and pervasive effect overall – then such interests would feel that an optimal strategy for political action would be to mobilize a collectivity of states and attempt to either stem the tide of globalization or provide some minimum of control over it. Assuming some degree of state autonomy, in other words assuming that the state is not merely captured by the forces of economic globalization (which seems a correct assumption to make), state authorities could co-operate to control those forces. This is the European Social Democratic project for the EU.

The Challenge of Bilateralism

Alternatively, political (state) authorities could seek control at a level corresponding to the globalization process, that is at the global level and through some international regime with wide, multi-regional membership. Examples of institutions at this level are the 34 international agreements or organizations dealing with FDI, and above all the WTO. But there is a lot of scepticism as to how effective such institutions may be to effectuate some degree of control over globalization processes. The test of the WTO will be the results of the series of dispute-settlement cases (panels) which are expected. The TRIPs agreement of the WTO, for instance, appears to give 'globalizing' interests a stronger hand *vis-à-vis* state institutions when it comes to controlling the effects, in particular distributive effects, of international technology flows (Hveem, 1995).

The strength of multilateral global institutions is at the same time their weakness. The resources it takes to negotiate them could be less than it would take to negotiate a corresponding network of bilateral agreements or regional arrangements. But the resources it takes to police the global agreement could be greater than in the case of the latter arrangements. Even regional arrangements could, however, lose to bilateral ones as political and economic actors consider their options. The problems associated with multilateral global institutions could also apply to regional ones. Bilateralism is an alternative to both of them because it has shown considerable strength not the least during the 1980s.

The strength of bilateral institutions – there are some 400 investment treaties and a great number of trade agreements concluded and managed on a bilateral basis – is their capacity to discipline parties (Yarbrough and Yarbrough, 1988). In a separate project it was found that some 375 bilateral trade regulating agreements were in operation during the whole or some part of the 1980s (Hveem, 1992).

The problem of large numbers is that it requires considerable resources to negotiate and monitor dozens or hundreds of agreements separately. Transaction costs may be very high. But the advantage is not the least that monitoring is more feasible and the probability of efficient control higher than in a multilateral agreement. Relatively resource-rich actors, such as the economic great powers of the Triad, can thus make a relative gain on bilateralism. The latter represent an advantage in that it offers the option of being selective. The great power does not need to control all other actors, only those which it perceives to be a threat to its own strategy. Also, global arrangements appear to be weakened by the fact that it takes a lot of effort to negotiate deals which are acceptable not only to all concerned national governments, but to their respective domestic interest group coalitions. Trade and industrial policy is domestic politics. It is often easier to accommodate domestic interest groups in bilateral than in multilateral global arrangements. This represents another argument in favour of bilateralism. The mechanism at work here is likely to be the following: the more parties are involved at the international level, the more issues and sectors must be involved to make a solution that is acceptable to all parties. But the more sectors which are involved for that reason, the more complex is the bargaining that has to be done at the domestic level.

These rather general observations offer an explanation of the seemingly paradoxical co-existence of bilateralism and multilateralism in the contemporary system (Gilpin, 1991). It also explains why it is so difficult to make GATT and its successor, the WTO, work effectively and why those countries who can benefit from the bilateralist option, in particular the major economic powers, will feel tempted to use it before the multilateral institution. Even in relations among themselves, such as in the G-7/G-5, the major powers appear to prefer bilateral deals over arrangements which co-ordinate *à sept ou à cinq*.

Options for Regionalism: The General Case

Could regionalization represent a compromise between the global and the bilateral options? In particular many observers believe that a combination of regional clustering, particularly in the Triad, and bilateral arrangements between the Three would be an optimal solution for the present problems of co-ordinating policy and managing the globalization process. Or put differently: regionalism may be perceived as a second-best solution when everybody considers his or her individual interests, but as a first-best solution when, as a next step, everybody realizes that compromising is necessary.

The fact that many observers, and not the least many political actors, appear to perceive regionalism as a compromise may make it a favoured political strategy. This is a cognitivist prediction. The present preoccupation with the Triad among and within the Triad members themselves is in itself a good reason to act: any one of the three would want to lead in the process of putting its act together in order not to lose out in the 'Struggle for the global product' (Schmidt, 1974) or 'Struggle for relative efficiency' (MacKinder, 1904). Such an explanation of regionalism does, however, have an overtone of realism, of geopolitical determinism, that may not be very fruitful. Not surprisingly Japan has already voiced concern that the increased emphasis on regionalism in international trade will represent a road towards protectionism. Since WTO does not contain clear rules to monitor regional

FTAs, the Japanese government urges such rules to be worked out within the G-7 and the WTO (*Nikkei Weekly*, 10 April 1995).

What seems relatively certain, and thus fruitful, is that regional political entities may come to play a role as a compromise between globalism and unilateralism or bilateralism, but that it would do so for *certain* purposes, not for all. If regional projects were to be dominated by the Triad members and they would remain preoccupied with their interrelationship, then the developing and the transition countries may lose.

Again perspectives on such an outcome will differ. Realists, even hegemonic stability theorists, may in fact shift from the latters' emphasis on hierarchy as a stabilizing factor to emphasise some sort of balance of power among regional 'blocs'. Idealists may see regionalism as a response to the vacuum left after the end of the hierarchy of the cold-war system.

I believe that developments in three particular areas will determine the future character of the international system with respect to the issues that I have dealt with:

(1) the evolution of the international financial system, in particular the policy on capital movements and the ability or disability of the main actors (those representing internationally important currencies) to control against potentially destabilising agents, in particular speculators, in the financial market (Strange, 1986);

(2) the evolution of competitiveness in terms of who will be leading or not the race in hi-tech industries and the mastering of the new technologies which are at the front of industrial modernization; and

(3) the outcome of the 'competition' among global multilateralist, regional free trade arrangements and the bilateralist tendencies in the major economic powers, mainly the USA.

It is anybody's guess what the outcome of these three trends will be in the 1990s and beyond. In follow-ups to this chapter I shall present some scenarios.

Implications for Development

Does regionalism have a real chance among developing and transition economy countries? And is it an instrument for development? Or rather: under which conditions could it be such an instrument?

In a globalized world no regionalism project can be completely isolated from the influence of factors and agents outside the region. The relationship within the Triad is in itself proof that a large part of the agenda for regionalism projects deals with the issue of how to handle reciprocity demands in matters arising from interpenetration (for example, through cross-investments) and exchange. The issue here is briefly put: how much regionalism agents can define the project in terms of 'we–they' mechanisms in order to shape an identity within a region in juxtaposition to some exogenous entity, or how much they will be obliged or forced to moderate the use of such a mechanism.

Research on the relevance of this issue for developing countries is being multiplied and is also well reflected in the contributions of other authors in this volume and the other four related collections. A tentative and very summary-like overview of the issue would probably begin by emphasizing the following structural factors, formulated here as three mainstream and two radical–critical propositions, as likely to determine the answer:

(1)   the type of initiative and/or agents that are behind the project, that is the goal and interests which it is meant to serve;
(2)   the resource base available for the project to be launched and carried through (economies of scale, manpower, infrastructure, institutional capacity not the least);
(3)   whether or not the countries concerned are complementary to each other or compete in terms of production and export profiles (Chime, 1977); and, *more radically*
(4)   exogenous political conditions such as geopolitics or the presence of strong major power stakes in the region (strategic resources, and so on); and
(5)   the presence of strong and dominant transnational actors who dominate or 'confiscate' the regional integration project (Girvan and Jefferson, 1977).

Received wisdom is that regionalism as a successful political strategy is a phenomenon of the structurally and economically developed industrialized world. Although most regional institutions at the inter-state level in fact have been set up among developing countries, few of them appear to have been more than just formal organizations with little practical effect. From this observation some have inferred that the level of development is a prime condition for success. Haggard makes this case in more general and global terms when he argues that:

(6) the lower the level of development the less inclined are countries to prefer 'deep integration', commitment to multilateralism in investment and trade (Haggard, 1995).

There appears to be a case against the assumption that complementary exchange is conducive to integration (point (3)). Much of the economic integration in Europe has taken place not because of comparative advantage, that is Ricardian exchange, but because of intra-industry trade. But to put much emphasis on this factor would probably be wrong.

According to Haggard, those developing nations which can point to some achievements or a potential for future achievement in this matter, are the newly industrializing countries. The proposition should hold as much for regional integration as for global schemes like the WTO which is the main object of Haggard's analysis. But is the proposition (point (6)) tenable?

I believe it is, but that it cannot explain most or even a large part of the variance in regional integration schemes. If in addition to level of development is added a positional argument then the weight of the argument becomes stronger. In several studies a neorealist perspective emphasizing positional behaviour has been proven to have a point. SAARC appears to be blocked by fear of Indian domination by the other and smaller members (see Muni in volume 3 of this series). On the other hand the entry of South Africa into the SADC in 1994 has created expectations that it will act as a 'benign' hegemonic state and lead the rest of the region onto a road towards higher development. One cannot thus say that there is consensus on a clear position in the literature about the role of regional hegemonic powers in the regional integration project.

Even with respect to exogenous hegemonic powers – states or transnational actors – there appears to be a diversity of views. Whereas some authors see it as a *contradictio in absurdum* that exogenous powers could create a benign regional integration process, others believe this to be possible, even the most effective means for creating a regional development process. The so-called 'flying geese' thesis is a case in point. It argues, briefly put, that the South East Asian region is led into a successful national development process in large measure because the countries of the region chose (or rather were forced) to follow the leadership of Japan (Akamatsu, 1960 [1934]). For reasons which will not be detailed here, Bernard and Ravenhill (1995) reject the thesis as a general proposition and argue that it is applicable only – and only partially – to the first tier, early industrializing country cases.

The African PTA has more than anything else been inefficient in stimulating South–South trade because members were pursuing a positional strategy: they feared that some members, such as Zimbabwe, would gain comparatively more than they would themselves from liberating trade flows. One country which first took a sceptical, but later turned to a positive view of the liberalizing integration schemes in the Southern African and the Indian Rim regions is Mauritius. It is obvious that part of the reason is the recent manufacturing success of that country. Level of development, or the 'sophistication' and diversity of the production and resource base, is important but still only one among several factors that determine the outcome of integration attempts.

The regional chapters in the present set of volumes offer a detailed survey of the various regional experiences. Only a few of the experiences and institutions surveyed have apparently produced tangible results in terms of directing trade or investment flows, promoting industry co-operation, or establishing procedures for policy co-ordination and conflict resolution. Why is that so? Is it for reasons that have been laid out so far and largely discussed in those papers? Or is it rather

(7) lack of clear goals and/or commitment by the parties?

Are structural factors as important as is widely believed, or are institutional ones underestimated? Is there a lack of not only cohesion or consensus among parties – a normal situation – but also:

(8) lack of proper procedures to settle disputes?

If by 'level of development' is meant also level of *institutional* development, the emphasis on level of development also probably becomes more tenable. And again it is submitted that a major factor is:

(9) whether a regional identity of some sort is present and makes itself felt in social and political institutions at the national and regional levels.

Institutional capacity and regional awareness may thus compensate for low 'achieved' level of economic development. The role of institutional factors may be seen in the case of SADC turning from a very decentralized to a more centralized system of decision-making recently (in the transformation into SADC). And South Africa's decision to join SADC appears to have initiated a process which may eventually undermine the PTA or absorb it into the SADC. Finally, countries in the less developed category may simply not have discovered and/or exploited the true potential for regional co-operation in non-economic issues. Dokken argues, for instance, that lack of regional integration in West Africa is due to an overemphasis on economic and neglect of the potential for co-operation in promoting greater ecological security (water management and so on) in the region (Dokken, 1996).

I do not believe that theories on regionalism and regionalization which have been worked out on the basis of experience among industrialized countries are *a priori* inapplicable to the rest of the world. But how applicable it is would still appear to be a matter for research. It is, in other words, only after having proven how the new regional projects initiated in the 1990s work that we may pass a final verdict. Mexico's integration into NAFTA may remain a special case, one of a North–South project integrating countries at different levels of development (widely defined). But it could also be repeated in other regions. As we compare the experience with such projects with that of others such as ASEAN and its proposed FTA, as Mercosur (also an example of integration among big and small economies at different levels of development) and as SADC, we will have a better basis for evaluating the validity and global applicability of a more general theory of regionalism.

CONCLUSION

This chapter has argued that the relationship between globalization and regionalism is not a straightforward unidirectional causal relationship. My concern has been to demonstrate that regionalism is more an attempt to direct economic internationalization according to some political goal rather than the other way round. But regionalism processes may of course – in some concrete cases, during some periods of history – be directed by private economic agents working through the channels of the state, corporatism and lobbying practices, and so on. A growth in intra-regional trade patterns or patterns of investment that show clusters of concentration on particular regions are not necessarily caused by regionalism. These patterns may be simply the effect of production and trade decisions and practices of firms.

Of the three theoretical perspectives, I believe that some patterns show up more often than others. States use international institutions to promote their interests: neo-realist explanations could therefore dominate institutionalist ones; intergovernmentalist theory takes prominence over neofunctionalist. But institutional aspects may in the process come to dominate the particular interest that led to the creation of institutions in the first place. Those who believe that the politics and bureaucracies of Brussels have taken over the direction of matters within the EC/EU could have a point, although generally speaking they would not be right until eventually the Maastricht treaty is implemented. That becomes a more and more distant prospect. And cognitivist factors should also be given some prominence in cases where leadership is exercised to create regional identity and awareness without necessarily or primarily being led by national or other particular interests.

Focus should be on the motives behind and the conditions for political action to be able to affect internationalization and globalization processes. More studies will have to be made, and better synthetization of available insight may also have to be done before a more solid theoretical basis has been found. It is my hope that this chapter has contributed to that endeavour.

Notes

1.   One should make a distinction between 'regionalism', which is the word for the general phenomenon, and 'regionalization', which represents the active pursuit of a strategy aimed at creating a regional system in a specific area. In this chapter I refer the two concepts to international regions, not subnational or cross-national regions.
2.   *Trade creation* refers to the replacement of higher-cost domestic production by lower-cost imports from countries within the region, whereas *trade diversion* refers to replacement of lower-cost imports from third countries by higher-cost imports from within the region.
3.   Hirschman's study has been criticized for either overstating the case or overlooking the fact that the type of strategy pursued by Nazi Germany is quite commonly used by great powers throughout history. It has for instance been argued that the high dependence of Central European nations on exporting to Germany in the late 1930s could be explained as a result of default, not design: Germany's industrial (and military)

expansion required raw materials which it could not obtain in sufficient quantities under stable conditions, thus it was pushed to seek new sources elsewhere and in areas to which it had safer access. It was not the character of the regime (Hirschman's point) as much as sheer need which directed it to Central European sources. (See for example, Baldwin, 1985 for a good critique, and Hveem, 1992 for a comparison with other hegemonial trade systems).

4. According to information obtained from sources in the Norwegian Ministry of Industries.

References

Akamatsu, K. (1960) 'A Theory of Unbalanced Growth in the World Economy', *Weltwirtschaftliches Archiv*, **86**, (2) (originally published in Japanese in 1934).

Baldwin, D. (1985) *Economic Statecraft* (New York, Columbia University Press).

Bernard, M. and J. Ravenhill (1995) 'Beyond Product Cycles and Flying Geese: Regionalization, Hierarchy, and the Industrialization of East Asia', *World Politics*, **45**, (2).

Bhagwati, J. (1992) 'Regionalism versus Multilateralism', *World Economy*, **15**.

Busch, M. L. and H. Milner (1994) 'The Future of the Trading System: International Firms, Regionalism, and Domestic Politics', in R. Stubbs and G. R. D. Underhill (eds) *Political Economy and the Changing Global Order* (Basingstoke: Macmillan).

Buzan, B. (1991) *People, States, and Fear* (New York/London: Harvester Wheatsheaf) 2nd edn.

Chime, C. (1977) *Integration and Politics among African States. Limitations and horizons of mid-term theorising* (Uppsala: The Scandinavian Institute of African Studies).

Deutsch, K. W. *et al.* (1957) *Political Community and the North Atlantic Area* (Princeton NJ: Princeton University Press).

Dokken, K. (1996) *Environment, Security and Regional Integration in West Africa.* (University of Oslo, Department of Political Science).

Fouquin, M. (1993) *Regional and World-Wide Dimensions of Globalisation* (Paris: Centre d'Etudes Prospectives et d'Informations Internationales) document de travail no. 93–04.

Funabashi, Y. (1993) 'The Asianization of Asia', *Foreign Affairs*, **72**, (5): 75–85.

Gilpin, R. (1991) *The Transformation of the International Political Economy* (Florence: The European University Institute).

Given, N. and Jefferson, O. (1977) *Corporate or Covillean Integration* (Kingston: Institute of Social and Economic Research).

Gourevitch, P. (1978) 'The Second Image Reversed', *International Organization*, **38**, (4) (Autumn).

Haas, E. B. (1964) *Beyond the Nation-State: Functionalism and International Organization* (Stanford, Calif.: Stanford University Press).

Haggard, S. (1995) *Developing Nations and the Politics of Global Integration* (Washington, DC: The Brookings Institution).

Hettne, B. (1994) 'The New Regionalism: Implications for Development and Peace', in B. Hettne and A. Inotai *The New Regionalism. Implications for Global Development and International Security* (UNU/WIDER).

Hettne, B. and A. Inotai (1994) *The New Regionalism. Implications for Global Development and International Security* (UNU/WIDER).

Hirschman, A. O. (1980) *National Power and the Structure of Foreign Trade* (Berkeley: University of California Press).

Hveem, H. (1973) 'The Global Dominance System', *Journal of Peace Research*, **9** (4).

Hveem, H. (1992) *The International Bargaining Economy* (Oslo, University of Oslo, Centre for Development and the Environment) mimeo.

Hveem, H. (1994) *Internasjonalisering og politikk* (Internationalisation and Politics). (Oslo, Universitetsforlaget).

Hveem, H. (1995) *Power, Promises and the Potential of WTO* (University of Oslo, Centre on Development and the Environment).

Jones, E. (1994) 'Asia's Fate. A Response to the Singapore School', *The National Interest*, (35): 18–28.

Kahler, M. and J. Odell (1989) 'Developing Country Coalition- Building and International Trade Negotiations', in C. Hamilton, and J. Whalley (eds) *Developing Countries and the Global Trading System* (London: Macmillan).

Kennedy, P. (1987) *The Rise and Fall of the Great Powers* (New York: Random House).

Keohane, R. O. (1989) *International Institutions and State Power. Essays in International Relations Theory* (Boulder: Westview).

MacKinder, H. (1904) 'The Geographic Pivot of History', reprinted in *Democratic Ideals and Reality* (New York, Norton, 1962).

Milner, H. (1988) *Resisting Protectionism: Global Industries and the Politics of International Trade* (Princeton, NJ: (Princeton University Press).

Mitrany, D. (1966) *A Working Peace System* (Chicago: Quadrangle).

Moravcsik, A. (1991) 'Negotiating the Single European Act', *International Organization*, **45**(1): 19–55.

Nye, J. N. (1992) 'What New World Order?', *Foreign Affairs* (Spring).

Ohmae, K. (1985) *Triad Power. The Coming Shape of Global Competition* (Singapore: McKinsey).

Ohmae, K. (1993) ''The Rise of the Region State', *Foreign Affairs* (Spring).

Putnam, R. D. (1988) 'Diplomacy vs Domestic Politics: The Logic of Two-Level Games', *International Organization*, **45** (3): 427–460

RIPE (Review of International Political Economy) (1994) *Editorial*, **1** (1).

Rosenau, J. N. (1990) *Turbulence in World Politics* (Princeton, NJ: Princeton University Press).

Schmidt, H. (1974) 'Struggle for the World Product', *Foreign Affairs,* **52** (April).

Seers, D. (1983) *The Political Economy of Nationalism* (Oxford University Press).

Simai, M. (1994) 'Preface' to B. Hettne and A. Inotai, *The New Regionalism. Implications for Global Development and International Security* (UNU/WIDER).

Stopford, J. and S. Strange (1991) *Rival States, Rival Firms* (Cambridge University Press).

Stranger, S. (1986) *Casino Capitalism* (Oxford: Blackwell).

Tyson, L. d'Andrea (1992) *Who's Bashing Whom. Trade Conflict in High-Technology Industries* (Washington, DC: Institute of International Economics).

UNCTAD (United Nations Conference on Trade and Development. Program on Transnational Corporations) (1993) *World Investment Report 1993. Transnational Corporations and Integrated International Production* (Geneva).

UNCTAD (1994) *World Investment Report*.

UNCTC (United Nations Centre on Transnational Corporations) (1991) *World Investment Report 1991. The Triad in Foreign Direct Investment* (New York).

Vernon, R. F. (1971) *Sovereignty at Buy* (New York: Basic Books).

Viner, J. (1950) *The Theory of Customs Unions* (New York: North-Holland).

Waever, O. (1990) 'Three Competing Europes: German, French and Russian', *International Affairs*, **66** (3).

Waltz, K. (1979) *Theory of International Politics* (Reading, Mass.: Addison-Wesley).

Wendt, A. (1994) 'Collective Identity Formation and the International State', *American Political Science Review*, **88** (2).

Yawrough, B. V. and Yawrough, R. M. (1988) *The Western Economy: Trade and Finance* (Chicago: The Dryden Press).

5 The New Regionalism: Impediment or Spur to Future Multilateralism?[1]

Percy S. Mistry

INTRODUCTION

A growing worldwide drive toward regionalism was expected to moderate in the wake of a successfully concluded Uruguay Round (UR). Instead it accelerated. That suggests, *prima facie*, a weakening in the power of orthodox international trade theory to explain the impulses behind the regionalism of the 1990s. It is now beyond dispute that the new surge in regionalism is influencing the post-cold-war global economic and political order. But it raises questions which have yet to be answered. These questions are not new. They have resonated since the first incipient steps were taken toward the formation of what has evolved into the European Union (EU) over a period of more than 40 years; but they have assumed a particular pungency in the last five.

Why are so many countries in every part of the world pursuing regionalism with renewed vigour? Are there non-trade, and non-economic reasons for explaining the post-1990 surge towards regionalism, which is occurring as if there was previously unnoticed repressed demand for it? Is the orthodox Vinerian framework for analysing the costs and benefits of *regionalization* adequate of itself to assess the costs and benefits of *regionalism*? Will the new regionalism impede multilateralism?

The conflict between regionalism and multilateralism caused particular concern during UR negotiations, especially when their successful conclusion seemed to be in doubt. Committed multilateralists became anxious about the competitive threat of regional initiatives to the multilateral objectives of the UR (Bhagwati, 1993). Since then some of the more artificial, contrived arguments against regionalism, which portrayed it as a spectre endangering the multilateral system, have been moderated (Mistry, 1994).

116

Today the debate about regionalism versus multilateralism (referred to hereafter as the RvM debate) has taken on a different complexion. It has broadened from a consideration of their respective effects on trade liberalization *per se*, to encompassing a more diverse range of dimensions – political, social, cultural, economic and security (Hettne, 1994). Potential trade gains have become a smaller, and perhaps not the most important, part of the new RvM debate. Increasingly, the new regionalism appears to be more a response on the part of national governments to manage, collectively, new political and economic risks and uncertainties which confront them in the post-Cold War era.

To comprehend the impulses behind the *new regionalism*, it is perhaps necessary to step back and consider what has been (and is) happening in the world since the collapse of communism. Two features appear to stand out.

The Global Distribution of Political, Military and Economic Power

This has changed dramatically since 1990. It will continue to change well into the new millennium. The relative stability provided by *bipolar* competition between two established superpowers – which resulted in the geopolitical equivalent of neutral equilibrium in physics – has given way to systemic instability in a *multipolar* world. Earlier competition between two superpowers in exerting global influence has been succeeded by unforeseen, disorganized and rapid transition from *concentrated bipolarity* in global regime management to *diffused multipolarity*.

That phenomenon is resulting in global economic and political power devolving rapidly – more by default than design – to emerging littoral giants: for example, China and India in East and South Asia respectively, Nigeria and South Africa in sub-Saharan Africa, Egypt and Israel in the Middle East and North Africa, Brazil in South America, Russia in Eastern Europe, and so on. In some instances, new emergent powers (China for instance) are consciously extending and consolidating their regional hold through the exercise of political and military muscle in attempts to assert doctrines of eminent domain and manifest destiny. In most other instances the devolution of global power is occurring less through conscious pursuit of a pre-ordained global or regional strategy and more as a consequence of nature abhorring a vacuum. Whatever the reason, each twist of the global kaleidoscope results in a changed pattern of relationships among nations at a faster pace than national or multilateral institutions can assimilate. That phenomenon is heightening uncertainty and risk for most nation-states which were formerly patronized by, or sheltered under the umbrella of, one erstwhile superpower or the other.

Whether that state of affairs will be temporary – until a new stable pattern of relationships among a larger number of regional powers has been established – or longer-lived, remains to be seen. What is clear is that with the demise of bipolarity, Cold War mechanisms and institutions for enforcing global stability and keeping client states under control have atrophied. And they have not yet been replaced by universal mechanisms which are broadly subscribed to, durable or effective.

Exigent multilateral arrangements attempted since 1990 in Angola, Bosnia, Cambodia, Haiti, Liberia, Rwanda and Somalia were inadequately cobbled together. They were inherently fragile, unstable and unenforceable. More disconcerting is the reality that even when multilateral intervention (occasionally supplemented by regional involvement as in Liberia) did succeed in arresting fratricidal conflict (Somalia and Cambodia) it could not assure the emergence of viable nation-states thereafter. The relative certainties which governed competition between two opposed political creeds (communism vs. democracy) and economic systems (market-capitalism versus command-socialism) have thus been replaced by a number of unforeseen uncertainties.

The post-Cold War world is now characterized by *convergence* toward a singular economic paradigm – universal capitalism[2] – accompanied by increasing *divergence* in the management of domestic (national) political regimes despite concerted efforts by the West (that is, the OECD club of countries) to promote multi-party, parliamentary democracy. The wave of liberalization which characterized the 1980s was mainly *economic* liberalization. In the 1990s, after the collapse of communism, it has become a package infused with both economic *and political* dimensions.

The West's push for global democratization seems premised on the belief that market economies, which require a degree of freedom in the functioning of price mechanisms, cannot function properly without equivalent political freedoms. Democracy is being propagated under the banner of good governance in other countries, both developing and in transition. Unfortunately, most such economies are unfamiliar with the limited freedoms which the functioning of markets implies and openly uncomfortable about linkages between economic and political liberalization which they perceive as spurious. Increasingly, Western insistence on democratic norms and inherently adversarial parliamentary procedures, are being seen as threats to different cultural norms elsewhere and to hard-won competitiveness in the trade arena. The Western push for the rapid liberalization of polities and expansion of democratic rights, commensurate with the pace of economic liberalization, is therefore meeting resistance from various quarters, not least in the most successful and competitive part of the world (East Asia).

That reaction can be explained in part by interpretations put on the different experiences of China, India and Russia in handling these two distinct liberalizations. Rapid political liberalization in Russia, even before economic liberalization began, has led to systemic chaos with the risk of a backlash in the form of communist resurgence. Most of the gains of *laissez-faire* marketization, which has been ineffectually regulated, have been captured by a powerful class, operating outside of the still unformed legal framework. By contrast, China has managed to capture significant gains from economic liberalization in an environment of continued political repression albeit less severe than it was previously. On the other hand, India has been politically liberal (in theory, much less so in practice) but economically repressed for half a century. The process of economic reform and liberalization being undertaken there is being severely impeded by the way in which its democracy functions resulting in a massive dissipation of gains.

In all three countries economic liberalization has unleashed corruption on a scale unimagined before. It has exacerbated the aberrant behaviour of their dysfunctional political classes and thrown up fundamental questions about the immediate suitability, and indeed even the workability, of parliamentary democracy in developing or transitional regimes. In the face of evidence in these three large countries, as well as evidence across Africa, the claim that democracy (as it is organized and practised in the West) is an essential concomitant to a market economy has little resonance; except perhaps in Latin America with its unique history of governance by military *juntas*. Moreover, experimentation with democratization is introducing its own new set of internal economic risks which governments are finding it more difficult to manage.

The Impact of Changes in Dynamic Comparative (Economic) Advantage

This is having global repercussions with the cause–effect cycle not yet being fully understood. Not so long ago, *comparative advantage* was used to explain patterns of international trade and the success of some countries over others in world markets. More often than not, such advantage was seen to accrue mainly to countries which had natural resources, particular qualities of human capital, a surplus of financial capital, and an advanced economic infrastructure by way of functioning markets and institutions.

The notion of *static comparative advantage* based on these endowments (of what economists call production factors) has given way to a different notion of more rapidly shifting *dynamic competitive advantage* which is based less on factors of production as such, and more on the possession of: market share, global brands, sophisticated process and information technology capabilities, access to global media and communications, facility with global image-making, the ability to access and interpret knowledge (in the most comprehensive sense of the word), and systemic dexterity which requires considerable flexibility in labour and factor markets.

These new determinants of competitive production and trade superiority have become particularly important in determining patterns of global production and, therefore, in patterns of world trade as well. The relative share of labour and raw material costs in the value added to final products continues to decline. At the same time, the value added share of information and service-inputs (the cost of technology content, marketing, distribution, transport, packaging, financing, information, post-sale servicing and so on) in the final product continues to rise. These structural shifts in the relative costs of global production tend to reward nations which are able to make instantaneous adjustments to changes in global market conditions and preferences. In an increasingly competitive and open global marketplace they favour the location of production (and thus of investment and employment) in those countries which are adaptive; that is, countries in which the costs of continuous dislocations caused by exogenous changes (mainly in terms of monetary and technological shocks) can be quickly absorbed domestically without incurring too high a risk of social or political rupture.

The unprecedented mobility of high-level human capital, as well as of financial capital, results in investment-orientated capital movements responding very quickly to, and reinforcing, enhanced competitiveness – to countries with responsive labour, capital and technology markets such as those in East Asia and the USA – rather than moving in the direction of countries which might be more advantaged in having either:

- an abundance of natural resources (for example, Africa, Australia or Canada); or
- a large stock of physical productive assets or of trained human capital in traditional mass-production manufacturing (for example, Europe or the former Soviet Union).

Taking these two major factors into account, national governments are beginning to experience the increasing difficulty of maintaining *domestic* political and economic equilibrium over any length of time purely through the manipulation of policy levers under their sovereign control. Traditional training in *national* politics or governance and the need to cater to national constituencies for their continuance in office, ill-equipped political leaders or governments to cope with the new challenges they face in assuring job security, income stability or sustained increases in prosperity.

Global competitiveness now depends on:

- continuous renewal and change of human skills and the composition/quality of human capital; and
- the even more rapid re-configuration of productive assets and capabilities.

The ability to accommodate such changes flexibly and quickly, without incurring the risk of social and political disruption each time a major adjustment has to be made, differs enormously across nations. Yet political leaders rarely appreciate what competitiveness actually entails and what needs to be done to enhance it; especially in those societies which have developed rigidities in their labour markets as a result of high in-built social costs.

National leaders and policy-makers thus face greater *uncertainty and risk* than they did before in dealing with exogenous influences and exigencies which have a larger impact on their domestic economies than those policies over which they believe they might have some control. In such circumstances of heightened political and economic risk, with a sudden diffusion of political and economic power on a littoral basis, it is not unnatural for nations to look to their immediate neighbourhoods (that is, regionalism) for safety in an attempt to widen the economic space over which policy-makers can collectively exert more control and retain a degree of dynamic equilibrium.[3]

This line of reasoning provides the backdrop for exploring in this paper further thoughts on whether adopting a *risk-management* approach in viewing the RvM debate would require some generally accepted tenets of orthodoxy to be reconsidered including, *inter alia*, the following:

- In the world which is emerging, is it still appropriate to portray regionalism and regionalization (or more appropriately *plurilateralism*) as a second-best (inferior) option to an increasingly dysfunctional multilateralism in managing the new economic and political risks that individual nation-states now confront in the global arena?
- Will the *new* regionalism be conducive to more effective multilateralism in the future? Or, going even further, is the new regionalism an essential *prerequisite* for the emergence of a new multilateralism?
- Has present (old) multilateralism become sufficiently dysfunctional as to need overhaul? Does it permit the satisfactory and smooth accommodation of the kaleidoscopic economic and political transformations that are occurring in the world? Are its institutional structures geared toward adapting to new realities or are they geared to thwarting and impeding the manifestation of these realities by protecting a pre-Cold War global power structure which no longer reflects global economic and political realities?
- Does a *new multilateralism* need to emerge before it can offer a superior alternative to the *new regionalism* in terms of **national** risk management?
- Is the current preoccupation with regionalism a healthy, rather than counterproductive, response on the part of nations to a world in which the fabric of multilateralism has been overstretched and where its processes and structures may need time in which to revive and adjust?

In attempting to answer these questions, it is necessary to dwell on: (1) what the new regionalism is; (2) emerging trends in global economic interactions between 1996 and 2025; and (3) the conditions under which the new regionalism is likely to support and facilitate, rather than impede, the emergence of a new multilateralism.

WHAT IS THE NEW REGIONALISM?

A review of recent literature on regionalism and regionalization[4] reveals a distinction between *old* (pre-1990) regionalism and *new* (post-1990) initiatives aiming at different types of regional integration arrangements (RIAs). These range from the loosest forms of co-operative association to much more tightly binding agreements leading eventually toward economic union. Yet it is clear that, despite the distinction, there is as yet no clear definition of the *new regionalism* which is commonly subscribed to. There is only some convergence of thinking in emphasizing its difference from the old.

One all-embracing definition of the new regionalism provided by the international relations school is: 'a multidimensional process of regional integration which includes economic, political, social and cultural aspects' (Hettne, 1994), emphasizing the non-economic, political and security dimensions of RIAs. It sees regionalism as a package rather than as a unique phenomenon or a single policy concerned with economics or foreign affairs. Such a definition goes well beyond notions of free trade areas and the integration of several national markets into a single functional unit. It views geographical identity, political convergence, collective security and regional coherence as being the more important features. Under this definition, the new regionalism is viewed as spontaneous and *from below* that is, driven by the demands of firms, industries, consumers and markets. In contrast the *old* variety of regionalism was seen as imposed *from above*; that is, by the dictates (fiat) of technocrats, bureaucrats, and political visionaries with grand designs and, therefore, as being necessarily more limited in scope, lacking in popular support and prone to the kind of failures from which grand designs inevitably suffer.

At the other end of the scale, the economic school (typified by the World Bank, for example) overtly acknowledges the importance of non-economic dimensions, but nevertheless defines the new regionalism in a more limited fashion; that is, as an economically *enhanced* free trade concept which is open, outward-looking and inclusive rather than the old variety which was protectionist, inward-looking and designed to exclude (Braga, 1994). Pre-1990 RIAs, especially among developing countries, were defined by the nature and height of the barriers which members erected to thwart non-members from economic participation. In post-1990 RIAs the aim is almost the opposite: that is, to have differential barriers in favour of members but in a context of progressively lowered (internal and external) barriers to the point where they become almost insignificant. The economic *enhancements* characterizing the new regionalism include: liberalization of intra-regional trade in services and intellectual property; free movements of capital and labour; and the harmonization of regulatory regimes. The economic school also notes a distinctive feature of the new regionalism being the incidence of North–South arrangements as opposed to the North–North and South–South arrangements which characterized earlier RIAs. North–South arrangements may well become the rule rather than the exception in the future.

Thus from both the political and economic angles, the definition of the new regionalism is clear about two things: first, that it is decidedly different from the old in encouraging greater porosity of interaction between the *region* and the rest of the world, rather than inhibiting it; and second, that the visible trade-related aspects of the new regionalism are much less significant than its other economic (especially investment, human capital development and technology transfer) and political/security dimensions.

EMERGENT REGIONALISM AS A PREREQUISITE FOR EFFECTIVE MULTILATERALISM

Taking these new features into account, why has regionalism become so fashionable so quickly again? Will that trend damage or strengthen the cause of multilateralism?

One explanation offered for regionalism becoming endemic in the post-1990 era is that the USA, in a departure from long-held traditions, has become a convert to regionalism (Bhagwati, 1993). From being a free-trader committed to multilateralism to the exclusion of other arrangements, the USA has in the post-Cold War regime developed a more regionally-orientated dimension. That impulse appears to have resulted from its anxiety:

- to consolidate dominance in its own hemisphere through NAFTA; and
- to counter the threat of competitive regional blocs emerging in Europe and Asia which challenge its primacy in dominating global economics and politics.

Such reasoning, however, is too US-centric to be satisfactory in explaining what is happening elsewhere.

A *second* explanation is that what has been happening with the evolution of the European Union has had powerful demonstration and follow-the-leader effects – both positive and negative – throughout the rest of the world, but especially in Latin America, Africa and

Asia, but also in Central and Eastern Europe (CEE) and the former Soviet Union (FSU). Most countries liberated from the former Soviet empire suffered a massive economic dislocation with the loss of their common economic space in COMECON. The European parts of the erstwhile Soviet empire, and in its zone of influence, are now scrambling to join, or associate with, the EU in one form or another on both the economic and security fronts. The Asian parts are adrift.

At the same time, the threat of competition from newly impoverished CEE/FSU countries being given preferential access to the EU is being seen by other (developing) countries as being potentially damaging to their own economic interests resulting in defensive impulses to regionalize in order to cope with these new risks. Developing countries with established preferential access to the EU (that is, the ACP countries) as well as those with bilateral arrangements with the EU, are accelerating their efforts to cement some form of RIA (NAFTA-like) with the EU (for example, Turkey, the Maghreb, some African RIAs and CARICOM). The successful countries of Asia and South America, seeing themselves at a disadvantage *vis-à-vis* EU and NAFTA, have triggered their own initiatives to regionalize in the two fastest growing regions of the world in an attempt to give themselves bargaining power with both these two large blocs.

A *third* factor which may explain the drive toward the new regionalism is the emergence, for the first time, of a universal market ethos (referred to earlier) resulting from: (1) the collapse of communism and the discrediting of socialism which has resulted in strengthening the hand of market-oriented policy-makers throughout the world; and (2) externally imposed structural adjustment (mainly by the World Bank and IMF) involving sweeping economic liberalization in the aftermath of the developing country debt crisis and the economic collapse of Africa, south of the Sahara. Both of these influences are likely to induce more enthusiastic opening of borders to the movement of goods, services, people and capital than has been the case before. That will result in enlarging of markets beyond those that most individual nations can provide within their own borders for domestic firms to be competitive and, indirectly, compel contiguous economies to converge and, possibly, unify in the longer term.

Fourth, whereas the cold war may have necessitated accommodating eccentricities of behaviour in the leaderships of some client states, its breakdown has led to a loss of that tolerance. Thus several nation-states whose economies were artificially propped up by superpowers anxious to retain influence at whatever cost (for example, in Asia, Africa, the Middle East, Central Europe, and the Caribbean) have begun to confront new realities in attempting to survive on their own. Most of these countries, whose economic sovereignty has been severely compromised, will inevitably need to engage in RIAs of some sort in order to bolster their prospects of economic survival.

To these four more or less widely accepted reasons might be added a *fifth* which, when viewed in the context of arguments for traditional multilateralism, appears heretical. In the RvM debate, regionalism is invariably portrayed as suboptimal and antithetical to the proper functioning of the multilateral system, whether the argument is made in the limited confines of the world trading system or across the broader canvas of the global economic and political system. Such argument obscures the reality that multilateralism has itself become dysfunctional. It is increasingly uncertain, cost-inefficient and, judged by results, ineffective. Its institutions are stale and sclerotic; the recent conversion of GATT into WTO notwithstanding. They seem more concerned about protecting their own institutional interests by veering either toward:

- continuing their traditional roles despite a changing world – as seems to be the case with the UN system; or
- becoming *de facto* extensions of the policy-making machinery of more powerful (OECD and G-7) shareholder governments rather than remaining neutral fora with genuinely multilateral perspectives and interests. This has already happened to a large extent to the two BWIs.

That multilateral institutions of some sort are needed is beyond dispute. Whether the ones which exist today, and the way in which they function, reflect the needs of the international community as a whole, is a more vexatious matter. Decision-making power in these multilateral institutions continues to reflect obsolete Cold War power balances – with a few modifications to accommodate the reclaimed economic power of Germany and Japan. It does not yet reflect the significant regional redistribution of global power which has occurred in the aftermath of the cold war's demise. Old multilateralism is dysfunctional because it is dominated by, and serves the interests of, faltering powers (mainly the G-7) which are unable or unwilling to afford fully the costs of exercising global responsibility. The multilateral system thus reflects the world of 1945–89 rather than the world of the 1990s and beyond. For that reason, the multilateral system's capacities are focused more on obstructing than constructing; on resisting change rather than accommodating it.

In short, the old multilateralism is no longer adequately structured nor is it sufficiently responsive to the needs of a rapidly changing global order in which obsolete rules of engagement have yielded to new uncertainties in political and economic relationships. Present-day multilateralism and the machinery which supports it is, for that reason, gradually but inexorably grinding to a halt. There is no longer a universal belief in the efficacy of, or even the need for the United Nations (UN). More than half the world believes (perhaps with some justification) that the operations of the Bretton Woods institutions – the World Bank and IMF – serve to detract from, rather than enhance, global welfare. There is much *prima facie* evidence to suggest that these two institutions, in particular, have become powerful vested interests in their own right at a time when the UN system is crumbling. They often seem more concerned about self-preservation, exemption from normal principles of transparency and accountability, maintenance of crypto-imperial operating styles, and preservation of the rights and immunities of staff, than with the progressive evolution of their mandates and functions to adapt to new, changing global economic and political circumstances.

It is therefore a plausible hypothesis that the new regionalism is being embraced with enthusiasm because the old multilateralism does not work any longer; at least not for the betterment and benefit of most of its members. Such a hypothesis is contentious and needs to be subjected to scrutiny. If found to be valid then the new regionalism may not only be conducive to the emergence of a more functional and useful model of multilateralism it may be a *prerequisite* for reconstructing a new multilateralism on *regional* building blocs which reflect the changes that have occurred (and will continue to occur for some time) in the global redistribution of power after 1989.

THE DEFICIENCIES OF PREVAILING MULTILATERALISM

In giving this sweeping hypothesis more specific dimensions, several avenues need to be explored in understanding better why the old multilateralism has become obsolescent.

Fundamental Design Flaws in its Architecture and Construction

The present structure was built primarily by the USA to serve a visionary purpose of progressively integrated and rule-based global governance which has been eroded and now virtually abandoned; perhaps nowhere more so than in the USA itself. Whereas at one time the USA was benevolently supportive of a multilateral system in which its role as a global hegemon (at least in the non-communist world) was implicitly accepted, it has become increasingly intolerant of demands for a more genuinely multilateral framework in which its role is reduced to that of being *primus inter pares* rather than a hegemon which is exempted from the global rules which it believes should apply to others.

For that reason it appears to have forsaken the supposedly more democratic UN system while attempting to consolidate its (and the G-7's) grip over the weighted-voting Bretton Woods Institutions. In the process it has made them virtual extensions of its own governmental policy-making machinery. In the process, both the UN and the BWIs have been damaged. They are no longer seen as being able or inclined to protect genuinely multilateral (as opposed to US or Western) interests; nor are they seen as being capable of achieving goals which enhance global welfare.

Although it remains the only military superpower left, the USA is paradoxically no longer the overwhelmingly dominant global force that it once was. Though a few recent interventions may imply the contrary, the USA can no longer impose its will on the world unilaterally by either persuasion or force. It has no domestic constituency for such engagement in any event. Its actions, whether in the Gulf War, Bosnia or the Taiwan straits, need to be legitimized (and invariably paid for) by others. While the Soviet threat has disappeared, the former client states of the USA – whether in Western Europe, East Asia or Latin America – have become powerful economic competitors even as they remain (for the time being) political and military allies with continued dependency on its nuclear umbrella. Countries that were mildly adversarial and are still developing (for example, China) are being perceived as, and have actually become, significant military threats.

In the face of these shifts in the balance of power the USA has remained unwilling to cede its multilateral power organically and share it with others under a more genuine set-up. While invariably requiring other nations to take up more of the obligations (in particular the expense) of maintaining and improving *global governance systems* – which is what multilateralism is all about – the USA remains unwilling to share the privileges conferred by the power (especially over systemic decision-making) which it has enjoyed for so long within extant multilateralism. Nor have any other nations developed the capacity to fill the vacuum that the USA's withdrawal and growing incapacity are inevitably leaving.

Reluctance to relinquish the prerogatives of global supremacy, understandable as that may be from the USA's viewpoint, poses severe problems for the progressive evolution of constructive multilateralism. So does the widening gap between positions taken by successive US administrations on the one hand, and the US Congress on the other, on a variety of issues that profoundly affect the rest of the world. The deepening rift between these two poles of political power directly influences the effectiveness of the existing multilateral framework. Conflict between them is something which, for the multilateral system, is becoming increasingly difficult (if not tedious) to accommodate.

Yet, civil society within the USA does not appear to be aware of, or sufficiently concerned about, the problems created for the rest of the world, from the carry-over effects of its domestic political infighting, as much as it perhaps should. Unfortunately, when the USA disengages and chooses not to exert itself in the multilateral system – as was the case in the early stages of the Yugoslav crisis and remains the case in paying its obligations to the UN or to the multilateral soft-windows for concessional financing of the poorest countries – it leaves a 'catch-22' type of void which cannot be easily filled.

The multilateral system therefore suffers from the worst of two worlds – it accommodates neither the USA's diminishing ability to undertake global responsibilities constructively, nor acts effectively in the face of US reluctance (or incapacity) to do so. The *burden-sharing* principles and rules which serve to define the roles and obligations of individual nations in multilateralism have been disregarded by the USA in a manner which has weakened the entire multilateral edifice. That peculiar characteristic reflects perhaps the most crippling flaw of present-day multilateralism. The system has had its foundations eroded by becoming inured to the exercise of hegemony by the USA for far too long. When such hegemony can no longer be exercised legitimately it leaves a void in the workings of multilateralism which is not easily filled.

There has been no experience over the last 50 years with any other nation, or group of nations, filling that void in a way that would be seen as legitimate or acceptable by the rest of the global community. Thus the present multilateral system is trapped in a nether world. It is unable to make the transition it needs to make because its structure is neither robust nor flexible enough to adjust to the changes in geopolitics and geoeconomics which are taking place. Reluctance on the part of the USA to cede power gracefully as part of a deliberate and properly worked out process of rule-based transformation is mirrored in the reciprocal reluctance and inability of Europe and Japan to exercise their proper share of global responsibility. Present-day multilateralism has thus been reduced to a depressing state in which:

(1) the USA still attempts to retain control over key multilateral decisions in the UN system, WTO and the BWIs, while
(2) Europe and Japan bear the brunt of the multilateral system's extraordinarily high (and increasing) operating costs, and
(3) the rest of the world remains unempowered and dispossessed in the multilateral arena even as its real geopolitical power and weight in the global economy increase.

Europe's Role

A second reason for the dysfunctionality of present-day multilateralism concerns the role that an increasingly regionalized, yet paradoxically still fractured, Europe plays in it. Western Europe taken as a whole (represented broadly by the members of the European Union and the enlarged Economic Area) presently pays the largest share (roughly 35–40 per cent) of the costs of the multilateral system and a much higher share of its non-security related part. Yet Europe has shown neither the ability nor the inclination to provide any direction or to set a more appropriate agenda for the multilateral system. On issues of *cross-border* trade, capital flows (whether official, aid or private), and movements of people, Europe remains an excessively inward-looking, self-constrained, protective and defensive part of the developed world. Whereas on most economic and social issues Europe is becoming increasingly unified, on global issues it still insists on speaking on the multilateral stage with too many voices in a number of tongues.

In a world of universalized market economies, Europe (with the exception of the UK) also remains the most *dirigiste* and statist part of the world. Its incongruent preoccupation with obsolescent socialism (albeit progressively diluted) sits uncomfortably with the realities of an unprecedentedly competitive global market place. Europe's main aim appears to be to deploy multilateral means to hobble the competitiveness of other countries and regions rather than to improve its own. In the global arena, Europe is thus emitting a confused set of signals arising from four pre-occupations:

(1) the resurgence of nationalism and ethnicity which threatens to slow down the widening and deepening of integration within Europe;
(2) increasing confusion about the meaning and application of subsidiarity within the Union at different levels of governance;
(3) discord between the voices of individual nation-states and that of the European Commission in key multilateral fora on issues concerning free trade, capital flows, and labour mobility; and
(4) the protection of its highly developed but increasingly unaffordable social welfare system within European walls.

In other words, a more integrated Europe is having a problem with translating its growing unity into coherence at the multilateral level because its members insist on both speaking separately, as well as with one collective voice, simultaneously. There is no choreography to ensure that those voices are consistent. That, of course, creates its own problems for multilateralism and does little to strengthen it. If Europe is to contribute towards building a new multilateralism it must lead the way in doing so by finding a way to express itself on a singular regional basis on issues other than trade. Until it does so, Europe's role in shaping the new multilateralism will be compromised.

Japan

A third problem with the old multilateralism concerns Japan. Until it was recently battered by a relentless series of (interrelated) internal political, financial and economic crises, Japan and the rest of the world were convinced that the centre of global economic gravity had shifted decisively from the North Atlantic to the North Pacific resulting in the dawn of the Pacific century. Having exerted every sinew to assume second place in the system after the USA, its domestic difficulties over the last five years have resulted in Japan suddenly becoming a weak and shaky part of the multilateral nexus.

This can be explained partly by the transformation which Japan's domestic political system is undergoing. From a one-party dominated system with established stability, predictability and internal party discipline, the corruption scandals which have rocked the Liberal Democratic party are leading to Western-style parliamentary democracy which is more fractious, confrontational and histrionic. That internal transformation is not being handled particularly well; largely because it is so uncharacteristic and unfamiliar. It is adversely affecting Japan's ability to play its proper role in the multilateral system as it is presently constructed or to influence the future shaping of it.

The emergence of Japan as a global power has of course been accompanied by that of other Pacific Rim countries – mainly China and in East Asia – as significant players in the global economy and as the most competitive capital-surplus countries in the world. But the multilateral system has yet to recognize the reality of East Asia's emergence as a globally significant region in its structures and decision-making processes. The difficulty which Japan confronted in taking its place in the present set of multilateral institutions reflected well the system's in-built sclerosis and its unwillingness to change from being largely a trans-Atlantic, mainly Anglo-Saxon club. Astonishing as it seems in retrospect, it took nearly 15 years (from 1970 to 1985) for Japan's position as the world's second-ranking economic power to be recognized fully within the rigid structures of established multilateralism. It is unlikely that other East Asian countries will be willing to go through the same tortuous routines. They are, instead, concentrating on regionalizing before exerting their power on the multilateral stage *en bloc*.

The Implosion of the Former Communist World, 1995–6

This has changed the traditional 'free-world' composition and character of multilateralism. Inconveniently, multilateralism has been shaped by global contours which have altered radically. Institutions established to deal with military security, international finance, global development and commons, and international trade, were designed to accommodate a pattern of political power relationships which no longer hold. Yet, they have not adjusted satisfactorily to new realities. As already observed, decision-making power in these institutions continues to be aimed at accommodating the economic and security interests of a few developed countries; interests which were framed in the context of the cold war and have not adapted significantly since then. Such multilateralism is neither appropriate for, nor conducive to, encouraging the evolutionary emergence of a post-1990 order in which greater power devolves quickly to new members and to newly industrialized developing countries whose economic and political weight, as well as military capability, is now much greater than it was before.

Who Benefits from Existing Multilateralism?

Fifth, across the more successful regions of the developing world (primarily in East Asia) and among the larger, more powerful, non-OECD littoral powers (for example, Brazil, China, India, Nigeria, Russia and South Africa) serious questions are being raised about whether they either need, or even benefit significantly from, the kind of multilateralism which exists today. To be sure, all of these countries may need to rely for back-stopping support on institutions such as the IMF and WTO for some time yet. That is inevitable given the high risks of occasional policy or market failure occurring in both their internal developmental trajectories and in the way in which their expanding economies relate with the world's rapidly evolving financial and trading regimes. But continued reliance on the IMF and WTO will pose new multilateral difficulties given the circumstances in which such recourse is likely to be arise.

Already these countries are relying less on other multilateral institutions for finance, technology, or for security. Their independent access to private sources of capital has grown dramatically between 1990 and 1995; it will grow faster still in the new millennium despite the possibility of hiccups like the Mexican crisis of 1994–5. Moreover their bilateral capabilities and influence in world markets and geopolitics is evolving at an entirely different and altogether more rapid pace than was previously possible.

Developing countries in Asia, Latin America and the Middle East (much less so in Africa) are therefore no longer constrained by previous multilateral rules in deploying the tactics of *realpolitik* to define and achieve their national interests and regional ambitions. They are pursuing these differently and more aggressively than they could before, unconstrained by the checks and balances of a bipolar world. They are unwilling to accept the kind of multilateralism in which their rapidly growing economic and littoral power is neither adequately recognized nor sufficiently reflected. For them the emergence of a regional presence is a *sine qua non* in staking their claim to be taken seriously as partners and equals by the developed world rather than continuing to be patronized, and remaining second-class or third-class citizens under a multilateral regime which still works to diminish and marginalize them.

EMERGING TRENDS IN GLOBAL TRADE AND FINANCE

The following realities need to be superimposed on these five trends – which are forcing shifts in the tectonic plates which underlie multi-lateralism – for a clearer perspective on the unfolding of the future.

- **Between 1945 and 1985** the most rapid growth in world production, trade and in other economic transactions (finance, technology transfer, investment, the importance of transnational brands) occurred *within the North*.
- In the first two of those decades (**1945–64**) such growth was between Anglo-North America and Europe. The centre of economic gravity was firmly located in the North Atlantic.
- In the next two decades, **1965–85**, the growth in cross-border trans-actions was more widespread – it embraced USA–Japan, Europe–Japan, and intra-Europe – with positive and negative spillover effects for the rest of the world. The centre of global economic gravity had already begun shifting.
- **Between 1985 and 1995** a new trend has emerged which will con-tinue into **2005**. The fastest growth in world production and trade in goods, services and financial transactions is now *between* the North and the South. This is already occurring in:

— Asia (between Japan and East Asia, *within* East Asia, and between East and South Asia);
— Europe where there has been explosive growth in transactions between Western and Eastern/Central Europe and increasing growth between Europe and the Middle East and Europe–Africa; and
— the Western Hemisphere, where the same surge is being seen in transactions between Anglo and Latin America.

- If incipient indicators are reliable guides, **between 2005 and 2050** the fastest growth in production and trade transactions will be *within the South*, involving growth of production and trade *within and across* Southern regions. The centre of global economic gravity will thus shift inexorably again from transactions within the North to transactions *within the South* as the South begins to account for the bulk of world output and trade.

— If present growth trends continue for the next decade and moderate slightly thereafter (especially in the five or six most populous economies of the developing world) the South will account for over 60 per cent of real global production and 40 per cent of global trade by **2015** and slightly more thereafter.
— This contrasts with the South having accounted for less than 20 per cent of real global production and less than 6 per cent of global trade in 1950; and only around 40 per cent of global production and 25 per cent of world trade in 1985.

• The relative proportions of output and trade accounted for by the North and South (as they are defined today) should begin to stabilize **after around 2050**.

Seen against this backdrop, it is not unreasonable to suggest that the unresponsiveness of the present multilateral system in accommodating the new role that developing countries and RIAs are playing in the world economy may provide a larger part of the explanation for increased experimentation with more fluid, imaginative *plurilateral* arrangements. These are likely to be *intra-regional* in the first instance, and will inevitably become *interregionally*-orientated in their next evolutionary phase. To some extent the second phase is already overlapping with the first under arrangements aimed at linking regions together across the Pacific (APEC) and Indian Oceans (the IOR initiative) and across the Mediterranean Sea (EU–Maghreb arrangements); these are discussed further below.

CAN PLURILATERALISM FILL THE VOID CREATED BY DYSFUNCTIONAL MULTILATERALISM?

The suspicion is growing by the day that the kind of multilateral framework (and machinery) needed to cope with the new, and still evolving, global situation in a manner which enhances future global welfare – not just in a limited economic sense but in a wider sociopolitical context as well – may be quite different to the obsolete framework which is currently in place. Yet the belief among developed (that is, OECD) countries is that any significant redesign of multilateral architecture is unnecessary. Needed changes can be wrought simply by tinkering at the margins of the present system. Moreover, the tinkering is being left to multilateral institutions themselves. Yet, these institutions have established demonstrable vested interests which are less inclined towards meeting the needs of the world around them than to guaranteeing their perpetuation (and their immunities and privileges) in as little-changed a form as possible.

The belief that multilateralism needs only marginal changes is not shared by the non-OECD world which is acting to fill the void which a dysfunctional system has left. What is being resorted to instead is experimentation with plurilateralism aimed at tackling the common concerns of smaller groups of contiguous nations pragmatically, rather than being guided by protective ideological foundations, as it was earlier. It often appears that such initiatives are being taken impulsively without forethought or foresight. But their proliferation around the globe raises questions about whether they represent expedient responses to the acute frustrations caused by exclusion and dispossession, or whether they reflect efforts (perhaps driven subliminally rather than consciously) on the part of non-OECD countries to achieve global empowerment through plurilateralism.

Such self-help initiatives may not just be a matter of temporal convenience. They are not likely to be quickly reversed when their limitations are exposed and the expectations on which they are based are frustrated. They may instead turn out to be essential stepping stones to constructing a stronger multilateralism built on plurilateralism (involving a 'pooling of sovereignty' among contiguous states) in a region, rather than on nation-states (whose sovereignty is becoming increasingly ineffectual), as the legitimate member 'units'. Mooting these possibilities is, of course, necessarily an exercise in indicative speculation at the present time; it is still premature to answer definitively the core questions which have been raised.

If the sustained upsurge of regionalism that is taking place around the world proves durable, then strong regional institutional arrangements will inevitably emerge. These will result in progressively deepening regionalism being translated into effective supranationalism. If that happens, the present machinery of multilateralism will need to be transformed to accommodate a new set of political and economic interactions *among regional entities* rather than among nation-states; unless of course these states happen to be of regional dimensions themselves.

The example at the cutting edge of this issue is represented by the case of the EU. At the present time the EU appears to be at a difficult moment in its transition because it is becoming clear that the EU can no longer escape the logic of supranationalism under a federal structure. Can the monetary union which is being aimed at in the EU under the Maastricht Treaty be sustained and stabilized if accompanying fiscal policy across the EU cannot be negotiated and applied in a consistent manner across all member states? If the answer to that question is in the negative then such a requirement could not be met without a single overarching political framework under which fiscal policy and its application could be agreed. Assuming that were to happen, it would be odd if European representation in global (and some regional) multilateral institutions continued to be through the presence of each individual member state as a member in its own right, rather than through singular representation by the EU as an entity representing their collective federated interests. That anomaly was glaringly obvious in the case of the UR negotiations and in the formation of the new WTO. It will become even more obvious as time goes by in the UN system and in the BWIs.

What holds for the EU will hold equally for other regions if, or when, they develop the same degree of depth in their integration arrangements. If they do not, their bargaining power with EU-sized blocs (or even with countries the size of the USA, India and China, for example) will inevitably be weakened and compromised. Following that line of reasoning, the building blocks of a new multilateralism are already being constructed. Yet the extant multilateral machinery remains impervious to, and uncertain about, the future adaptations that must be made to accommodate exertion of regional influence.

If the new regionalism is not to be antithetical to multilateralism but instead help to shape multilateralism in the future, what characteristics must it have? The economic studies[5] which have been done (Mistry, 1994) suggest certain specifications for the kind of regionalism which would be compatible with existing multilateralism. They propose for example that new RIAs should:

- reduce simultaneously their external tariffs *pro rata* to the progressive reduction and elimination of internal trade barriers;
- be consistent and compatible with WTO rules and regulations;
- employ simple, straightforward and easy to monitor rules of origin;
- be non-discriminatory in the treatment of foreign enterprises; and

- incorporate effective dispute settlement mechanisms which are consonant with those used in multilateral arrangements.

These particular specifications are useful only in the limited context of visible-trade relations. Similar specifications are necessary for multi-laterally-friendly regionalism embracing other interactions such as: trade in services; investment and capital flows; labour market and human capital flows; and technology flows; as well as non-economic dimensions such as those covering security, environmental and ecological commons, other global commons, and political as well as international sociocultural exchanges. A careful analysis of the studies on regionalism which have been done by political scientists and international relations experts would enable such specifications to be extruded; but that is an exercise which is perhaps best left to another paper.

Apart from multilaterally-friendly characteristics being embedded in the plurilateral arrangements which have been devised since 1990 there are other reasons for believing that the new regionalism is more likely to support the emergence of functional multilateralism rather than to thwart it.

(1) There is comforting evidence that new RIAs already incorporate built-in features which will make more likely the emergence of effective multilateralism; in particular their openness and inclusivity.

(2) By strengthening plurilateral processes, even small weak nation-states have some say in decision-making at the regional level. The new regionalism is more likely to encourage the kind of multi-lateralism in which a relatively small number of larger and more-equal regional blocs will have more bargaining power with each other. They will therefore be more obliged to listen to and accommodate one another. This might result in small sovereign nation-states *indirectly* having a more influential effect on the three large *reserve-currency* nations (the USA, Germany and Japan) which dominate the dysfunctional framework under which multilateralism presently operates. Interaction among a smaller number of regional blocs, dealing with each other on a more equal footing, is likely to curb the multilateral power which these three nations have, and often abuse, when they are unable to handle their domestic political problems. As the events of 1990–5 have demonstrated, the USA, Germany and Japan have

each passed on to the rest of the world the costs of delaying their
internal economic, political and social adjustments resulting from
an inability to handle the domestic political implications of
addressing their internal imbalances and fiscal-monetary policy
twists.

(3) The new RIAs are multilaterally friendly because they are driven
by:

- market forces rather than by fiat;
- strategic alliances between governments and between transnational
corporations;
- technological innovation and information which is enabling regional
and multilateral integration to occur in parallel;
- convergent demands of regional and global consumers of goods and
services which are being traded competitively in a global marketplace; and
- technologically driven shifts in production which are breaking down
conventional patterns of vertically integrated mass-production
enabling much greater flexibility in global component sourcing
and localized assembly without losing the economic advantages of
scale (Oman, 1994).

Thus successful regionalization is dependent on lowering barriers to
successful globalization.

Paradoxically, the resurgence of regionalism is both a result as well
as a cause of the process of globalization. It has *resulted* from that
process because technologically-induced structural changes in the
globalization of production have made RIAs for market enlargement
more attractive and viable. It is also a *cause* of that process because
regionalism has reinforced and strengthened globalized production
through a positive feedback mechanism. What would have been considered anomalous even a decade ago is commonplace today. The UK
(because it is an efficient platform for exploiting the EU market) is
now competing with Malaysia and India for Korean investment in
semi-conductor manufacturing plants. Similarly the USA is competing
with Mexico for locating Japanese automobile and electronics assembly and manufacturing facilities.

Firms from developing regions are likely to become much larger
sources of foreign investment in the developed world in the next few
decades to establish and secure their global market shares for goods
and services in developed markets. Conversely, and at the same time,

firms in developed countries will expand their investments in (and export jobs to) developing regions in order to remain cost-competitive in their production of goods, and even in the provision of certain kinds of high-value services (for example, much of the information-processing for back-office support for the global banking industry is now being done more economically and efficiently in India). Obviously, in a world of globalized production possibilities for firms intent on developing a global consumer base, nation-states are becoming irrelevant (if not inconvenient) as entities of jurisdictional focus. All productive firms of almost any size (and not just established large transnational corporations) are open to possibilities anywhere which will reduce their costs, increase their consumption base, and enhance their profits.

Richer countries and regions will naturally resist and delay the economic and social adjustments which are necessary to accommodate market-driven shifts in patterns of global competitiveness. Yet the capacity for resistance and procrastination by their low-quality political leaderships, will be limited by the realization that the future growth and welfare of wealthy countries depend increasingly on sustaining demand in poorer countries. In globally open markets where the real costs of investment capital are being equalized, and where transfers of capital and technology (as well as of highly skilled workers) are instantaneous, richer countries will be compelled to make long-delayed internal adjustments to their uncompetitive costs for unskilled and semi-skilled labour, and of their social welfare systems, in order to compete against countries with much lower effective costs of labour than their own. Poorer countries on the other hand will have to:

- make long-delayed adjustments to antediluvian policies which have prevented their markets from functioning properly;
- revamp their ineffectual and counterproductively imperfect systems of political governance; and
- overcome their significant disadvantages in terms of their relative endowments of physical and social infrastructure as well as of high-level human capital.

Such adjustments might be deferred by both rich and poor countries – with significant costs for the long-term welfare of their national economies as well as that of the global economy. But they cannot be avoided indefinitely. The longer essential political, social and economic adjustments are delayed, the more painful and expensive the eventual dislocations are likely to be. In many cases these adjustments are likely to be more successful if undertaken in a regional rather than national context (Mistry, 1996) allowing national firms in these economies to become regionally competitive and financially viable before they can become globally competitive.

The transition from the old to the new multilateralism via pluralism, albeit inevitable in the long run, is likely to be fraught with various pitfalls. As temporary setbacks with the EU suggest, regional experiments of various kinds will evolve and be refined (or even reversed in some instances) over a period of time. Multilateralism based on the participation of regional rather than national entities, will therefore take a considerable period of time before it can become a practical reality. The EU is likely to be at the forefront of such a development if and when it occurs.

REASONS FOR OPTIMISM ABOUT THE FUTURE OF MULTILATERALISM

Despite the difficulties that will arise, there is room for optimism that the new regionalism with lead to more effective, functional multilateralism leading eventually to rule-based global governance of most international and interregional transactions. It took several centuries for the sovereign nation-states which exist today to evolve. The collapse of communism has resulted in a new impulse towards nationalism with the formation of new nation-states. That process may well spill over into other regions of the world as nation-states in Asia and Africa, forged under the pressures of colonialism, gradually re-assert pre-colonial ethnic identities. These new nations will need to enter into regional arrangements to survive economically. Seen in historical retrospect, the few decades it will take for nation-states to coagulate into larger regional entities through pooled sovereignty will appear to have taken a mere moment.

Reason 1

One reason for hope that regionalism will give way quickly to more functional multilateralism is that, as observed earlier, regionalism in the 1990s is being driven by forces which are essentially *global and private* rather than governmental, national, or regional, in nature.

Nation-state governments are seeking to lower the risks and uncertainties they face through: (1) the enlargement of their immediate economic and political space and (2) voluntary pooling of their sovereignty. Seen in that way the forces which are propelling regionalism in the 1990s and beyond are, at the same time, compelling regionalism to be globally compatible and multilaterally friendly.

Regionalism *per se* will not impede multilateralism any more than nationalism would. The real difficulty with the transition from the old to a new form of multilateralism may be a different one. Breaking down the old multilateralism – in which individual nation-states and their governments are the key actors – will result in uncomfortable dislocations before a new multilateralism can emerge in which regional institutions and private actors play a determining role. There is no easy or smooth way in which such a transition is likely to be achieved. It will be resisted strongly by vested interests who gain the most, in terms of their personal and official agenda, from the incestuous nexus which exists between key officials in national governments and the managements of multilateral institutions.

Reason 2

Regional arrangements themselves are attempting to coalesce at unanticipated speed through the emergence of overarching agreements which already embrace two or more reasonably well-established regions. APEC and the Indian Ocean Rim (IOR) initiatives are classic examples of such arrangements. APEC aims to embrace RIAs which have already been formed in North America and in Asia and may also come to embrace emergent RIAs which are achieving deep integration relatively quickly in Latin America. The IOR aims to embrace RIAs formed in Eastern and Southern Africa with those in South Asia, East Asia and the Antipodes through the membership of countries in IOR which are linked to more than one of these other arrangements. Similarly a Baltic community initiative linking the former Baltic States to Europe and the Nordic communities is taking shape. And, a new Atlantic Free Trade Area is being mooted to link RIAs in North and South America, along with those in the Caribbean to the EU (but not yet to those in Africa).

These *supraregional* umbrellas are being created and are attracting political and public support even before the more confined regional arrangements that they cover have been fully formed, or evolved sufficiently, to ensure that the basic principle of ever-expanding inclusivity is not compromised. They suggest that inclusivity reflects adherence to a new principle of regionalism – that is, avoiding the prospect of making any regional bloc a static, defensive, and closed entity with a membership which is fixed for all time. The emphasis has shifted from regions being exclusive clubs to becoming flexible and porous. RIAs now permit multi-speed and variable-geometry approaches to encourage inclusiveness. These two terms, of course, are shorthand for arrangements which permit some members of RIAs to take bolder and more rapid strides toward deep integration while leaving the door open for others to meet established criteria as and when their domestic political circumstances and constituencies allow.

Reason 3

As with GATT, there are now explicit provisions (Article 24) in the WTO and other multilateral organizations (for example, the regional development banks) not just to accommodate but to encourage the process of regional integration. There are also provisions in the NAFTA, EU and new Asian RIAs to establish association agreements with non-members. Moreover, the regional arrangements which are developing, are taking into account security and political considerations to a much greater degree than before; perhaps nowhere more so than in Europe and the Middle East.

In East Asia, ASEAN, which is generally regarded as one of the more successful and least bureaucratic RIAs in the developing world, started out as an association to anchor peace and stability among its members, through renunciation of the use of force for settling disputes, rather than to foster economic integration *per se*. Laudably, it has managed to achieve both security and prosperity for its members. In South Asia, however, SAARC has achieved neither, largely because of the implacable hostility of its two largest members towards each other; a situation which the rest of the world has done little to diminish through effective inducements or sanctions. The increasing resort in new RIAs to linkages between inclusivity and the achievement of economic *and security* objectives, provides further ground for optimism that such arrangements will eventually lead to a more effective multilateral framework under which regional economic and political achievements can be permanently enshrined, enforced and expanded.

Reason 4

There is now a discernible proclivity even on the part of large federal developing or transiting countries with continentally-sized internal markets – for example, Brazil, China, India, Indonesia, and Russia – to view RIAs as a serious alternative to the autarkic approaches they have pursued in attempting to achieve rapid national development. They do not see RIAs simply as vehicles for anchoring their domestic reforms and securing their new-found openness – reasons which were given by Mexico in NAFTA and by Greece, Portugal and Spain in Europe. Instead there is now a general belief in these and other developing countries that the notion of what constitutes *a market* – in a world which is globalizing rapidly at a rate which even inward-looking, self-obsessed national governments can do little to thwart or hold at bay without incurring severe punitive costs – has changed beyond recognition.

These subcontinental and largely self-sufficient economies, to which economy-of-scale arguments for regionalization have been unimportant, are now worried about becoming uncompetitive, and thus unattractive to foreign investment capital, if they do not become active and enthusiastic members of both their immediate regional, and the wider global, market regimes which are inexorably taking shape.

Reason 5

There is no evidence to suggest that the new regionalism binding countries through deeper *intra-regional* integration – a process which is only about five or six years old – is in any way thwarting *interregional* interaction. Take the example of trade: while trade *within* regions has grown dramatically during the last five years (especially in Asia and Latin America), it has not grown at the expense of trade between regions. That is one sign that the new regionalism may bolster rather than impede multilateralism. Another is that the same feature is true of both direct and portfolio investment capital flows. While private intra-regional capital flows have also grown dramatically since 1991, that has not happened at the expense of growth in interregional capital flows.

EVALUATING THE NEW REGIONALISM

A major difficulty that arises in evaluating the new regionalism is the absence of a sufficiently rigorous methodology for capturing, or even understanding fully, the essence of all of its costs and benefits. What is missing is an analytical framework (Mistry, 1994) for assessing RIAs in a more holistic manner than the Vinerian analysis, which is confined specifically to the limited issue of trade in goods. This approach – based on the now-familiar constructs of trade creation and trade diversion – has been the main plank, used for the last 45 years, for assessing whether RIAs are beneficial to potential members. But such analysis, while rigorous, is too partial, confined, and even misleading, to be satisfactory for drawing conclusions about *all* of the costs and benefits of a regionalism which attempts to achieve more than just enhanced trade opportunities. Vinerian analysis does not accommodate a reasonable assessment of either: (1) the *dynamic* economic effects of regional integration; or (2) the non-economic – that is, political, security, social, and so on – benefits and effects of regional integration.

Thus there is an imbalance between the sophisticated quantitative analysis which can be undertaken to assess the trade implications of RIAs and the less-rigorous, almost elusive, *qualitative* basis on which the case for assessing the non-trade effects of RIAs must rely. A further anomaly arises in that although Vinerian analysis involves mathematical sophistication, and is therefore perceived (by economists) as being 'hard', it relies on information/assumptions about the relative competitiveness of firms and on tariff and trade data which are imperfect and often without empirically validated foundations. The same type of rigorous mathematical analysis cannot be undertaken to evaluate other benefits that might flow from investment, policy co-ordination, or from security and political arrangements under RIAs. Evaluation of these benefits is invariably undertaken qualitatively, relying more on subjective judgement than on objective indicators.

Clearly this lacuna in intellectualization about regionalism, and the imbalance between the use of hard methodology to assess net trade benefits and comparatively soft methodology to assess all of the other dimensions of regionalism, leaves analysts and policy-makers in a difficult position when the case is made either for or against closer regional integration. They have little option except to react to such arguments on either judgemental or political-preference grounds.

Developing a holistic methodology for assessing all the advantages of regionalism in general, or even of specific RIAs in particular is, of course, easier mooted than achieved. There is no obvious precedent which suggests the viability of a single all-embracing approach to evaluating the costs and benefits of a phenomenon with multiple effects of a quite different nature (economic, political, military and social). Nor is it easy to contemplate how a meaningful interdisciplinary effort – bringing to bear all of the necessary expertise required in economics, political science, international relations, military and security matters, environmental and ecological sciences, as well as the social sciences – might be organized to develop a more appropriate methodology.

Even so, these obstacles do not provide sufficient reason for failing to undertake a search toward an approach which, however imperfect, might yet yield more valuable insights than either the Vinerian model, or the qualitative-judgemental alternative. For obvious reasons, the latter is often perceived as being based more on emotion than on reason and placing a premium on rhetorical articulation than on analytical incisiveness.

In carrying forward this argument it is interesting to observe that when it comes to preferences for multilateralism there is generally very little analysis demanded to *prove* that it is the best approach to resolving problems raised by cross-border interactions whether of an economic or political kind. It is simply assumed to be best for a variety of instinctive and intuitive reasons as well as for reasons founded in economic theory rooted in abstruse mathematics. Yet when it comes to preferences for regionalism the demands made to prove that regionalism can offer benefits (against a backdrop of general sentiment that regionalism is invariably second-best) are far greater.

This asymmetry, on reflection, raises questions of its own; especially when it is recalled that the nation-state – an entity whose legitimacy and sanctity is now taken for granted and whose intrinsic worth is much overplayed – was itself the product of an evolutionary historical (and invariably involuntary) process of territorial and tribal assimilation and aggregation. Regionalism through the formation of regional identities seems only to be the next natural and logical step in that same evolutionary process. The main difference appears to be that whereas nation-states were formed mainly through conquest, regions are taking shape through voluntary pooling of sovereignty.

A second and quite different concern in evaluating the benefits of the new regionalism is the threat that successful *macroregionalism* (the formation of supranational identities comprising several economically integrated member states) may trigger a simultaneous reaction towards *microregionalism* (the splintering of extant nation-states into constituent ethnic subregions). The combination of those two processes could, in some instances, obliterate the identity of many nation-states as they are presently constructed and, retrogressively, could undo the coherence which nation-states have managed to achieve. The UK provides a hypothetical example. If the evolution of the EU succeeded in providing a common currency, a common monetary policy, an agreed continental fiscal regime, a common foreign policy, and a common defence policy, with supranational institutions being created to implement all of these, it is difficult to see why a central government in the UK would need to exist. Applying the principle of subsidiarity to the pressures for devolution which already exist within the UK, it would be possible for its individual ethnically-identifiable components (England, Scotland, Wales and Northern Ireland) to fragment and operate as independent sub-sovereign entities sheltered under the broader regional framework provided by the EU. These mini-states could then easily undertake those functions of governance which were relegated to a lower level and thus taking care of the lingual, education, health, social welfare, policing and other local preferences of their populations.

This hypothetical possibility applies not just to the UK but to almost every EU member country which has clear internal fault-lines (for example, Catalonia in Spain, the North and South of Italy, the Flemish and the French components of Belgium, and so on). It also applies to other nations (with similar internal divisibilities) which are presently involved in regional formations on other continents (Quebec in Canada, the provinces of Mexico and so on). *What regionalism may spawn under enlarged economic spaces, is a proliferation (and possible realignment through reorganization) of smaller political spaces.* Such fragmentation would result in the governance of those aspects of life not catered for specifically at the regional level to be undertaken by more homogeneous ethnic entities; thus deploying the principle of subsidiarity more fully and at a lower level of political unit than is presently being contemplated, for example, in the EU.

The possibility thus exists that the new regionalism may result, unintentionally, in redefining yet again the notion of the residual nation-state. That could have a fall-out similar to the disintegration of the former Yugoslavia and Soviet Union where over 20 nation-states have emerged in the place of two. In these instances, the nations which have emerged have reinforced their ethnic identities at considerable cost in human lives and economic *disintegration*. In doing so they have compromised their immediate economic and political prospects – because of their significantly diminished bargaining power with the rest of the world – precisely because of the dissolution of the regional economic arrangements which formerly bound them.

In very few studies of the new regionalism have these possibilities, of redefining the future nation-state and coping with a new set of relationships among them, been envisioned or accounted for. It is difficult to establish a priori whether such a fall-out should be seen as a cost or benefit of regionalism and from which viewpoint. It would clearly be seen as a serious danger and an unacceptable cost by those anxious to retain extant national identities while subordinating their constituent ethnic identities. It might be seen as a benefit by those ethnic minorities (or even majorities) in extant nation-states which feel that they have been discriminated against and subordinated unfairly within their existing unitary political structures. Nonetheless, for those to whom the new regionalism means building on the blocks provided by existing nation-states, the distinct (and paradoxical) possibility of those very units being fractured by the success of such regionalism can only be a cause for justifiable anxiety and discomfort.

CONCLUSION

The various points made in this chapter – about the new regionalism, the global forces impelling its frequency, intensity and direction, and about whether regionalism constitutes a threat to multilateralism or a renewed opportunity to make multilateralism work better – need no summarization. What is behind these forces is encapsulated in two insightful observations made by Oman (1994) and Henderson (1994) respectively:

> Economists tend to see globalization as a good thing and, in looking at regionalization, economists have therefore tended to focus on the question of whether regional groupings are likely to constitute building blocks or stumbling blocks for globalization. Many other people, on the other hand, including national policy-makers and their constituencies, especially in the OECD, see globalization as threatening. They see it as accelerating the pace of change to which they must structurally adapt, and over which they seem to have less and less control. Even more than in the past, globalization tends to foster both *de facto* regional integration and *de jure* regional agreements among governments. Regionalization, in turn, tends to foster globalization in so far, and only in so far, as it is allowed to

stimulate the forces of competition within a region. The challenge for policy-makers is to pursue regionalization as a means to weaken the powers of entrenched natural oligopolies and rent-seekers while responding to the growing need, engendered by globalization, for deep international policy integration. And deep international policy integration is unlikely to occur without deep regional integration occurring first.

In the face of increasing regionalism, two questions can be asked about the future of the world trading and investment system. First, will it become more open and liberal? Second, will the extent and influence of regional trade blocs increase? Contrary to what is often suggested, these two questions are distinct. The future of the multi-lateral trade and investment system, and of international economic integration, will not depend on the extent to which regional inte-gration arrangements *per se* become more extensive or deep-rooted, but rather on how far liberal rather than interventionist influences will affect the evolution of external economic policies in the leading nation-states and trading entities, in particular the European Union and the United States. Regional agreements will largely reflect this balance – i.e. the balance between liberalism and intervention either at the national level or in the world as a whole – rather than determining it. That part of the current debate which portrays regionalism, on the one hand, and multilateralism on the other, as warring principles is misguided. A truer and more fundamental antithesis is the conflict between liberalism and interventionism, whether it be national, regional or global.

These two quotations, taken in context, summarize the essence of this chapter. If progress is to be made toward a more stable and prosper-ous world, regionalism and multilateralism cannot be seen as antag-onistic. They have to be seen as interwoven strands of the same continuum in the overall process of historical evolution in a political sense. The kind of multilateralism attempted in 1945 was a noble quest with objectives that remain valid. They should not be compro-mised despite the disappointing failure of multilateral institutions and processes to achieve them fully. Those failures have as much (if not more) to do the way in which nation-states have behaved in a multi-lateral context as with the defaults of the multilateral system itself.

Yet, much has been achieved through both regionalism and multi-lateralism. It is moot, if not mischievous and even pointless at this juncture, to try to compare which of these two processes has achieved more between 1945 and 1995. The achievements of neither should be trivialized. Yet, a dispassionate appraisal of regionalism and multi-lateralism, as practised thus far, would suggest that much that is desirable, from the viewpoint of global safety and human welfare, has not yet been achieved by either process.

In those areas where a perhaps premature thrust toward multi-lateralism may have failed to accomplish key objectives – in terms of both global prosperity and security – it is reasonable to explore whether regionalism, as an intermediate way-station, might not offer a better approach at the present time. It might offer a superior route to achieving more functional multilateralism in the future, rather than relying only on the marginal improvement of extant multilateral machinery that is demonstrably not working well.

Part of the reason for multilateralism being dysfunctional is that it depends on interactions among nation-states which are politically and economically so unequal (in their capacities, endowments and their future potential) that they have ceased to be meaningful constituent units on which multilateralism can rely for its functioning. Integrating individually insignificant national units into more influential regional economic and political entities may therefore be a prerequisite for multilateralism to function more effectively.

This does not mean that further progress with multilateralism must be deferred until regionalism has run its full course. Greater integra-tion through regionalism can be pursued in parallel with improving the functionality of multilateralism without the two processes being sequential. The efforts of policy-makers and analysts, at the national, regional and multilateral levels, must be focused on how the forces of globalization can be channelled towards eventually achieving fully functional multilateralism – however imperfect and elusive that desti-nation may seem at the present time.

Regionalism, globalization and multilateralism all seem to be por-trayed as potentially threatening to many national governments and their electorates in the developed world. They are seen as resulting in dilution or loss of sovereignty and power. They are also seen as compromising entrenched rights and expectations accumulated over a period of time – for example, the expectations of rising real incomes, total social security, free access to public education, health care and social services, and the right to secure jobs for life on the strength of an acquired skill or professional qualification. Governments and peo-ple in poorer countries which have not yet enjoyed these privileges may conversely see these same processes as a means towards acquiring them and towards achieving greater empowerment in the international arena.

Obviously, regionalism, globalization and multilateralism are not, in themselves, dangerous. They seem threatening only because they stimulate global competition and transmit its impact into national economies. But the world is inexorably becoming a single global market with or without regionalism. When the impact of competition is transmitted across national borders it inevitably compels societies, institutions and individuals to adapt more rapidly to global circumstances which are continually changing. The forces of global competition are therefore bound to cause painful domestic dislocations and adjustments as *dynamic competitive* (rather than *static comparative*) *advantage* shifts kaleidoscopically across firms and nations; and as the demands for remaining competitive (at the level of the firm, county, province, nation or region) requires continual retooling and investment in physical and human capital.

In a world that is globalizing regardless of whether national governments (or even regional organizations or multilateral institutions) and electorates may want it to, the challenge for national (or local) policy-makers is to ameliorate and accommodate the domestic dislocations caused in a politically acceptable fashion; that is, without incurring the risk of societal destabilization and the disruption of effective governance. Seen in that context, it is an exercise in futility for national politicians and governments to decry the disadvantages of further regionalization or of continued multilateralism. No matter how much they may wish to, it is now well beyond the capacity of any single government or nation to stop the world because it wants to get off. The genie of reliance on the market mechanism is now out of the bottle and has been provided free global access. It will be difficult, if not impossible, to put it back in the bottle and reverse the tide of universal capitalism without a global cataclysm of extraordinary dimensions.

The efforts of national governments and politicians would therefore be more productively expended on tutoring, leading and preparing their electorates for the reality that is materializing, whether or not they embrace regionalism and/or multilateralism. Political responsibility requires that national leaders pay more attention to convincing their electorates about the importance of shedding long-cherished, but no longer valid, beliefs about their *rights* and expectations, and shift political focus instead to their obligations and the efforts required of them to ensure that their societies can indeed compete against other societies with different attributes and advantages/disadvantages. It would be more constructive for the new regionalism to be portrayed as a voluntary pooling (rather than an involuntary surrender) of sovereignty, undertaken to increase collective bargaining power over a wider economic space, simply because national sovereignty is of diminishing value and of decreasing import and significance.

As Oman and Henderson incisively observe globalization is now a reality. The choice is therefore no longer one among nationalism, regionalism or multilateralism. These are all approaches to the end of societal betterment rather than destinations in themselves. The real choice is between a liberal market approach at the national, regional and global levels or an interventionist approach which attempts to keep the market at bay at all of those levels. It has become impossible to have the market work at any one of these levels but not the other. In 1990, history made a choice in favour of markets offering the dominant economic paradigm for the world economy for the foreseeable future. There is no going back. For the next few decades, regionalism offers a better approach than either nationalism or multilateralism in the interregnum between the era of the nation-state, which is about to end, and the era of global governance which is still some distance from materializing in effective form.

Notes

1. This chapter is based on some rough ideas first unveiled in a speech delivered at a Fondad Symposium on Regional Integration in Latin America and the Caribbean which was held in Santiago, Chile on 1–2 March 1995. A modified version of that speech was published in J. Teunissen (ed.) *Regionalization and the Global Economy: The Case of Latin America and the Caribbean* (The Hague: FONDAD, 1995).
    Throughout this chapter the term 'multilateralism' is used as having *global* connotations (that is, as in the UN or the Bretton Woods institutions or the WTO). 'Regionalism', while multilateral in nature (that is, in that it involves a set of multilateral relationships among a more confined group of usually, but not necessarily, contiguous countries) is often referred to as 'plurilateralism' to make a verbally convenient distinction from multilateralism. It must be recognized however that, while regional

arrangements are invariably plurilateral, it does not follow that plurilateral arrangements are necessarily regional (in a geographic context;
although they may be in an economic context).
2. This term is meant to denote an economic system based on the primacy
of free markets and prices in determining resource mobilization and
allocation at every level from national to global. Although the market
system has established its supremacy over the command economy, three
distinct market *models* appear to be emerging in the new era of universal
capitalism. The first, and least *laissez-faire*, is the *European social-market*
model where market economics and relatively free price-signalling are
broadly embraced in the economy but with a heavy overlay of social
compensatory arrangements and an intricate web of internal transfer
payments for a variety of purposes (education, health, welfare, unemployment, retirement and so on) which make labour markets more rigid,
less responsive and much less adaptable to rapid changes in dynamic
global comparative advantage. The European model has resulted in very
high social protection from dislocations but also in much higher levels of
structural unemployment in a world of globally freed capital flows. At the
opposite extreme is the *East Asian competitive-market model* where
markets are governed (but not replaced) by governments anxious to
achieve national competitiveness as a strategic goal, where full democracy is voluntarily suborned to the need to make rapid economic progress, and where social safety nets are neither as comprehensive nor as
expensive as in the European case. Asian labour markets, unrestrained
by excessively protective legislation, are extremely flexible and responsive although at the expense of job and social security. In between these
two market models lies the *American mixed-market model* which com-
bines some of the competitiveness of the Asian market model with some
of the social security arrangements of the European model, but not on as
comprehensive or expensive basis; thus leaving American labour markets
less rigid and more adaptable than European ones to changes in global
competitiveness but not in being quite as flexible as Asian labour markets.
3. Their response, in that sense, is not entirely dissimilar to those of global
investors who undertake portfolio diversification through holding a
wider range of assets in mutual funds and hedge on price movements
through risk management instruments.
4. There has been an impressive volume of work done on regionalism and
regionalization over the last five years, emanating from various sources
including: UNU/WIDER, OECD, GATT/WTO, FONDAD, the UK's
Royal Institute for International Affairs (Chatham House), UNCTAD,
the regional UN economic commissions and the regional development
banks, to mention but a few. These of course exclude ongoing academic
efforts as well as work being done by various strategic, specialized policy-

research institutions around the world on the regionalism phenomenon (see Mistry, 1994)

5. Unfortunately most of the work done by economists on regional integration is dominated by trade economists and is highly trade-focused although some recent work is beginning to cover non-trade dimensions.

References

Bhagwati, J. (1993) 'Regionalism and Multilateralism: An Overview', in J. de Melo, and A. Panagariya (eds) *New Dimensions in Regional Integration*, (CEPR, Cambridge University Press).

Braga, C. (1994) *The New Regionalism and Its Consequences* (Washington, DC): The World Bank).

Henderson, D. (1994) 'Putting Trade Blocs into Perspective', in V. Cable and D. Henderson (eds) *The Future of Regional Integration* (London: The Royal Institute for International Affairs (RIIA), Chatham House).

Hettne, B. (1994) *The New Regionalism: Implications for Development and Peace* (Helsinki: UNU/WIDER).

Mistry, P. S. (1994) 'Regional Integration and Development: Panacea or Pitfall?', paper prepared for a FONDAD Symposium on The Future of Regional Economic Integration, The Hague (4–6 Sept.).

Mistry, P. S. (1996) 'Regional Integration and Structural Adjustment in Southern Africa?' Paper prepared for a FONDAD/DBSA Conference on Regional Integration in Africa, Johannesburg (7–9 Feb.).

Oman, C. (1994) *Globalization and Regionalization: The Challenge for Developing Countries* (Paris: OECD).

Teunissen, J.J. (1995) (ed.) *Regionalization and the Global Economy: The Case of Latin America and the Caribbean* (The Hague: FONDAD).

6 New Regionalism in Southern Africa: Part of or Alternative to the Globalization of the World Economy?[1]

Bertil Odén

INTRODUCTION

There are several reasons for the revived interest in regionalization[2] as an analytical tool and potential instrument for development in the post-Cold War world (dis)order. Most of them are related to the globalization[3] of the world economy and the new global political economy where the political and economic power pattern is changed.

The literature on the changes at the global political level after the Cold War is mushrooming. Stubbs and Underhill (1994), Shaw and Korany (1994) and *Third World Quarterly* (1994) are recent sources for a good overview of the main issues of interest to countries in the South. In this context, I will not elaborate on the issue. Suffice it here to list some of the main features:

(1) the general level of trade tariffs is much lower and the trade regime in general much more liberal than, for instance, 30 years ago, in spite of the plethora of non-tariff barriers that have been introduced especially by the OECD countries to protect their producers against competition from developing countries. The liberalization trend will be further strengthened as the GATT/ WTO Marrakesh agreement is implemented;

(2) the hegemony of the market economy concept and the strong influence of neoliberal economic thinking in international financial institutions;

155

(3)   the proliferation of new states in the wake of the collapse of the Soviet Empire;

(4)   the technological breakthroughs in the areas of communications and information, revolutionizing financial and information systems of the world;

(5)   the increasingly evident pattern of three major trade blocs, dominating world production and trade and the increasing uncertainty as to the relations between them, giving various options for countries outside those blocs;

(6)   the increasing stratification among the countries outside the three main trading blocs, with a rapidly increasing gap, between the 'fastgrowers' in East, South East and South Asia and most of the SSA countries;

(7)   the emerging pattern of North–South regional co-operation and integration.

The strong economic and social stratification during the neoliberal era since 1980 has also created more evident core-periphery situations *within* both core, semi-peripheral and peripheral countries. This means that the previous world system categorization has to be developed from using only territorial perspectives into more complex categories.

When 'new regionalism' is used in this new and continuously changing global setting, the 'new' element, compared to some 'old' regionalism, is partly used to indicate just that the external framework has changed. But there are also other factors, distinguishing the old and new regionalism. The transformation from 'old' to 'new' regionalism is described for instance in Palmer (1991).

While new regionalism as a term is now used frequently in the discussion, the definition of what is meant by this term is ambiguous. All agree, however, that there is a need to distinguish old integration and regionalization projects from the ones that are discussed in the 1990s, for instance well articulated by James Mittelman in Chapter 2 in this volume.

> While this is not the place to rehearse a critique of each variant, all of them are deficient inasmuch as they understate power relations and fail to offer an explanation of structural transformation. In some ways a break with this tradition, the new regionalism approach explores contemporary forms of transnational co-operation and cross-border flows through comparative, historical and multilevel perspectives.

Although there are various implicit or explicit definitions of new
regionalism, I suggest that it is possible to distinguish between two
main lines. One is mainly based on a modernized and broader version
of trade integration theory and is focused on the relation between
trade regionalization schemes and 'multilateralism',[4] or globalized
trade liberalization. The theoretical framework is taken from neoclassical economics, mainly from trade integration theory.

The main example of the other concept labelled 'new regionalism'
is the UNU/WIDER project, of which this book is one output, the
'WIDER approach' for short.

The main issue in the first category is to analyse the relations
between trade integration schemes and the ongoing globalization
process in the post-cold war, post-bipolar world economy. The normative point of departure is that regionalization should not be
allowed to prevent the globalization process. Regional co-operation/
integration is seen as a second-best solution that should be designed
to avoid delaying the process towards an open global economy and the
globalization process. At the national level, this is also the ideological
basis of the structural adjustment programmes carried out by many
Third World countries, supported or imposed by the IMF and the
World Bank.

The second category of new regionalism can with Amin (1994) be
seen as a building block for constructing a different global system than
the present globalization, which by triumphalist neoliberal economists
is labelled 'the only way'. It can also be an alternative, where regionalism is a modifying factor in the globalization process.

Especially for groups of Third World countries, this category of new
regionalism can be seen as an alternative to continuing globalization
of the economy, in which process they individually are linked to the
North along the lines of a centre–periphery model. Not in the sense
that they delink themselves from the North, but with increased regional interrelations and interdependence on a regional level, rather than
directly to the core countries in the North. This alternative can be
looked upon as an adaptation of the 'collective self-reliance' concept
from the 1960s and 1970s to the global political economy of the 1990s.

Both concepts were introduced in the late 1980s (see, for instance,
Riesenfeld, 1989), while the main part of the literature using them has
been published during the 1990s. The aim of this chapter is to compare the two alternative concepts and investigate the degree to which
they are compatible or antagonistic. In order to concretize the discussion, Southern Africa is used as a case.

NEW REGIONALISM AS PART OF GLOBALIZATION – OPEN REGIONALISM

One part of the present discussion on open regionalism can be considered as a rebirth of that on the pros and cons of what is now called 'old regionalism' during the 1950s and 1960s. The focus of the discussion in both cases is on whether regionalism, defined as trade integration, is a step on the way towards multilateralism or whether it slows down this process, compared to international negotiations. This is discussed by Bhagwati. He argues that in this context two major questions must be answered. One is whether the immediate impact of preferential trade blocs is to reduce or increase world welfare. The other is whether, regardless of the immediate impact effect, regionalism will lead to non-discriminatory multilateral free trade for all, through continued expansion of the regional blocs until universal free trade is reached, or if it will fragment the world economy (Bhagwati, 1993, pp. 31–2). It is sometimes argued that regionalism as a path to multilateralism is a quicker, more efficient and more certain method than international negotiations with participation of a large number of individual countries. Bhagwati argues strongly against this perception. This was also his position when the issue was discussed 20 years ago.

At that time this was also the position of the US administration, while in the present global political economy it has shifted from a strongly 'multilateralist' attitude towards one in which regionalism is accepted, at least for the Americas as exemplified by NAFTA. Bhagwati argues:

> If America's regionalism is not to turn into a piecemeal, world trading system-fragmenting force, it is necessary to give to it a programmatic, world trade system unifying format and agenda. One possibility is to encourage, not to discourage, Japan to line up the Asian countries (all the way to the Indian subcontinent) into an AFTA, with the US lining up the South Americans into the NAFTA, on a schedule, say, of 10 years. Then Japan and the United States, the two 'hubs' would meet and coalesce into a larger FTA at that point finally negotiating with the European Community and its associate countries to arrive at the Grand Finale of multilateral free trade for all in Geneva. (Ibid., p. 45)

The World Bank discussion as it is developed in two recent documents, IBRD (1994) and Hallet and Braga (1994), does not explicitly take its point of departure in the new world order, but in the major regional trading agreements, stating:

Perhaps the two single most important recent developments that have brought regionalism into new prominence are the further integration and enlargement of the European Community (the European Union since the ratification of the Maastricht Treaty) and the establishment of the North American Free Trade Agreement (NAFTA). (IBRD, 1994, p. i)

According to the World Bank, the basic features of traditional trading agreements such as free trade areas and customs unions still continue to define new regional arrangements also, but that a number of more recent regional agreements have three additional elements. This is called 'new regionalism' in the World Bank studies.

(1) The agreements extend beyond conventional arrangements addressing trade in goods. They often also cover the liberalization of trade in services, movements of labour and capital, harmonization of regulatory regimes and co-ordination of domestic policies.

(2) North–South arrangements are based on reciprocity as opposed to one-way, unilaterally defined preferences, as in the Lomé convention. The recent example most commonly referred to is NAFTA.

(3) There is a shift of emphasis in South–South agreements, whereby free trade areas and customs unions seek to build on national trade liberalization efforts and complement outward-orientated trade strategies.

The IBRD study recognizes that there are also non-economic motives for regional integration agreements (RIAs), the instruments for new regionalism, according to the study. Apart from a formulation that 'countries may feel a political need to act in concert' those 'non-economic motives' belong to the economic policy field. 'Non-economic' motives in the World Bank language, means that regional integration arrangements are sometimes reached in spite of not being the optimal economic solution, which by definition is global liberalization, based on multilateral and as wide-reaching agreements as possible, such as the GATT Uruguay Round. The study thus recognizes that sometimes a number of countries may form an RIA to integrate deeper than a multilateral framework permits, or that participation in a RIA may be seen as an 'insurance' against the possibility that another regional bloc will turn protectionist, or to 'lock in' trade reforms at a national level to counter domestic pressure to reverse ongoing liberalization. Mainstream economists have in recent contributions underlined the importance of this 'locking in' argument for foreign investors, as the governments credibility through such arrangements is improved among potential investors. See for instance Gunning (1995) and Lyakurwa (1996).

The analysis in the IBRD report is focused on the costs of any RIA 'bearing in mind their intrinsically discriminatory character', both for outsiders and in terms of their effects on efforts to achieve non-discriminatory unilateral and multilateral trade liberalization. The premise of the study is the assumption that globalization is always the preferable development, that traditional comparative advantage trade theory also functions in a transnationalized global economy. 'Evaluating world welfare in strictly economic terms, economists believe that RIAs are second-best means of achieving trade liberalization, and there should be no complacency about their discriminatory effect' (IBRD, 1994, p. iv). The study excludes all factors except economic ones. What it calls 'non-economic factors' are actually 'suboptimal economic factors', if the perspective of the document is accepted. Later in the study the main theme is further elaborated:

> For the most part, unilateral liberalization with respect to the rest of the world and multilateral liberalization make better economic sense than liberalization built upon regional exclusivity. For this reason, non-economic arguments are often necessary to justify a regional approach....where the objective is to increase relatively low levels of trade among contiguous countries, emphasis may be more usefully placed upon the development of infrastructure and communication networks than upon trade preferences.
>
> (IBRD, 1994, pp. 31–2)

Logically following from this conclusion is the following recommendation as to future World Bank support to RIAs: 'Support for regional initiatives, in turn, has not been a priority. The analysis developed in this paper suggests that this strategy should be contained, given the second-best character of these arrangements' (ibid., pp. 33–4).

It seems as if the study is mainly an ideological text with the main aim to warn Third World countries not to involve themselves in regional arrangements not consistent with further globalization.

'Outward integration' and 'open regionalism' are key words. Regional economic policy contrary to the ongoing structural adjustment programmes at the national level is not accepted by the study. It can be noted that the recommendations of the study are more hostile against regionalization than the present position of the USA administration seems to be.

Without using the term 'new regionalism', the arguments of the World Bank studies can be found elsewhere in recent literature. It is the red line in the contributions to de Melo and Panagariya (1993), as well as in an article by the two editors (de Melo and Panagariya, 1992). See also, for instance, Bergsten (1994) and Hormats (1994). Davies (1992) labels this World Bank version of new regionalism 'neoliberal market integration', which is quite accurate.

Peter Robson argues in an article (Robson, 1993) that some recent policy-orientated appraisals of regional economic integration schemes among Third World countries have been unsympathetic or hostile. He uses the World Bank conference documents, which were later published in de Melo and Panagariya (1993), to exemplify this. According to Robson, the static allocation effects of regional integration on which the 'World Bank approach' is founded, overlooks the administrative, efficiency and transaction cost savings, that should be considered and which have been much emphasized in the EU discussion. Substantial gains can be expected in areas like interstatal roads, railways, ports, telecommunications, water supply and energy.

Other Examples of Open Regionalism

As already mentioned, Palmer (1991) is one of the scholars who have discussed the 'open regionalism' concept.[5] He associates himself with a discussion on regionalization in South East Asia, where this term is used to emphasize that the regional co-operation/integration envisaged will be outward-looking and take place within an open framework. Other authors using this concept are Drysdale (1991), Fine and Yeo (1994), Oman (1994), Gunning (1995), Mistry (1995), and Lyakurwa (1996).

The general content of open regionalism, as used in the discussion on East and South East Asia, is close to the new regionalism concept, used in the Hallet and Braga (1994) study. However, open regionalism in South East and East Asia has not been linked to organized trade integration schemes, such as free trade areas or common markets, but to regional interaction in selective areas, notably cross-border investments and a flexible and well-functioning financial system. The option to formalize the co-operation as a free-trade area or common market is sometimes discussed, mainly as a contra-reaction to NAFTA and the broadening and deepening of the European integration. See for instance Elek (1992), Kim (1992) and Panagariya (1994).

Open regionalism (*'regionalismo abierto'*) has also emerged in the Latin American discussion, for instance in a recent document from the UN Economic Commission for Latin America and the Caribbean, ECLAC. It distinguishes between open regionalism and general liberalization/globalization in the following way:

> What differentiates open regionalism from trade liberalization and non-discriminatory export promotion is that it includes a preferential element which is reflected in integration agreements and reinforced by the geographical closeness and cultural affinity of the countries in the region. A complementary objective is to make integration a building bloc of a more open transparent international economy. (ECLAC, 1994, p. 12)

As pointed out in a review article by Hettne (1994), apart from being a recognition of the fact that the global economy in the 1990s is different from the one in the 1960s, this is also a cautious strategy in a situation where there is a great uncertainty about the future development of the world economy. The ECLAC open regionalism thus can serve as a bridge to the alternative new regionalism concept.

NEW REGIONALISM AS ALTERNATIVE TO GLOBALIZATION

In this category two main options are available, both included in this volume. The most radical one is that of Samir Amin, which totally denounces globalization, because of its polarization effects. The WIDER approach is a more modest one, accepting that regionalization projects will take place within the framework of globalization, but constituting permanent parts of a global system, rather than being temporary sequences in the globalization process. Both are represented in this volume and it would therefore be repetitive to penetrate them in this chapter. To be able to discuss the two alternatives in the case of Southern Africa a brief presentation is, however, necessary.

Samir Amin

I argue that Samir Amin's chapter in this volume is based on a slightly different new regionalism concept than most of the others, and perhaps especially Björn Hettne's, which I call the 'WIDER approach'. In his recent writings, Samir Amin has expressed concern at the polarization of the global political economy and argued that the building of large integrated regions in the Third World – particularly in Africa and the Arab world, but also in Latin America and South East Asia – is the only efficient response to the challenges of a deepening polarization generated by the capitalist globalization processes. Amin is the scholar, whose perspective for the 1990s is closest to that of the 1960s and his arguing is similar to the general delinking debate 20–25 years ago, although he takes into consideration the deepened polarization as the core countries, in his analysis, exploit their five monopolies: technological, financial, access to the planet's natural resources, the media and communication monopolies and the monopolies of weapons of mass destruction. According to Amin, the restoration of the periphery to a *comprador* role is an accomplished fact and the World Bank structural adjustment policy is its manifestation.

Amin's alternative is based on three radical changes of the present global political economy, regionalization being one of them, as can be seen in the following quotation from Chapter 3:

Globalization, that is, the unilateral submission to the so-called rationality of the global market, is not really an alternative. It does not go beyond management of the crisis, and does not offer ways and means to overcome it. Therefore the only realistic alternative should proceed from combining:

(1) positive changes at the 'grassroots' (that is, the national levels), encompassing their ideological and political dimensions, opening the way to labour–popular social hegemonies;
(2) regionalization with a view to creating reasonable frames efficient for the political and social management of negotiated interdependencies going beyond the strait-jacket which the nation-state represents today with respect to the challenge of the 'five monopolies' generating polarization; and
(3) the progressive building of a global political truly democratic system, far away from the concept of hegemony, offering a

frame to the operation of interregional interdependencies. (Amin, 1994, p. 25; and Chapter 3 in this volume)

Amin's analysis lacks among other things a discussion of which social forces would be the bearers of the suggested radical changes of the present political economy, in the present hegemony for openness. Irrespective of the degree of utopia, it is clear that Amin's view of the role of new regionalism differs more radically from the open regionalism alternative. Amin regards it as a building block for constructing an entirely different global system and thereby an antagonistic alternative to the ongoing globalization. The WIDER approach, as exemplified by Björn Hettne, is more modest. New regionalism is a modifying factor within the globalized world. It shares, however, Amin's view that regional blocs, including those in the periphery, can constitute permanent parts of the world order and not temporary, second-best phases in the globalization process, as is the view of most supporters of open regionalism.

Open New Regionalism and the WIDER Project

This book and the related set of volumes give a good picture of where the new regionalism concept is positioned at present. In this section I shall briefly compare the WIDER concept with the open regionalism concept, in order to apply the two concepts to Southern Africa in the next section.

As the previous discussion showed, open regionalism is firmly based on neoclassical economics, particularly foreign trade theory including a type of enhanced trade integration, in which the static trade creation/trade diversion analysis still plays an important role. A main aim when launching the 'new regionalism' concept is to avoid regionalization among countries that may limit the scope for global economic liberalization. The 'WIDER approach' (or what has already been referred to as the New Regionalism Approach), on the other hand, is based on a broader perspective which includes economic, political and cultural aspects. It is a package rather than a single policy. It goes beyond the free market idea. The political ambition of creating territorial identity and regional coherence is important.

The ideological content of open regionalism is part of the worldwide domination of neoclassical economy, leading ultimately to a global market. In the new regionalism, as I understand it, regional constellations of states could constitute building blocks in the world order, and some of those would do not necessarily have to be linked to one of the three dominating trading blocs.

A third distinction, related to this, is that the new regionalism has as one point of departure a scepticism about the ideology of economic globalization, due to its polarizing effects at both a global and a national level. According to Hettne (1992), Polanyi's scepticism towards the 'hazards of planetary interdependence' associated with free trade corresponds to that of contemporary neomercantilists. Hettne argues that the end of the Cold War era led to a hegemonic position for the market, which would indicate that the stage is set for the second phase of Polanyi's famous 'double movement'; that is, when the self-protection of society is activated. Polanyi based his discussion of the double movement on the development during the second half of the nineteenth century and the double movement growing as a counteraction against the 'Utopian principle of a self-regulating free market' (Polanyi, 1957). His level of analysis was the leading countries of that era, thus the national level.

One hundred years later, it is clear that the principle of a self-regulating financial market is utopian. The self-protection of society in this case has, however, to take place at the global level, where it is difficult to see social forces corresponding to Polanyi's 'human and natural components' of the society. The international financial institutions are not playing this role and it is also difficult to define them as 'society'. Rules and regulations for the trade of goods are negotiated within GATT/WTO and through other international negotiations, which means international rules and regulations are more common in this field. An interesting issue – outside the scope of this chapter – is whether Polanyi's 'double movement' concept can be transformed from the national to the global, or at least regional, level.

Under open regionalism there is only room for three main trading blocs, which should be 'outward-looking'. In recent years the debate has increasingly focused on North–South integration, of which NAFTA is the main example. The ongoing negotiations between the EU and South Africa is another. These may well be the first signs of a general attitude in the North towards demanding reciprocity in trade agreements with countries in the South. The new regionalism differs also on this point, as it claims that there is room for weaker regional blocs emerging in the periphery, as permanent parts in interregional discussions and negotiations.

Mistry (1995), in comparing Hettne with Hallet and Braga (1994), concludes: 'It is becoming increasingly apparent that the non-trade aspects of regionalism – which have invariably been underplayed by trade economists who have monopolized debate on regional integration since the invention of Vinerian analysis in the early 1950s – may even be more significant than the trade related aspects of the process.' Mistry suggests that one reason for the emerging new regionalism is that 'the multilateral system as presently constructed is functioning with an increasing degree of imperfection, uncertainty, inefficiency and ineffectiveness.' He goes as far as to suggest: 'Open regionalism may not therefore just be a conducive to more effective future multi-lateralism, it may actually even be a prerequisite for building a new multilateralism of the kind that more properly reflects the changes that have occurred in global balances of geopolitical and economic power.'

When it comes to the balance between inward-looking and outward-looking regionalism, the WIDER concept is still ambiguous. As it is so multifaceted it is obvious that the level of openness is much more difficult to define than when trade integration or rules for cross-border investment are discussed.

This issue is implicitly discussed by Hettne: 'The new regionalism is emerging in the grey area between the free trade area model [trading blocs as a 'decentralized' GATT system], on the one hand, and the Fortress model on the other. The new regionalism is also a Third World phenomenon and may in fact provide solutions to many problems for the South' (Hettne, 1993a, pp. 8–9).

Among the issues to be further elaborated upon, Hettne (1993b; and Vol. 5 in this series) mentions:

- self-reliance was never viable on the national level, but may be a feasible strategy on the regional level (collective self-reliance);
- collective bargaining on the level of the region could improve the economic position of Third World countries in the world system;
- collective strength could make it easier to resist pressures from the North;
- certain conflicts between and within states may be more easily solved within a regional framework.

NEW REGIONALISM IN SOUTHERN AFRICA

In this section the discussion on the two main new regionalism concepts is applied to the case of Southern Africa, in order to investigate to which extent they are compatible, in spite of their covering two different concepts.

Initially, it should be noted that the label 'new regionalism' has also been used to discuss Southern Africa regionalization by, for example, Martin (1991) and du Pisani (1993). None of them, however, seem to use the term as a new theoretical concept, but rather to label the normative alternative among their scenarios for the future development of Southern Africa. With the IPE levels of analysis they discuss at the regional and national level, while the open regionalism and WIDER also include the global level. Martin's and du Pisani's perspectives, although focusing on the intra-regional factors in the Southern African region, are broader than the enhanced trade integration analyses used by the World Bank. In spite of their use of the term 'new regionalism', they fall outside the discussion in this context.

The ongoing discussion on new regionalism in Southern Africa is mainly based on the open regionalism concept, with the theoretical framework taken from trade integration and direct investment theory.

In Southern Africa most countries[6] have undergone formal SAPs, including a strong trade liberalization and more open rules and regulations towards foreign investments. Since 1993 the Crossborder Initiative, CBI,[7] has been under implementation, which further strengthens the liberalization of regional trade and capital movements. Both these activities are carried out at the national level, and can be reversed by decisions at the same level. An increasingly popular argument for regional integration among trade theory economists is that it will 'lock in' the trade liberalization decisions, due to the increased costs for an individual country of reversing them. Gunning (1995) takes this argument one step further by suggesting that the locking-in instrument should take the form of North–South integration, which would also promote the credibility of the participating countries' trade liberalization towards international investors.

In Southern Africa there is one long-standing example of relatively successful asymmetric trade integration in the form of Southern African Customs Union, SACU. The dominance of South Africa over the other members[8] has been very strong and South African institutions have been administrating the union without any particular SACU institutions. This will be changed in the new SACU agreement which is under negotiation in 1996.

Meanwhile the region, excluding South Africa, has had 15 years' experience of project co-operation within the SADC[9] framework, which during 12 years deliberately avoided trade integration and focused on co-operation around project investment and functions.

Some previous suggestions on regionalization in Southern Africa, have been based on a development integration model. See for example, SADC (1993) and Davies (1993). That model contains also trade integration, but the degree of openness is less, compared to what the strong forces behind the open regionalism demand.

Increasingly it has become clear that the Marrakesh agreement and GATT's transforming into WTO will make it very difficult for any inward-looking regional trade agreement to emerge. The worldwide hegemony of globalization puts a strong pressure also on the countries in Southern Africa to liberalize further and open up their economies to the rest of the world, both at the national and the regional level.

The trade integration discussion is totally dominated by this view and the scope for inward regionalization is very limited. Therefore at the trade and investment level anything else than open regionalism is probably excluded for Southern Africa.

It is difficult to find any mainstream economist in Southern Africa who argues for anything else than open regionalism or no regionalism at all in order to avoid disruption of the globalization process. However, some trade unions in South Africa and owners/managers in, for instance, threatened textile companies argue for a slower pace than decided upon in this ongoing trade liberalization process. The argument is that too strong unrestricted competition will de-industrialize important labour-intensive parts of the South African manufacturing industry. On the other hand, within the Department of Trade and Industry it is argued that the choice for labour intensive South African manufacturing industry, such as textiles, is either to move the production to neighbouring countries where the labour costs are significantly lower or to be wiped out by imports from China and South East Asia in a few years' time when the transition period of gradually reduced protection under South Africa's agreement with GATT/WTO is over.[10]

In Southern Africa, the trade flows have increased significantly, while the trade regime has gradually been liberalized in a number of countries, but not as part of formal trade integration scheme. SACU has continued to exist along the previous lines, waiting for the result of the ongoing negotiations on a new agreement. SADC has not been able to decide upon a trade regime, in spite of several efforts by its Trade and Industry Sector secretariat. The reduction of the PTA/ COMESA tariffs are only carried out by a few of its members and above all the SACU countries, with the dominating share of the intra-regional trade, are not affected.

In Southern Africa, as in many other regions, the two processes of economic globalization and political regionalization are going on simultaneously. How compatible are they in Southern Africa, and which are the main forces that will support the two models?

The new regionalism has not explicitly been discussed with Southern Africa as a case. But a similar broadly-based, regional project taking the economic globalization into consideration in a Southern African context can be found in some SADC documents. They contain, however, some features that distinguish them from open regionalism:

(1) they are much broader sectorwise than the enhanced trade integration model in the open regional integration;
(2) they are modes of regionalization outside the trade integration pattern;
(3) there is an emerging common view on main policy issues, not only macroeconomic ones. This trend is however still fragile, and can be broken over specific issues;
(4) they involve regional security; and
(5) they involve environmental issues.

The official SADC line may thus be interpreted as close to the 'WIDER approach' to new regionalism, although SADC documents are not formulated very clearly on this point (SADC, 1993 and 1994). They do not refer to any contradictions between trade integration and what is called development integration, including both environment and security issues. SADC can be said to avoid this question, mainly because it is not perceived as contradictory.[11]

Within SADC, which according to its treaty and other policy documents should be closer to the new regionalism concept, an interesting change is taking place. During the last few years, including 1996, the importance of the private sector for creating growth and development in the SADC countries has been emphasized. The objective of the whole presentation in the theme document at the 1996 SADC Consultative Conference, seems to be to convince the private sector to invest in and trade with SADC countries.

The easing of regional trade barriers, enlarging regional markets and promoting investment are most useful when used as strategies to marketing a particular region as an attractive option for international trade and investment'   (SADC, 1996, p. 20).

To unleash the private creativity and entrepreneurship, investment incentives such as guarantee against nationalization of private enterprise, the right to repatriate capital, profits and dividend, lower corporate tax rates, including tax exemptions, have been employed to attract local and foreign investment. The direct role of governments have been minimized whilst their management capacity, as well as that of providing infrastructural support, have been enhanced.   (Ibid., pp. 20–1)

During the conference open regionalism was the dominant perspective, strongly argued by many donor agencies, the representatives from large international and South African firms, as well as from private sector interests in other SADC countries, criticizing South Africa for having a too protectionist trade policy.

As long as the focus is on trade of goods, investments and capital flows the pressure for open regionalism will be strong. To what extent this is compatible with SADC activities along the 'development integration' pattern suggested in previous SADC policy documents, with important state intervention in order to avoid increasing the inherited regional imbalances, remains to be seen. It may be that SADC develops into a two-track organization: on the one hand following open regionalism in the areas of trade, investment and capital flows; and on the other, following more regionally-based activities in regional goods sectors, security, environment, culture etc.

The SADC comprehensive agenda is a new feature in the history of regionalization in Southern Africa. SADC most often calls it development integration, although with market integration included as well as the flexibility of 'multi-speed' and 'variable-geometry' features that are suggested in the African Development Bank study (ADB, 1993). The comprehensive SADC perspective may be categorized as a variant of new regionalism. To what extent implementation of regional issues in Southern Africa will follow such a pattern is another question.

One feature of the new regionalism which is consistent with the development taking place in Southern Africa is the within and below perspective. Not that SADC is a popularly-based organization, although during 1994 and 1995 it organized a number of workshops and conferences aiming at mobilizing NGOs and other popular groupings. But co-operation is taking place and organized by interests outside the government structures, supported by SADC. One example is the Southern Africa Power Pool, organized between public electricity companies and formalized in a SADC Protocol on this issue. Variable-geometry co-operation in the fields of tourism, transports and so on should also be noted as consistent with the 'from within and below concept'.

The most interesting point in this case, as well as at the more general level, is if the 'WIDER approach' to regionalism and the open regional integration concept are compatible in the sense that they can be implemented on parallel tracks. The economic forces arguing for the open regionalism concept are obviously much stronger than those interested in the WIDER concept, but are there any major reasons why they should be against it, as long as it is perceived as a complement and not 'a stumbling block'. Partly, this is a parallel discussion to that on the compatibility between an open trade and investment regime and functional co-operation in sectors like water, energy, transport and communication.

The level of protection that is envisaged in the new regionalism is of course crucial to its compatibility with the open regionalism. On this point the 'WIDER approach' so far is vague at the general level and has not been applied in any specific case. My impression after being able to follow the discussion is that during the project it has developed into a gradually more open direction, partly as a reflection of the increasing hegemony for global openness in the field of trade, investments and financial flows.

In South Africa discussions on regionalism are taking place from both the open new regionalism and the broader new regionalism perspective, with the proponents of the former dominating the debate. Representatives from the private sector and mainstream economists belong to this group, which also is supported by external institutions such as the World Bank, IMF, aid agencies, especially the USAID and the UK. There is a risk that trade and investment considerations reduce the scope for any other type of regionalization.

SOUTH AFRICA AS BENEVOLENT REGIONAL HEGEMON?

New regionalism as well as other regionalization models do not explicitly take into consideration a situation as in Southern Africa, where one partner is a strong dominant in the region. On the contrary, normally regionalization models implicitly assume more or less equal partners.

However, an analysis of the regional political economy in Southern Africa that ignores the hegemonic position of South Africa would be futile. This leads to the question of what type of hegemonic regime could be developed in the region: benign or exploitative. This is not the place to elaborate profoundly on the issue, which should be discussed as a topic in its own right (Odén *et al.*, 1995).

For a hegemonic regime to emerge in Southern Africa at least two minimum conditions have to be fulfilled:

- South Africa must have the capacity and the will to create and maintain a mutually beneficial hegemonic regime; and
- The other countries in the region must be willing to let South Africa play the role of benign hegemon and they must have sufficient capacity to be able to participate within such a regime.

There are at least four dimensions of these two requirements:

(1) political will
(2) economic capacity
(3) institutional capacity
(4) nation-building and political stability.

In Southern Africa the most dynamic regionalization forces are often to be found among actors (private and public) in the economic field. They will often act faster than intergovernmental forces, which have a tendency to negotiate over long periods of time before they come to conclusions on how regional co-operation and integration should take place. It should also be added that the over-all capacity of the states in the region to implement regional integration is weak, which further restricts the capability of governmental action.

Furthermore, if the nation-building process has to be completed before governments and other actors are prepared to embark upon genuine regionalization, then it is difficult to envisage any quick progress in Southern Africa.

This may significantly reduce the possibility for the emergence of a benign hegemonic regime. However, it also entails that the potential for hegemonic regionalization varies between different sectors. The asymmetric interdependences existing in Southern Africa, notably within 'regional' goods sectors can be utilized to create and maintain mutually beneficial relationships.

The political will to integrate is stronger in these 'regional' issue-areas than in those sectors where the prospective benefits and their distribution are more diffuse and matters are more politicized. Even though economic and institutional capacity are unevenly spread in the region, there appears to be enough capacity from which to start, given that a sufficient degree of political will and stability exists in the region.

The pressure from the international level to continue liberalization in the areas of trade, capital and investment are strong and the institutional framework has been increased by the Marrakesh Agreement. Meanwhile the World Bank and the IMF continue to police this development at the national level, strongly committed to the idea that it should not be disturbed by more ambitious regional initiatives. This reduces the scope for the kind of regionalization that SADC policy documents envisage. SADC's weak capacity and the real, as opposed to the rhetorical, backing by the member states has so far been modest.

There may exist two very different types of hegemonic regime in Southern Africa. In the first, the regional hegemon seeks to create a regime that serves its own myopic short-run national interests, through the exploitation of its partners. In order to do so the hegemon is relying mainly on authoritarian control, coercion and negative sanctions. This is the exploitative hegemonic model of regionalization. In the second, the regional hegemon is facilitating the emergence of mutually beneficial relationships between itself and its partners. It is applying a long-run perspective on the definition of its national interests and the interests of the regime. Regional benevolence is not interpreted as contradicting the facilitation of long-term national interests, but mutually supportive to it. This may be categorized as the benevolent hegemonic model of regionalization in Southern Africa.

What type of hegemonic regime emerges in Southern Africa will depend on the balance between market and political forces. This can also be expressed in terms of balance between open regionalism and multidimensional new regionalism. A stronger benign hegemonic regime will support an emerging new regionalism and that in turn will improve the conditions for benign hegemonic regime. On the other hand, a more exploitative hegemonic regime will be based on a stronger degree of open regionalism. Against this background two interesting questions emerge.

(1) The modest question is whether it is possible to combine a continued open regionalism in the sectors of international goods

with some type of alternative new regionalism in the regional goods sectors, including also environment and security?

(2) The more ambitious question is whether it is possible to create a regional regime also in the areas of trade, investment and capital that aims at developing the region into one more permanent building block in an international world order, strong enough not be be forced into the role of backyard of one of the three major economic blocs.

CONCLUDING REMARKS

I have tried to summarize the differences between the 'open new regionalism' and the 'WIDER approach' to new regionalism in Table 6.1. While the former is a formally economic project, the latter has much more of explicit political content. The political effects of open regionalism are still strong, as it puts severe constraints to the regionalization process in many areas. In passing it can be mentioned that one reason for the low level of success of regionalization schemes in Africa may be that, while they are highly political projects, their aims are often expressed in the form of economic (trade) integration, which is based on assumptions regarding the economic structure and development level that are far away from that in the participating African countries.

In recent years the open regionalism concept has grown stronger, and is backed up by main international institutions, not only the World Bank and the IMF. This trend has been further strengthened by the establishment of the WTO and the Marrakesh Agreement.

One issue which merits further research is to what extent the two open regionalism and the WIDER new regionalism concepts can be used simultaneously, in various politico-economic areas. Here Southern Africa could be a good case to study. At the national level SAPs have created open, liberalized and still liberalizing trade regimes in a number of countries in the region. Important influences from South East Asia affect the political and economic debate, including advice for further liberalizing of the rules and regulations for trade, investment and capital flows. South Africa is gradually liberalizing its foreign trade, investment and foreign exchange regimes. External forces, including the IFIs and bilateral donors support these activities. The broad SADC regionalization concept, called development integration

Table 6.1   Two concepts of new regionalism

	Part of globalization* – 'Open regionalism'	*Alternative to globalization* – 'WIDER regionalism'*
Focus	Consistence with 'multilateralism'. Temporary stage, as a second-best solution	Alternative to bilateral linking to core countries More permanent part of world order
Normative content	Globalization superior to any other world order and gives highest global welfare.	Globalization not the preferred world order Regionalism one instrument to avoid increased global polarization
Discipline from which main perspectives are taken	Neo-classical economics (trade theory)	International relations International political economy International security studies
Relation to world market	Open, outward	Less open, but not inward
Political initiative	Reactive – outside From above	Active – inside From below
Main proponents	World Bank IMF Neo-classical economists 'Open-regionalism' IR scholars writing.	UNU/WIDER project IR, IPE and peace research scholars, such as Amin, Buzan and Hettne
The role of periphery countries	Subordinated partners either in a globalized world order (multi-lateralism) or linked to the core countries of one of the three main trading blocs (North-South integration)	Regionalized groups of periphery countries subordinated but with more autonomy in the global political economy

* What is labelled here as globalization is often called multilateralism in documents, for instance from the World Bank and GATT.

and with some features similar to that of WIDER's new regionalism is less in focus both in the discussion and in real life.

Will SADC policy be able to survive the globalization trends in the fields of trade, investments and finance capital? Is it possible to develop a more coherent Southern Africa, which as a region can play a role in an emerging world order? Will an end-1990 revival of Karl Polanyi's second movement contribute to get the unleashed market forces under a certain control at the regional level? This depends on political commitment, economic and institutional capacity and level of national maturity and long-term perspective in the countries concerned. The forces in the region supporting such a development are at present not very visible. There is however an awareness at the policy level and among individual politicians, private company executives, scholars and others that may be able to enhance this perspective and also give it stronger organization.

A further argument would be that new regionalism as an alternative to globalization seems to be relevant for Southern Africa because trade integration is not the driving force; because of its inside, from-below perspective; because its wide coverage allows the inclusion also of such obvious existing or potential conflict issues in the region as migration and utilization of water resources; because the 'SADC feeling' to the extent it exists, can be utilized; and because the potential improvement of the region's position in the international division of labour.

As already stated, such a development may be significantly simplified with a benevolent hegemonic regime in the region. This would imply that South Africa has the commitment and capacity to play the role of regional hegemon and that the other countries are prepared to accept such a role.

Notes

1. I would like to express my thanks to professor Björn Hettne, Hans Abrahamsson and Joakim Öjendal for constructive comments on an earlier draft of this chapter.
2. The distinction between 'regionalism' and 'regionalization' is that the former refers to the general phenomenon while the latter refers to the process, either through implementation of a strategy aimed at creating a regional system or as result of more spontaneous forces. In the literature several terms are used, which sometimes are not clearly defined

and partly overlap each other. Hettne suggests 'a normative meaning of regionalism by using it primarily with regard to regional integration as a political project, while using substitutes such as "regional cooperation", "regional initiatives" and "regional integration" in a more positive (i. e. descriptive) context' (Hettne, 1992, p. 6).

3. 'Globalization' is defined in various way, depending on discipline and school of thought. The military/security realists refer to the technological developments which make weapon and communication systems 'global'. Others refer to the increased universality of rules, regulations and institutions, decided within the UN, GATT or other frameworks. Still others focus on the spread and commonization of ideas and information, often referred to as 'the Global Village'. My focus is on the increased movement of finance capital and the new pattern of trade and production resulting from the new information technology, giving scope for economic actors to act at the global level, while political actors still live in an international world.

4. In the jargon of the international organizations the expression 'multilateralism' is often – somewhat inadequately – used to cover both the political and the economic spheres. I shall occasionally use this expression as an alternative to 'globalization', particularly when the text refers to the World Bank and its discussion of the relation between 'regionalism' and 'multilateralism'.

5. A good definition of 'open regionalism' is suggested in a footnote to an article by Frank Gibney: 'This is best defined as a policy furthering removal of trade, investment and technology barriers, with an eye on GATT disciplines, expanding subregional trading agreements and working towards mutual, nondiscriminatory access to economies elsewhere' (Gibney, 1993, p. 23).

6. Seven of the twelve SADC countries have had or have formal SAPs, based on agreements with the IMF and the World Bank. The macroeconomic and debt positions of South Africa, Botswana, Namibia, Mauritius and Swaziland have not made it necessary for those countries to introduce IMF/World Bank-backed programmes.

7. *Regional Integration and Cooperation in Africa.* Crossborder Initiative. Eastern and Southern Africa and Indian Ocean. (Supported by ADB, EC, IMF, WB) (Jan. 1995).

8. Botswana, Lesotho, Swaziland and *de facto* from its independence 1990 also Namibia.

9. SADC, Southern African Development Community was established in 1992, as a transformation of the Southern African Development Co-ordination Conference, SADCC, which was formed in 1980. SADCC focused on project co-ordination as method of co-operation, while SADC aims at a much more ambitious level of regional integration. SADC has twelve members: Angola, Botswana, Lesotho, Malawi, Mauritius, Mozambique, Namibia, South Africa, Swaziland, Tanzania, Zambia and Zimbabwe.

10. Personal communication, 7–8 Feb. 1996.

11. This view was confirmed in an interview with the executive secretary of SADC, Kaire Mbuende, 31 Jan. 1996.

178 New Regionalism in Southern Africa

References

African Development Bank, (ADB) (1993), *Economic Integration in Southern Africa* vols 1, 2 and 3 (Abidjan: ADB).
Amin, S. (1994) 'Regionalization in the Third World – In Response to the Challenge of Polarizing Globalization (with special reference to Africa and the Arab world)', paper prepared for presentation at the 16th World Congress of the International Political Science Association, Berlin (21–5 Aug.) Reprinted as Chapter 3 in this volume
Bergsten, C. F. (1994) 'APEC and World Trade. A Force for Worldwide Liberalization', *Foreign Affairs*, **73**, (3).
Bhagwati, J. (1993) 'Regionalism and Multilateralism: an overview', In J. De Melo and A. Panagariya (eds) *New Dimensions in Regional Integration.* (Cambridge: Centre for Economic Policy Research/Cambridge University Press).
Davies, R. (1992). *Integration or Co-operation in a Post-apartheid Southern Africa: Some Reflexions on an Emerging Debate*, Southern African Perspectives, no. 18 (Bellville: Centre for Southern African Studies, University of the Western Cape).
Davies, R. (1993) 'Emerging South African Perspectives on Regional Cooperation and Integration after Apartheid', in B. Odén (ed.) *Southern Africa After Apartheid. Regional Integration and External Resources* (Uppsala: The Scandinavian Institute of African Studies).
de Melo, J. and A. Panagariya (1992) 'The New Regionalism', *Finance and Development* (Dec.).
de Melo, J. and A. Panagariya (eds) (1993) *New Dimensions in Regional Integration* (Cambridge: Centre for Economic Policy Research / Cambridge University Press).
Drysdale, P. (1991) *Open Regionalism: A Key to East Asia's Economic Future*, Pacific Economic Papers no. 197 (Canberra: Australia–Japan Research Centre, Australian National University).
du Pisani, A. (1993) 'Post-Settlement South Africa and the Future of Southern Africa', *Issue. A Journal of Opinion*, **21** (1–2).
ECLAC (1994) *Open Regionalism in Latin America and the Caribbean* (Santiago: Economic Commission for Latin America and the Caribbean).
Elek, A. (1992) 'Trade Policy Options for the Asia-Pacific Region in the 1990's: the Potential of Open Regionalism', *American Economic Review*, **82**(2).
Fine. J. and S. Yeo (1994) 'Regional Integration in Sub-Saharan Africa: Dead End or Fresh Start?' paper presented at AERC Workshop on *Trade Liberalization and Regional Integration*, Nairobi.
Gibney, F. B. (1993) 'Creating a Pacific Community. A Time to Bolster Economic Institutions', *Foreign Affairs,* **72** (5).
Gunning, J.W. (1995) 'Regional Integration and Strategies for Trade Policy in Sub-Saharan Africa', paper presented at the 11th World Congress of the International Economic Association. Tunis.
Hallet, A.H. and C.P. Braga (1994) *The New Regionalism and the Threat of Protectionism* (Washington: The World Bank, Policy Research Working Paper, 1349).

Hettne, B. (1992) 'The Double Movement: Global Market versus Regionalism', paper for the UNU symposium on *Multilateralism and Images of World Order* (Oct.) (Florence: United Nations University).

Hettne, B. (1993a) 'The Future of Development Studies' (Padrigu Working Papers no. 29, Göteborg University).

Hettne, B. (1993b) 'Neo-Mercantilism. The Pursuit of Regionness', *Cooperation and Conflict*, **28** (3).

Hettne, B. (1994) Review in *Ibero Americana, Nordic Journal of Latin American Studies*, **24** (1).

Hettne, B. and A. Inotai (1994) *The New Regionalism. Implications for Global Development and International Security* (Helsinki: UNU/WIDER).

Hormats, R. D. (1994) 'Making Regionalism Safe', *Foreign Affairs*, **73** (2).

IBRD (1994) *The New Regionalism and Its Consequences*, Sec M94–234. (Washington: IBRD).

Kim, D.-C. (1992) 'Open Regionalism in the Pacific: A World of Trading Blocs', *American Economic Review*, **82** (2).

Lyakurwa, W. (1996) 'Integration of Trade and Finance in Africa', paper presented to FONDAD/DBSA conference on *Regional Economic Integration and Global Economic Cooperation: The Case of Africa*, Midrand, South Africa.

Martin, W. G. (1991) 'The Future of Southern Africa: What Prospects After Majority Rule?' *Review of African Political Economy*, 50.

Mistry, P. (1995) 'Open Regionalism: Stepping Stone or Millstone toward an Improved Multilateral System?' in J. J. Tenunissen (ed.). *Regionalism and the Global Economy. The Case of Latin America and the Caribbean* (The Hague: Fondad).

Morales, R. and C. Quandt (1992) 'The New Regionalism: Developing Countries and Regional Collaborative Competition', *International Journal of Urban and Regional Research*, **16** (3).

Odén, B. (1994) 'Regionalisation in Southern Africa. Three studies on regionalism in the post-apartheid, post-cold war era', Licentiate Thesis at the Peace and Development Research Institute, Göteborg University.

Odén B., M. Bøås, and F. Söderbaum (1995) 'Regionalism in Southern Africa: South Africa, the benign hegemon', Uppsala: The Nordic Africa Institute, The Southern Africa Programme, working paper no. 7.

Oman, C. (1994) *Globalisation and Regionalisation: The Challenge for Developing Countries* (Paris: OECD Development Centre).

Palmer, N. D. (1991) *The New Regionalism in Asia and the Pacific* (Toronto: Lexington).

Panagariya, A. (1994) 'East Asia: A New Trading Bloc?', *Finance & Development* (Mar.).

Polanyi, K. (1957) *The Great Transformation* (Boston: Beacon Press).

Riesenfeld, S. (1989) 'Pacific Ocean Resources: The New Regionalism and the Global System', *Ecology Law Quarterly*, **16**.

Robson, P. (1993) 'The New Regionalism and Developing Countries', *Journal of Common Market Studies*, **31** (3).

SADC (1993) *Southern Africa: A Framework and Strategy for Building the Community* (Gaborone: SADC).

180   *New Regionalism in Southern Africa*

SADC (1994) *Regional Relations and Cooperation Post-Apartheid. A Strategy and Policy Framework* (Gaborone: SADC).

SADC (1996) *Towards Enhanced Trade and Investment in the Southern African Development Community (SADC)*, SADC Consultative Conference on Trade and Investment, Johannesburg (1–3 Feb.).

Shaw, T. M. and B. Korany (eds) (1994) 'The South in the New World (Dis)-Order', *Third World Quarterly*, **15** (1).

Stubbs, R. and G. R. D. Underhill (eds) (1994) *Political Economy and the Changing Global Order* (Toronto: McClelland & Stewart).

Third World Quarterly (1994) *The South in the New World (Dis)Order* **15** (1) special issue.

7 Globalism and Regionalism: The Costs of Dichotomy

Ralph Pettman

In talking about world affairs we would seem to face the 'usual dilemma' of a 'trade-off' between 'analytical stringency' and the attempt to grasp reality 'in all its complexity' (Hettne, 1994, p. 2). Hans Morgenthau once likened this trade-off to stuffing jellyfish into pigeon-holes. It's a graphic image. Put in such terms the process is clearly difficult and messy. Morgenthau's metaphor depicts well, though, the dichotomy between the analytic ordering task and real-world chaos. On the one hand we have reality, in human terms uniformed and indeterminate. On the other hand we have our more or less stringent categories, constructed so as to give reality some meaning and shape (George, 1994).

Regionalism and globalism are two key concepts that supposedly bring such shape and meaning to our understanding of world affairs.

- As an ideology, regionalism says we ought to live in geopolitical domains greater than states, though not worldwide. Regionalization is the description of an empirical trend that ostensibly inspires or bears out this basic belief.
- As an ideology globalism says we ought to live in ways that unite people worldwide. Globalization is the description of an empirical trend that ostensibly inspires or bears out this basic belief.

Dichotomizing regionalism and globalism is used as a shaping tool too. The dichotomy is supposed to highlight these two key aspects of global reality, comparing and contrasting them, ranking and ordering them, as modernist discourse dictates.

It is never entirely clear to what extent the shape and meaning such concepts provide is made or found. Globalism, for example, or the desire to bring people together on a global basis, often masquerades as *globalization,* or the idea that people are coming together in this way regardless. Regionalism is likewise used as if it were the same as *regionalization.* The difficulty of sustaining the difference between analysis and advocacy (another dichotomy) is readily apparent here.

Such a difficulty suggests there may be difficulties with categorization/dichotomization *per se.* While dichotomies in general and this dichotomy in particular are standard analytic fare, the question does arise: how far is our understanding of world affairs furthered in the process?

Postmodernists consider dichotomous clarity to be too limited, too misleading. They argue that the current repertoire of categories has been bought at too high a price. They attend to the voices, hitherto silenced, they say, that come from outside dichotomous analysis. It is these voices that are now the more likely to further our understanding; these 'thinking spaces', they believe – the ones that marginalized speakers inhabit – that we now need to make or find.

Postmodernists point out, for example, how counterposing globalism and regionalism requires attributing an 'essence' to them both. Dichotomizing proceeds on the assumption that concepts like these are inherently knowable and definable. Acting as if their indeterminacy and contingency does not matter, we are supposed to get superior clarity, certainty and policy control. The question is: do we? Who cannot we hear because of this dichotomy? What aspects of reality are obscured by this analytic ploy?

Postmodernists find the assumption about 'essence' not only inappropriate but self-defeating. Postmodernism is not a single approach, but a postmodernist of any sort will look for the dimensions to reality that modernist dichotomizing conceals.[1] Postmodernism means looking, for example, for what the dichotomy – globalism/regionalism – silences or hides. Indeed, it means not 'looking' at all, since 'looking' is a methodology that only makes sense in terms of the modernist's objectifying mind-gaze. Postmodernists are much more likely to stand close and 'listen' instead.

LIMITS AND COSTS: EMPIRICAL REFERENTS

The idea that conventional analytic dichotomizing, whatever the benefits it brings, may have self-defeating limits and costs attached to it, is a contentious one. Though the postmodern position that such an idea promotes is now taken much more for granted, it is still somewhat unclear as to why counterposing globalism and regionalism, for example, should obscure more than enlighten our understanding of the politics of globalism, and of regionalism as well. Since this question of limits and costs is so contentious, and because its implications are so important and far-reaching, it deserves extended discussion. What follows is one such discussion.

Consider the environment. Though air-borne filth, atmospheric warming and ozone layer depletion are sourced locally, their consequences are both regional and global. Middle-class and upper-class members of society move to suburban annexes, for example, to escape the effects of high-density living in city cores, but they find melanoma induced by ozone layer depletion waiting for them when they get there. They withdraw into spatial enclaves, even employing their own police to secure their privacy and safety, but they breathe the same air as the populace who dwell beyond their wire-capped walls. At the other end of the sociological scale are the ocean atoll and river delta-dwellers, who may never have seen a factory or a car, but whose homes the rising seas that result from carbon dioxide emissions and global warming may inundate regardless. Along with the proliferating options that industrial capitalism makes possible, in other words, goes contracting scope for territorial 'escape alternatives'. This is a regional and a global development. It is also one so notable that it is said to represent a new and radical 'totalitarianization' of world space (Mlinar, 1992, p. 20).

Dichotomizing globalism and regionalism does not give us much purchase on questions of environmental degradation. The dispute over water resources in the region called the Middle East, for example, is not resolved by comparing and contrasting it with global dilemmas in this regard. This has to be done by state representatives trying to negotiate Palestinian access to West Bank groundwater or the Jordan river. Likewise those who come together to urge each other to co-operate in the making of laws to control atmospheric emissions; whether such conferences are global or regional ones, they are stubbornly statist ones too, perpetuating the idea that state-centricity is the preferred way to conceive of world affairs. They provide a theoretical and practical chance to privilege the Westphalian moment. They perpetuate statism, which is arguably a large part of the problem, and a key, *status quo* ideology which regionalism and globalism help to obscure. It is the constant making over of the global population in statist terms, in other words, that may cost those concerned the benefits of non-statist solutions. It is the dichotomizing of globalism and regionalism that may – paradoxically – limit awareness of this fact, by restricting the question to a statist one and by helping to legitimate it in statist terms.

Take another example – telecommunications and computers and the totalizing effects they currently have. 'In the context of the traditional, static society', Mlinar says 'territoriality was very clearly expressed in terms of exclusiveness of locations or 'communities' in space... In the context of flows'; however, just like the context of air pollution, 'certain ideas... can be present everywhere, without their presence or use in one location precluding that in all others. As accessibility increases, the importance of the location is thus both relativized and diminished. Indeed, with "perfect" accessibility... location would be irrelevant' (Mlinar, 1992, p. 25). Accessibility will never be perfect and location will never be irrelevant but Mlinar is highlighting here what globally connected computers can do.

The shift from a 'space of places' to a 'space of flows' that telecommunications and computers bring about is accompanied by a 'unification of time frames...'. Time discrepancies 'no longer exclude an area from the global system...' and organizations need no longer operate non-stop in 'global time' (ibid., p. 22). Electronic hyperspaces can be built wherever information can be stored. They can then be made accessible from anywhere, at any time.

What this means is that anyone with the technological means to do so can traffic information continuously and worldwide. The more advanced that capacity, the deeper and denser such networks become. This makes new modes of organization possible.

This leads to 'network' organizations, for example, that flourish on their skills in co-ordination alone. By integrating investment, design, production, distribution and sales, 'network firms' can closely monitor local markets. They can then create customized, standardized goods to fit those markets (in an industrial version of what sounds suspiciously like 'repressive tolerance').

It also leads to proliferating educational services. Despite a lack of library or other research resources, for example, the micro-circuits of local provider institutions or local students can be plugged directly into the macro-circuits of global data storage. Being remote can cease to matter as cores and peripheries become functional designations, not locational ones (Luke, 1992, p. 45).

It also allows finance to escape its conventional bounds. Money is moved in seconds around the world inside networked computers. It is downloaded into the Westphalian world, quickly depriving a government, for example, of the ability to determine 'basic fundamentals' like 'trade balances, the national market rate or even the money supply' (Neyer, 1994, p. 3). The networks themselves are well beyond single state controls. Short-term capital movements that take place within computer networks are much less evident than trade goods and services moving across state borders. Some would say that the 'real economy of goods and services and the 'symbolic' economy of money and credit' are now moving apart (Ibid., p. 14) and that the resultant competitive pressures are obliging capital-poor state leaders to push the 'social and ecological achievements' of their peoples down towards the global mean – if they are not on or below that mean already – so they have something to offer on the world market. The unemployment and the marginalization that follow are seen as unavoidable.

Again, concepts of globalism and regionalism of the conventional sort do not account well for what is going on here. Again, there are limits and costs to casting world affairs in terms of a dichotomy between the two. The way globalism and regionalism are described and explained in state-centric terms can prevent us once more from seeing how far the chains of cause and effect reach, and what our alternatives might be. State leaders are most likely at the moment to opt for 'free competition' and a marginal role for themselves in the telecommunications/computer revolution. The minimal state is seen at the moment as the most efficient state. It may well occur to state leaders to regulate the computer transactions across their borders, or to try to re-think how the world is coming to work in terms of linked cities rather than linked states, but regulation and rethinking of this sort is not common. It requires an appreciation of the politics of globalism not limited by dichotomizing the global and the regional in statist terms. It means making the attempt to understand the costs now incurred by such a dichotomy. Regionalism is mostly a distraction in this regard.

One last empirical example of the limits and costs of dichotomizing globalism and regionalism is provided by Hessler (1994) in his discussion of world trade flows. Hessler's summary of these flows suggests that globalism (understood in state-centric terms) is more important than regionalism (similarly understood), a suggestion that contradicts the argument that globalism comes after regionalism, as the end-product of a longer process of interstate consolidation.

Hessler sees regionalism as largely irrelevant to a discussion of globalism and he provides empirical reasons for doing so. Indeed, he sees the idea of a 'new regionalism' as something of a 'fiction'. His analysis of international trade reveals, he claims, a strong regionalizing pattern during the 1960s, after which there was a decade of 'stagnation and de-regionalization...'. He does highlight a large increase throughout the 1980s of inter-regional exports and imports around the Pacific rim. He also notes a 'slight' increase during this period in intra-Western European trade, though this increase he explains in terms of 'compensation' for a concomitant decrease in trans-Atlantic trade. But these were exceptions. They are not, he believes, the rule.

Add to his picture of deregionalizing trade blocs and growing global exchange the fact of burgeoning global financial markets – 'long and short term capital movements do not', Hessler concludes, 'follow geographical or regional patterns' – and we might reasonably ask, as he does, whether positing the existence of regionalism in Europe, America and Asia is either a 'realistic' or a 'practicable' assessment of what is going on in the world (Hessler, 1994, pp. 10–11).

Hessler would suggest, in other words, that we are going straight to globalism from statism, and that we are by-passing regionalism in the process. State-making is giving way to global exchange, not regional arrangements. Regionalism is neither a 'stepping stone' to globalism nor a 'stumbling block' in this regard. It is proving to be an irrelevance. This would suggest that dichotomizing globalism and regionalism is irrelevant too.

One problem with Hessler's conclusion is the extent to which it draws upon state-centric statistics. It does not, as a consequence, account for historical identities of other kinds that are equally definitive of world affairs. What, for example, of the identity represented by the 'overseas Chinese'? Hessler cites only nationally collected trade and investment figures. As such he fails to account for those aspects of world affairs that have little or nothing to do with nationally-orientated trade and investment.

As such, he overstates his case. To say that regionalism is not a notable aspect of world affairs, to say categorically that it is 'neither realistic nor practicable', could itself be neither realistic nor practicable. The globalizing of trade and monetary trends, cast in statist terms, may well overshadow regionalizing trade and monetary ones, accounted for in the same state-centric way. That need not mean, however, that people have no sense of being 'European' or 'Asian' or 'North American'. These regional identities do exist and, what is more, they seem to be stronger than cosmopolitan ones, though demonstrating as much empirically entails comparative testing of political identities that has not yet been done, and indeed, may not be do-able. Concepts like globalism and regionalism are multidimensional and what is happening in one dimension may be belied by what is happening in another. Peoples drawing together into a politico-strategic and politico-economic region called 'Europe', for example, may find themselves being drawn away from that region at the same time by such universalizing politico-cultural processes as consumerism or 'Hollywood'.

LIMITS AND COSTS: 'WHERE ARE THE WOMEN?'

As we saw in the previous section, our empirical referents invariably highlight some aspects of reality, obscuring others in the process. More to the point, the empirical referents most commonly used in the contemporary study of world affairs predispose a state-centric version of globalism and regionalism that has notable limits and costs.

A wide range of feminist critiques now draws attention to another neglected issue-area, however, and that is the issue of gender bias, or more particularly, male-centricity. One dimension concealed by the analytic 'pigeon-holes' of the conventional globalism/regionalism dichotomy is the gendering process that cuts completely across it. These categories conventionally preclude any awareness of gender (as well as any awareness of race, class, ethnicity, indigenous status, and so on). Does this matter? Perhaps these categories are irrelevant. To answer these questions, and to understand the limits and costs of such preclusions, we have first to ask who is being silenced, however, and by whom.

Consider, for example, the politico-strategic dimension to world affairs. As noted already, this dimension is most commonly described in state-centric terms. The usual analytic narratives tell us how the form of the European state was globalized, with notable success in some instances and with notable lack of success in others, and how the ideology of statism – the idea that we all ought to live in territorially bounded, centrally governed, sovereign entities called states – has now become a hegemonic world practice. Much of the politicking that goes on around the concepts of globalism and regionalism promote and protect the European model of 'the state'. Even where globalism and regionalism erode the sovereignty that constitutes the premise on which states are made, they endorse the idea of state sovereignty by default.

In international relations theory the making of states is commonly construed in Hobbesian, Grotian or Kantian terms. Each conception articulates a different view of human nature (competitive, co-operative and solidarist in turn). Each provides a different reading of globalism or regionalism and a different reading of the globalism/regionalism dichotomy.

Each one also articulates a masculinist conception of world affairs. Each serves to consolidate not only a state-centric world but a male-centric world as well. Dichotomizing globalism and regionalism tells us nothing about the statism germane to both, in other words, and the rendering of women as invisible as politico-strategic persons that statism entails. We are only just beginning to understand the limits and costs that this involves (Tickner, 1992).

Consider the politico-economic dimension to world affairs. We live in an industrializing capitalistic world, a world that can be read either as classical liberals do, in terms of the market practices of entrepreneurs; or as classical Marxists do, in terms of the capitalist mode of production and the competing class relations characteristic of it; or as neomercantilists do, as the defence of the state by other means. What remains obscured, however, unless we make a specific effort to highlight it, is the masculinist bias characteristic of all three perspectives. There is now a gender critique of each one. Unless a conscious effort is made to entertain this critique, however – to expose the male-centric nature of the world political economy (and hence of any conception of regionalism or globalism crafted in these terms, or any dichotomy between them) – then that radically significant fact will remain unrevealed and its limits and costs will stay hidden too.

Classical liberals and classical Marxists both see entrepreneurs advocating a world business civilization. They see the rules and arrangements of this civilization – rules about the status of contracts, for example, the sanctity of profits, the value of private property, and the significance of free, waged labour – as necessary for the workings of an open global market. They see the market as a socioeconomic and sociopolitical fact of premier importance, the liberals because it is supposed to provide a prosperous and peaceful world, the Marxists because it is exploitative and because the class conflicts it engenders are supposed to cause capitalism to collapse.

Neither confronts the radical socioeconomic and sociopolitical significance of sex and gender discrimination on a world scale. Neither is prepared to confront its own ideological shortcomings in this regard, or the limits it places on our capacity to see what an unpatriarchal world would look like – one, for example, where women no longer do two-thirds of the world's work for a tenth of the world's income and the right to own one-hundredth of its property, as they do today. I know of no analysis that dichotomizes globalism and regionalism that draws attention to the radical disparity at issue here.

Consider, finally, the politico-cultural dimension to world affairs, namely, the proliferating mind-set of Enlightenment modernism. Enlightenment modernism constitutes the mental context in which wealth-makers and those who build states currently behave. The rationalism they privilege, as well as the materialism, the secularism and the individualism that goes along with it, is the mental milieu modernists most diligently promote and protect. It is this milieu they see as the most appropriate within which to craft states, money and human consciousness.

Enlightenment modernism does not apprehend the extent of its own masculinism. Nor does it provide an appreciation of the gendering process that politico-acculturation involves on a global scale. Nor does it highlight the extent to which this process ensures the formal preponderance in the public sphere of people who are male. No one counts the costs. No dichotomizing of globalism and regionalism attempts such an accounting or argues the need for one.

LIMITS AND COSTS: THE 'REVOLT AGAINST THE WEST'

The global spread of the Enlightenment milieu has not gone uncontested. Not only do a wide range of feminists ask what the limits of rationalism might be and who it might be for, but diverse other groups are now questioning its epistemological, axiological, ontological, and spiritual predilections too. They are starting to count the costs, not only for themselves but for the planet as a whole, of this one way of knowing the world and of living in it too. And they are starting to find these costs prohibitive.

Thus we find the contemporary notion of Asian globalism – the conceptual complement to that of Asian regionalism – a notion that a number of analysts are now developing to draw attention to the Eurocentric nature of the conventional discourse on world affairs. Globalism is usually assumed to be Western globalism, and Western globalism is usually seen as the only kind of globalism worth talking

about. This claim is currently contested. It is not enough, such analysts
say, to dichotomize Western globalism and Asian regionalism. This
does scant justice to the breadth or depth of the difference.

Take epistemology, and the scientific method that privileges one
particular way of getting new knowledge, namely, rationalism. It is the
power of human reason that makes possible the objectified thinking
that the scientific method requires. Reason also makes possible
experimental procedures that can be used to check and compare the
results of such thinking, with cumulative consequences that are well
known to us all.

Though only a minority of Earth's people have mastered scientific
methods or have learned the contemporary significance of using
reason to such an extent, the relentless pursuit of a singular truth by
that minority has made it harder for others to live by the light of
alternative values like beauty or goodness, redemption or honour.
Most people do live by other values, but the totalizing effect of the
scientific culture of the 'West' is readily apparent in the burgeoning
desire by 'others' to learn how to do it and how to operate the
technologies already acquired from its primary producers. The world's
epistemological diversity, in other words, just like its ecological diversity, is under siege, and who is to say that what we lose in the process is
not what we need?

Rationalism does not just entail the use of a singular mental faculty
in the relentless pursuit of truth, it also entails – as indicated earlier in
the discussion of modernism – individuation (its ontological concomitant) and materialism and secularism (its spiritual ones). 'Objectifying
rationalism' is meant to arrive at the representation of an external
reality that is as close to that reality as humanly possible. Using the
mind this way, however, means creating a surveillant sense of the self
that is 'in' the world but is consciously 'set apart' from it. Using the
mind this way augments the sense of individual autonomy. It also –
and this is arguably its most important cost – has alienating and de-
sociating effects that are now quite marked.

From this mentally detached perspective the world is readily reified.
And while reification allows for abstract conceptual manipulation of
models of how the world works, it also leads to a sense of the world as
being materially contrived. So while reification may be necessary to
make science possible, it does predispose a sense of the world as
material and secular rather than divine. Rational mind-makers colour
the cosmos with their own instrumental purpose, finding in it no
'spirit' or 'presence', only 'things'.

The global success of scientific ways of knowing is not neutral, then, when it comes to aspirations, sensibilities and faith. As such, it inspires diverse antagonisms. Globalism as the spread of scientific culture, or as the promotion and pursuit of scientific culture, means the global endorsement of one set of values, one way of being, and one set of fundamental beliefs. It means the globalization of the intellectual preoccupations that since the Enlightenment have seized an influential number of people in Europe and in its cultural and intellectual dominions.

At one point in a discussion of the 'revolt against the West', Hedley Bull argues that the 'spiritual or psychological supremacy of the West' was at its 'highest point' at the end of the last century. This would suggest that it is now on the wane, though earlier in his analysis he says, rather confusingly, that the global impact of the West has been more far-reaching since that point in time (Bull, 1985, p. 219). Whether passed its peak or proliferating still, globalization of the modernist values that Westernization entails has been a marked feature of our times. It is a key measure of the success of Western globalism. Rationalism has never received universal endorsement, though. Indeed, diverse attempts to reject such values were notable from the beginning. Bull draws attention to a number of common 'themes' in this rejection process. He denotes these in turn as the 'struggle for equal sovereignty', the 'anti-colonial revolution', the 'struggle ... against white supremicism', the 'struggle for economic justice', and the 'struggle for ... cultural liberation: the struggle of non-Western peoples to throw off the intellectual or cultural ascendancy of the Western world so as to assert their own identity and autonomy in matters of the spirit' (Bull, 1985, p. 222).

The contest has taken many forms. It has been symbolic and pacific, for example, with the 'attribution of value' to a 'tradition' of some sort being no more than a claim to 'parity of respect' (Dore, 1985, p. 411). It has also been material and strategic, with oppositional claims even a cause of war.

The contest continues daily. It is a discernibly politico-cultural one, whatever its material or strategic concomitants. It compares the hegemonizing, globalizing impact of Western ways of knowing and being with other identities. It makes the parochialism of the West seem decidedly grandiose.[2]

Dichotomizing globalism and regionalism of any kind provides little purchase on this whole issue-area. Which would not matter if the issue-area itself did not matter. But few would dismiss the 'revolt against the West' as something of little significance. On the contrary, contemporary discussions of world affairs show a growing sensitivity in this regard. The failure of the globalism/regionalism dichotomy to contribute to what is arguably one of the most important dimensions of contemporary world affairs has to be seen in this light.

To recapitulate: the effects of rationalism in the West have been considerable and it was generally assumed (not least by Western social theorists) that the global spread of scientific knowledge and industry would mean the spread of the mores of the societies where they were invented. This, the 'convergence' thesis, was 'most influential', as Dore observes, 'in the late 1950s and early 1960s when it was possible to argue [for example] that the Japanese, poor souls, were not very efficient industrially because they somehow could not get their societies organised...' (Dore, 1985, p. 416) It was 'rather awkward' for the convergence idea, then, when Japan became the second most productive country on earth, and the Japanese got that way while remaining notably themselves.

Material achievements by state-makers and entrepreneurs in Singapore, Hong Kong, Taiwan and South Korea, in Indonesia, Thailand and Malaysia, as well as in mainland China's southern coastal region, has led one theorist (among many) to posit a 'different regional historic bloc with its own set of hegemonic features...', that is, a 'transformation' of the 'world-hegemony of liberal capitalism [predicated on *"homo economicus"*] into a regional hegemony of Asian Corporatism [predicated on *"patria economicus"*]' (Ling, 1994, p. 21).

This is not to deny the significance of the historic borrowings in Asia from the European Enlighteners and of the common effects, wherever it has been adopted, of industrial capitalism. Clearly there are 'norms, institutions and practices' that are now shared by industrial capitalists wherever they live. The editors of the *Far Eastern Economic Review* talk of 'Eastern' and 'Western' norms as being identical, for example, and of 'faithful adherence to the old verities: hard work, enterprise, family, thrift, responsibility. Today these values may be called 'Asian' but they are nonetheless the same 'Protestant work ethic' or 'Victorian virtues' that helped 'build' the West. This being the case, they say, the 'difference between Asia and the West is that Asia still respects the universal values that many in the West no longer seem to cherish' (*Far Eastern Economic Review*, 1994, p. 5).

Most analysts would see some difference at least in the 'social meanings' and 'respective contexts' of Western and Eastern capitalisms, however. It is this difference that interests those who believe in such ostensibly 'Asian values' as family cohesion, respect for education, and social solidarism. (All such values are respected in one Western society or another, of course, and some are not especially Eastern ones. The comparison between East and West is usually made in such general terms, however, as to render any particular exceptions anomalous.)

Indeed, a leading member of America's foreign policy establishment sees the difference as being so acute as to justify a macro-comparison in terms of 'civilizations'. Cold War I (an ideological and economic conflict between 'capitalism and communism') is turning, Samuel Huntington argues, into a kind of Cold War II (a cultural conflict between 'civilizations'). We may even, he hints, get a World War III along these lines. Indeed, the differences between civilizations and the awareness of such differences are seen to represent a significant new threat to the West (read: the USA). More specifically the threat lies in any non-Western civilization that modernizes without Westernizing. Huntington cites a number of (unspecified) 'Confucian and Islamic' states that he finds threatening in this regard (Huntington, 1993, p. 48).

From outside Huntington's strategic studies institute at Harvard these macro-patterns are read very differently, however. Asian commentators talk of a materially progressive, socially cohesive East, and of a West beset by crises of confidence and diverse communal disorders. They see the West itself, not some 'Islamic–Confucian connection', nor the modern-day descendants of the Muslim and Mongol hordes, as being responsible for intercivilizational strife. It is to the East, they say, that Westerners are now having to turn for positive examples of social repair. Westerners are urged not to act as if they were under siege, nor to close their mental gates on what they might learn elsewhere. Rather, they are urged to 'Go East, Young Man [*sic*]' (Mahbubani, 1994, p. 32).

The permanent secretary of Singapore's ministry of foreign affairs notes, for example, the soaring crime rates, divorce rates, teenage suicide rates, and declining educational standards that characterize liberal capitalism in the USA. Unlike the USA, where liberating the individual has 'imprisoned society', East Asia still enjoys, he claims, relatively high levels of social order and family cohesiveness. Freedom in Singapore, he concludes, is not to be compared with the licence that corrupts the West. It is rather the result of 'social order and discipline'.

In an editorial on 'Asian values', an international weekly with a more global audience (*The Economist*) pursues the same theme. It waxes lyric about the 'deep differences between the West and Asia, not in values... [so much as] in the way their societies work'. (Since how societies work has a lot to do with the values shared by those who work in them, this distinction would seem more apparent than real.) The editors of *The Economist* are well aware that 'Asia' contains '60 per cent of the... [global] population ... four or five major cultures, several distinct forms of social organisation, an ethnic mosaic of astonishing complexity, and three or four big religions'. This would seem to make it more sensible, as they point out themselves, to talk about 'Confucian values... Islamic values... [or] Japanese or Hindu values' rather than 'Asian values' *per se*. Given that Confucian, Islamic, Japanese or Hindu traditions are not monolithic either, one would not want to stop there. Despite their manifest appreciation of this diversity, *The Economist*'s editors still cannot resist sliding into the same simple distinctions used by the Singapore spokesman, however (*The Economist*, 1994, p. 10). Despite making all the appropriate disclaimers, the editors of *The Economist* counterpose 'West' and 'East' just the way the Singaporean does.

They provide in the process the same rationale for Singapore's less-than-democratic rule that the latter does. What should we deem 'less-than-democratic', however? The liberal values aspired to by the 'best of the West'? Rule 'by the people' that becomes progressively more indirect and elitist? Or the communitarian values aspired to in the 'East'? Rule 'for the people' that becomes progressively more patronizing and elitist?

A number of East and South East Asian state leaders have flourished by favouring the communitarian definition of democracy. It is compatible with the social hierarchies that still characterize their societies. It is also compatible with their own political ambitions. They are also beginning to see no reason (if only because their new-found wealth means power that can be, and is being, used to create moralities convenient to their cause) why those elsewhere should not agree with them. Those with might are usually wont to presume that they are right as well. East and South East Asian state leaders are no exception.

Communitarian democracy and the current prosperity of East and South East Asian states has made for new levels of self-confidence on the part of the state-makers and wealth-makers involved. By the end of the 1980s Singapore, Taiwan, South Korea and Hong Kong accounted for more than half of the world's exports in manufactures. Japan and Taiwan had the world's largest foreign currency holdings. This not only meant much greater global influence. It also made for a greater desire to define what gets considered to be the 'global good'. The historical precedents are compelling. It was the same sort of technological and commercial edge that made it possible for the people from a little island off the west coast of Europe, for example, to control large parts of the world, a control they did not lose until the middle of this century. It was the fact of Britain's empire that prompted the British to assume the sort of innate mental and moral superiority they still claim to enjoy.

While the manufacturing and marketing success of Japan, and of the other newly industrialized countries in the South East and East Asian regions, has not led, in the post-war period, to territorial imperializing of the British kind, it has lead to similar self-assessments of superior virtue. This is particularly so among elite groups who find such self-assessments politically advantageous.

A similar case is made by academic commentators who see 'industrial neo-confucianism' (the selection of meritocratic elites by rigorous exam procedures, group loyalty, a culture of self-cultivation that augments work skill – the learning of foreign languages, of computing, of foreign market practices, and the like) as a key cause of East Asia's spectacular economic growth (Vogel, 1991, p. 101). Hung-chao Tai, for example, posits an 'Oriental or affective model of economic development', which he believes emphasizes 'human emotional bonds, group orientation, and harmony'. All of which stands in stark contrast, he claims, to established Western models which stress rationality and individualism (Tai, 1989, p. 7).

Max Weber made the same distinction when he posited the 'Calvinist work ethic' as the key reason we have capitalism today. He saw a marked difference between the Protestants of Europe and the Confucians of China in this regard. Puritan rationalism meant 'rational mastery of the world' he argued, since sober industry was a sign of eternal salvation, and getting to heaven was the key reason for being alive. On the other hand Confucian rationalism meant 'rational adjustment to the world', since the value placed on being a scholar–official militated against profit-making and the acquisitiveness associated with commerce (Tai, 1989, p. 9).

However plausible Weber's argument sounds, we should be wary, in these post-colonialist times, of turning 'orientalism' (Said, 1985) on its head. Saying that those born and raised to the east of Suez are more diligent and responsible than those born and raised to the west of it is no more credible than saying (as the European imperialists did) that those born to the east of Suez, compared to those born to the west, are innately lazy and corrupt. Regionalist thinking can be a real trap in this regard.

The point is that positing any and all such distinctions is a political act, and it is to obscure, for example, the common effects of rapid economic growth in both 'the East' and 'the West'. This is not to deny that the Japanese, for example, are 'different' and that their version of capitalism is different too. Pinning that difference down in cultural terms is notoriously difficult too, however. Japanese modernizers borrowed a lot from Europe, but in a selective way. Most hoped that the social changes that were necessary for industrial development could be brought about without their ceasing to be able to formulate the meaning of being 'Japanese' for themselves. They wanted an industrial revolution but not an intellectual one. Industrial capitalism is changing what being Japanese means, however. The solidarist, sexist and highly hierarchic society of pre-war times has been giving way to a less insular, more rationalistic and more individuated one. Japan is 'internationalizing', though the process is slow, selective and still relatively superficial.

How much, we may ask, of this whole profound and highly political question do we find in the current literature on globalism and regionalism? Does the dichotomy between the two – even that between Western globalism and Asian regionalism – give us much to go on in this regard? In my reading of the literature, it does not. And as it does not, then we are warranted in raising the question of the limits and costs of this dichotomy, and how to transcend and mitigate them.

LIMITS AND COSTS: PACIFIC EUROPE BETWEEN 'ASIA' AND THE 'WEST'

Dichotomizing globalism and regionalism in terms of a regionalizing 'East' and a globalizing 'West' not only threatens 'Asian' senses of self (prompting a fight back in kind), it also puts the peoples of Pacific Europe in an ambiguous and potentially threatening situation too. Australia and New Zealand, for example, are settler societies whose populations, for historical/imperial reasons, are mostly Anglo-European. Until the Second World War they deferred very closely in every respect to the 'motherland' – the United Kingdom. With the end of that war, the rapid collapse of Britain as a globally significant power, and its move towards Europe, they had to reconsider their longer-term futures.

The rapid material changes in a number of Asian countries provided the peoples of Pacific Europe with close markets and new sources. Availing themselves of the opportunities these presented required a very different orientation, however. It meant learning Japanese, Chinese, Korean and Indonesian as second languages, for example, rather than French, German, and the even more anachronistic Latin. It meant coming to terms with non-modern cultures, and Anglo-European rationalism and individualism as cultural preoccupations of relative worth.

Delayed by the war in Vietnam and the policy choices on the part of Pacific European state-makers to side with the USA; pushed by politico-economic necessity regardless; pulled by a more culturally adventurous post-war generation that had no memories of such personally searing historical episodes as Japanese expansionism, Australians and New Zealanders sought to cultivate a greater awareness of and sympathy for things and people 'Asian'. They were inhibited in this respect by a radical sense of the 'difference' of Asian traditions. They were not helped by the 'tyranny of distance' and the sense of being a European populace far removed from their place of origins. These were only temporary inhibitions, however.

Ethnically more mixed, larger and more self-consciously a 'middle power', Australia moved first. A whole generation of post-war politicians with a nostalgic preference for all things English had to die off first. Only then was it possible to begin to proceed past the ethnocentric preference for the Western, and more particularly the British way of life, to another source of inspiration and money. Only then was it possible to begin acknowledging and engaging a rapidly changing, highly diverse, still alien part of the world, designated Eastern, but very different from the stereotypes Australians of non-Cambodian, Vietnamese, Laotian or Chinese origin typically associated with that word.

For various reasons, New Zealanders moved more slowly, but though it was longer coming, the urgency of their drive to acknowledge and engage 'Asia' was equally as marked.

The costs of having dichotomized West and East were very clear in both contexts. The prejudices that this dichotomization inspired made the process of acknowledgment considerably more difficult than it needed to be. The limits it placed on perception and understanding had as much to do with Eurocentricity as it did with the Asianness of the peoples Australians and New Zealanders were coming to engage. The fact that Australians and New Zealanders were themselves Pacific

Asians, a designation every bit as meaningful and realistic (given the diversity of the region where their islands lay) as the Pacific European one, began to make politico-cultural sense to them. Its politico-strategic and politico-economic sense had been plain for some time.

REGIONALISM AND GLOBALISM

East and West, North and South; some more than others, some more quickly than others; people are said to be globalizing or being globalized, regionalizing or being regionalized.

While regionalism remains tied firmly to a state-centric view of the world, and this includes the regionalism of the European Union, which has moved furthest to mute the significance of state sovereignty *per se*, globalism is changing, however:

> [C]ontemporary (post-modern) 'globalism' rejects [it is argued] 'older visions of world unity based on the spread of a single core area (the North). It emphasises instead the equal dignity of a wide plurality of cultures and civilisations, and enshrines cultural diversity and spatial equality... as basic features of the proposed world system.   (Strassoldo, 1992, p. 39)

Should the 'new globalism' prevail, then it will ultimately be possible to exalt many cultures in its name and not just the Western ones. The difference between regionalism and globalism will narrow to the point of insignificance and the dichotomy between the two will become analytically very uninteresting.

Should the 'new globalism' prevail, the politics of it will still be problematic. A global society made up of 'loose, competitive, hostile subsystems, as it was in pre-modern history' (ibid.) and centred on cultures and civilizations rather than states, will still be one of struggle and strife.

Should the 'new globalism' fail to prevail however, and a less pluralistic and more unified world come to pass, then globalism will entail many of those forms of diplomacy and alliance, trade and investment, ideology and identity that keep it going now. Regionalism will refer to eddies in the global pool, that is, to geographically more limited versions of the same thing. The limits and costs of dichotomizing the two concepts will remain as discussed.

Most analysts anticipate not a pluralistic postmodernist form of globalism but a unitary and modernist one. They tend to imagine it

in the conventional 'unitary' sense. Such a sense is said to be 'at least
as old as the rise of the so-called world religions two thousand and
more years go' (Robertson, 1992, p. 7), though the events of the last
500 years, and of the last 50 in particular, are also said to represent an
accelerating trend towards it.[3] Regionalism is seen in this respect as a
lesser version of the same thing, that is, all the jockeying for advantage
that goes on making confederal, suprastate institutions, a global market and a global mode of industrial capitalist production.[4]

Whether we are providing an objectifying judgement or voicing our
ideological intent – whether, that is, we are using globalism and
regionalism analytically to refer to globalization or regionalization,
or using it rhetorically to advocate such processes – the basic concepts, in the conventional sense, denote 'one world'.

This being so, we are back where we began, namely, with the
question: what's the point of dichotomizing regionalism and globalism
when they would seem to be points on a continuum, and not much
opposed? What's the point of heralding the dissolution of the state by
suprastate practices when both one and the other are becoming more
important, as seems to be the case today? Why look for the line where
national markets seem to divide into regional as opposed to global,
when both are becoming busier and more integrated, or if Hessler is
to be believed, regional markets do not exist at all? And why ask when
it is that people stop acting locally and start thinking globally, when
they are thinking more locally and acting more globally at the same
time?[5]

THE NEW REGIONALISM/THE NEW GLOBALISM

Recent work of Björn Hettne on the 'new regionalism' provides one
answer. In a WIDER monograph Hettne has defined regions as both
'historical formations' and 'political subject[s] with...[their] own
identity'. This identity evolves 'from within', he says, so the 'new'
regionalism of the post-cold war sort appears to be both more comprehensive and more spontaneous than the 'older' versions, that were
relatively specific and created 'from outside' (Hettne, 1994, p. 2). He
posits no precise threshold between nationalism and regionalism,
however, and there seems no reason, in his terms, to posit one
between regionalism and globalism either. At which point any dichotomy between the two falls to the ground again. Indeed, any such
dichotomy would seem to hinder an understanding of the historical

contingency and the highly politicized character of the practices involved, and of the sort of limits and costs already described.

Instead of trying to locate moving lines that do not exist, and counterposing categories that lie on either side of such lines, that do not exist either, we might be better off examining the dynamics of what is happening without expecting to come to conclusions of such pigeon-hole clarity and discretion. Consider 'international interdependence', which is one commonly cited global dynamic that can be cast in Hettne's terms. If we see this as what happens when attempts are made to maximize particular normative understandings internationally, while minimizing what is felt to constitute common threats to security, then the outcome of those attempts could conceivably be 'one world'. We do not need to decide in advance at what point regionalism gives way to globalism, however, and we do not need, as a consequence, to dichotomize them.

Perhaps this is all to the good. Out of a keener appreciation of imprecision may come a deeper awareness of how these questions are couched. This in turn may promote the discussion of what is not being said. This in turn may promote the inclusion of categories and concepts currently excluded, providing thereby for an awareness of globalism and regionalism, and of a kind of globalism and regionalism, that only the postmodernists have so far been prepared to countenance.

Notes

1. Positing a dichotomy between modernism and postmodernism is to endorse the superior efficacy of modernism. It is, in effect, to argue an essential difference between the two. This is a modernist ploy. Postmodernists would replace the 'either ... or' formula of modernism with a 'both ... and' one.

    'Modernism' in its most comprehensive sense refers to the contemporary privilege bestowed upon rationality. Prefigured by ancient Greek philosophers, this distinctive way of using the mind only works well if the assumption is also made that truth is singular. Those who would question this assumption are currently said to subscribe to 'postmodernism'. Postmodernists do not, on the whole, wish to reinstate the primacy of pre-modernist ways of using the mind – revelation, rhetoric and so on. They are concerned with what rationalism stops us knowing. While the 'light' thrown by the rational mind does illuminate, they say, it also blinds. It is this blinding effect that most fascinates postmodernists. It is the limits and costs of intellectually-induced myopia they strive the hardest to transcend.

2. Note, for example, the 1994 Asian Leaders' Forum, that brought together in Bali in September half a hundred politicians and business people from around the region to discuss 'Convergence and Asianization in Asia'. The Forum considered, in particular, the 'processes of globalization and convergence' which were perceived by many in both Asia and the West to be reducing the differences between both countries and cultures. This process was of concern to many in Asia who feared that their cultural and political attributes were being eroded by Western ones. Hence the regional interest in what was coming to be described as 'Asianization', a highly political process designed to define an 'Asian' identity and an emergent 'Asian' world-view (The Asia–Australia Institute, 1994, p. 2; also Funabashi, 1993).

3. 'Total' globalization, as Mlinar argues, 'would mean that local features would be the same as global ones... the whole world... [would] be found in each locality and at the same time each locality, region, nation... [would] be found all over the world'.

All parts of the world would manifest the whole, in other words, and the whole would be manifest in all its parts (Mlinar, 1993, p. 22). The globalizing process, that is, '... the interpenetrating processes of societalization, individualization, the consolidation of the inter-national system of societies, and the concretization of the sense of humankind', would be complete (Robertson, 1992, p. 104).

4. The 'politics of globalization' posits globalizing practices of many different kinds, and draws our attention to the politicking they entail. There is a reverse verbal formulation, however – the 'globalization of politics' – that posits the progressive replacement of 'parochial political battles' within states by the sort of global responses now deemed necessary to realize people's security and welfare. This latter phrase, the 'globalization of politics', draws our attention to what is said to be a changing global focus as political action shifts from the national to the international or the transnational domain (Luard, 1990). I discuss this here in terms of the concept 'international interdependence'.

5. It is worth noting Mlinar's attempt to eschew linearity here by opting for 'oscillation'. Regionalization occurs at the expense of globalization, he believes, and vice versa in an interdependent but antagonistic way. In line with what seems to be his cybernetic modernism, Mlinar sees this oscillation dying down, however, and the relationship between the two eventually changing from one of 'exclusion' to one of 'mutuality' (Mlinar, 1992, p. 24).

References

Asia–Australia Institute (1994) *Newsletter*, no. 5 (May) p. 2.
Bull, H. (1985) 'The Revolt Against the West', in H. Bull and A. Watson (eds) *The Expansion of International Society* (Oxford: Clarendon).

Dore, R. (1985) 'Unity and Diversity in Contemporary World Culture', in H. Bull and A. Watson (eds) *The Expansion of International Society* (Oxford: Clarendon).

Economist, The (1994) 'Asian Values' (28 May), pp. 9–10.

Far Eastern Economic Review (1994) 'Asian's Welfare: learning from the West's forgotten values' (23 June) p. 5.

Funabashi, Y. (1993) 'The Asianization of Asia', *Foreign Affairs*, 72 (5): 75–85.

George, J. (1994) *Discourses of Global Politics: a Critical (Re)Introduction to International Relations* (Boulder: Lynne Rienner).

Hessler, S. (1994) 'Regionalization of the world economy: fact or faction?', paper presented to the ISA Convention, Washington, DC.

Hettne, B. (1994) 'The Berlin Workshop: basic issues', paper prepared for the UNU/WIDER workshop on the *The New Regionalism*, Berlin (August).

Hettne, B. and A. Inotai (1994) 'The New Regionalism: implications for global development and international security', UNU World Institute for Development Economics Research (UNU/WIDER).

Huntington, S. *et al.* (1993) *The Clash of Civilizations? The Debate* (New York: Council on Foreign Relations).

Ling, L.H.M. (1994) 'Hegemony and the Internationalizing State: a postcolonial critique – China's internationalization into Asian corporatism' (unpublished).

Luard, E. (1990) *The Globalization of Politics: the Changed Focus of Political Action in the Modern World* (London: Macmillan).

Luke, T. (1992) 'From the Flows of Power to the Power of Flows: teaching world politics in the informationalizing world system', in L. Gonick and E. Weisband (eds) *Teaching World Politics: contending pedagogies for a new world order* (Boulder: Westview).

Mahbubani, K. (1994) 'Go East, Young Man', *Far Eastern Economic Review* 19 May p. 3.

Mlinar, Z. (1992) 'Individuation and Globalization: the transformation of territorial social organization' in Z. Mlinar (ed.) *Globalization and Territorial Identities* (Aldershot: Avebury).

Neyer, J. (1994) 'Structural changes in the world economy and the new shape of conflicts', a paper presented to the ISA Convention, Washington, DC.

Robertson, R. (1992) *Globalization: Social Theory and Global Culture* (London: Sage).

Said, E. (1985) *Orientalism* (Harmondsworth: Penguin).

Strassoldo, R. (1992), 'Globalism and Localism: theoretical reflections and some evidence' in Z. Mlinar (ed.) *Globalization and Territorial Identities* (Aldershot: Avebury).

Tai, H. (1989), 'The Oriental Alternative: an hypothesis on culture and economy', in H. Tai (ed.) *Confucianism and Economic Development: an oriental alternative* (Washington, DC: Washington Institute Press).

Tickner, J.A. (1992) *Gender in International Relations: a feminist perspective on achieving global security* (New York: Columbia University Press).

Vogel, E. (1991) *The Four Little Dragons* (Cambridge, Mass.: Harvard University Press).

8 Regionalization and its Impact on the Theory of International Relations

Kaisa Lähteenmäki and Jyrki Käkönen

INTRODUCTION

The end of the cold war has presented the field of international relations with an unparalleled challenge. Even if we take an anti-positivistic stand and do not expect the study of international relations to be most of all of prediction but of understanding and interpretation, it is obvious that as a research project international politics has become more difficult to manage. The apparent randomness and unpredictability of the events of the past few years have led many scholars to look for alternative modes of explaining international relations. Thus for instance chaos theory and postmodernism (see Chapter 7) have emerged in the agenda of international relations.[1]

In particular, the realist paradigm, for a long time the dominant paradigm of international relations, has been subjected to criticism and to some extent almost violent and absolute abandon. It is true that many of the core concepts and assumptions of the realist interpretation of the world have indeed lost their meaning altogether: what is the role of bipolarism in a world that is becoming at the same time increasingly integrated and fragmented? What is the relevance of traditional notions of security when armed security cannot be seen as an answer to most of the conflicts and problems in international relations? What can the dichotomy between war and peace contribute to our understanding of the world when internal conflicts, rise of nationalism and fundamentalism and so on have made absolute war or absolute peace rare or non-existent?

The post-cold war international system has been accompanied by the emergence of new phenomena such as regionalization from below. Often these phenomena are explained simply by referring to the end of the cold war. The idealism of peace research, peace through

203

204 Regionalization and International Relations Theory

co-operation, has encouraged us to understand regionalism in a positive way. Among the positive expectations is the assumption that regionalism weakens power politics and makes armed security impossible. Yet this does not change the fact that conflictuality is still one of the dominant factors in international relations. The emerging new regionalization is part of a process which aims at creating order when the old order, based on bipolarity and the balance of power, has vanished. Yet we must remember that the pursuit of order still remains; the difference being that instead of one overarching order there seems to be a tendency towards various smaller 'suborders'.

We shall attempt to present regionalization in its new forms in a realist framework; as an attempt to test how realism can be understood as something where states are not necessarily the only relevant actors. By doing this we want to offer some clarity into the debate on regionalism that appears to be interpreted in such a variety of ways that one gets the impression that a coherent interpretation of regionalism or even a meaningful debate on it is simply out of reach, since the points of departure when dealing with regionalization seem to be so different and so far apart.

One of the main problems with the debate is lack of coherence in the use of the concepts 'regionalization' or 'region' themselves. Some scholars have attempted to differentiate between traditional state-centric regionalism created from above in contrast to the new regionalism created from below.[2] Yet there is no consistency in using these concepts; many consider regionalism as a whole comprising all forms of co-operation between the regions, whether these regions are states, subnational or wider geographic entities. To make our point of departure more explicit, it is important to note that when referring to regionalization and new regionalism, we refer to subregional co-operation *created from below, not by states or supra-national actors*.

STATE-CENTRIC APPROACH IN INTERNATIONAL POLITICS

No matter how much the realist paradigm has been challenged, it has survived as the leading paradigm within the field of international relations. Until the end of the cold war it was difficult to talk seriously about a change of paradigm. In the realist approach *the state is the actor* in the international politics. According to Vasquez, the state always occupied a central role in the studies on international politics.

In their concrete analysis even approaches which have tried to challenge the realist tradition have used empirical material related to states.[3] K. J. Holsti has also come to the conclusion that the state-centric approach has not been threatened during the post-Second World War period.[4]

One important aspect is that states have *the monopoly of legitimate violence*. Internally they use it for maintaining peace in civil society. Externally states protect their own population against any foreign threat, and if needed by force. Force is also needed *to realize the national interests in relation to other states*. In that sense international politics always includes an aspect of power. In fact the aim of the states is to increase their power in relation to other states. *Power is a means and an end* for the states in their international activities.

The monopoly of violence is closely connected to war. The aim of states as well as that of international studies is to maintain or achieve peace in the anarchic international society. However, peace is subordinated to the continuity of the international society of the states. War is allowed for sustaining the independence of the state and the continuing existence of society in the state. According to the realist tradition state and war are interrelated in the Modern Ages.[5]

The last point we have to refer to in this connection is sovereignty. First, *states are sovereign in their internal jurisdiction* and other internal affairs. In principle no state has any right to intervene in other state's internal politics. States are also sovereign in their foreign politics which aims to secure the existence of the state and the nation. Therefore, even in international co-operation states implement their national interests and they are not submitted to any international authorities.

The central role of the state gives a crucial position for the governments, heads of state and ministries of foreign affairs and defence. These national authorities form the prism through which all the domestic interests will be turned into national interests in the international politics. According to a very strict interpretation, communities, national organizations or any other institutions cannot have independent international policies. However, non-state international connections have created the sector of the NGOs or even INGOs which has extended the reach of narrow realist approach. Also international economic conditions are seldom, except in former socialist and today still in some developing countries, controlled by the states. States are however responsible for negotiating the norms and rules of international economy.

Integration and interdependence theories revolve around states, as well. Co-operation takes place in a conflictual environment where competition between states, subnational and supranational levels persists. Usually co-operation emerges from a common conception of an external threat: this has been the case in creation of the EC[6] and of more recent regional co-operation in the form of trans-border co-operation which has emerged even between subnational regional entities. New forms of regionalization have emerged in order to tackle the new threats such as economic recession and instability or crime that is very much a 'trans-border' problem. Even if these problems cannot be solved without help from the state authorities, local cross-border initiatives can play an important role in bringing the problems into the domestic and international agenda, bridging or connecting together the local and national/international context.

THE WEAKNESSES OF THE REALIST PARADIGM

As we mentioned earlier, the realist approach has been challenged by alternative theoretical constructions. One dimension where the weakness of the state-centric approach was evident was economics. The post-First World War recession had already made it clear that states were not sovereign in the economic field. They did not have sufficient means to manage their national economies. Many important factors were outside their reach. After the Second World War, this became even more evident. Not only were the newly independent developing countries dependent on external factors, but also most of the rich states became dependent on resources far beyond their borders.

One solution for gaining political control was to create international organizations for managing the international economy. Another solution was the formation of multinational or transnational companies. Many multinationals controlled larger resources than most of the sovereign states. And, on the other hand, many states were not able to control the activities of the multinationals. This challenged the concept of state sovereignty in domestic but also in international affairs.[7] In the Western world the evolution of the multinationals and the restructuring of the international economic system gave birth to the so-called political economy of international relations. In this approach states were just one category of international actors.

From a historical point of view, the concept of the nation-state is very problematic. Hobsbawm[8] has shown that we can hardly talk about nation-states. Modern states were born in Europe in the sixteenth century. At that time they had very little to do with nations. Modern states were by origin and especially by their territory successors of the feudal states of the late Middle Ages. The increasing role of the central authority led to the creation of nations inside existing state borders. Within a certain territory the laws were codified, language unified and finally a nation created. In contradiction to this it is difficult to find a nation which would have manifested itself also as a state.

The remarks above are important in the sense that the state as a concept is not as central for the realist tradition as has been assumed. We do not say that the paradigm will collapse in the case that the state concept is weak according to some latest evaluations. The state is just one actor and one form of social and political organization of people.[9] However, the state can be replaced by another actor without losing the power-political aspect of the realist paradigm.

States are becoming less relevant as reference points for many people.[10] One reason is that states are too hierarchical. Networks are more egalitarian and provide more opportunities for direct participation. Therefore they are more relevant in the activities of people. This leads to the decline of the state authority as well as of sovereignty. One reason for this might be the close connection between the so-called modern nation-state and industrialism.

In the nineteenth century economic growth based on industrialization gave the means to construct a welfare state. The state was organized for industrial production. Industry and wide-scale paid labour were the basis of a taxation system that made it possible to aim at common welfare. The post-industrial society does not provide the same basis, and the state loses its meaning *vis-à-vis* the ordinary people. The people as well as the economy have to find new ways of surviving.

NEW OPTIONS FOR ORGANIZING THE INTERNATIONAL SYSTEM AFTER THE COLD WAR

Regionalization is a phenomenon which already existed during the Cold War. In the theories of international relations this was connected to economic integration and security. The EC as well as NATO were very much regional organizations. On the other side of the iron curtain there were CMEA and WTO countries. On the continental level there are organizations like the OAU or OAS which are regional by their character.

Although regionalism has for a long time existed as a phenomenon in international politics, there is a difference between old and new regionalism. Previously 'region' as a concept referred to continents or to limited geographical regions. From this point of view region has been more of a geographical concept. On the other hand, it referred to trade or military blocs which were formed by states geographically close to each other. In current regionalization geography does not, however, play an important role.

Even after the cold war there is a risk of confusing regionalization with something that could be called 'continentalization'. After the cold war there has been a visible geopolitical school in international studies which has launched a discussion about three more or less continental trading blocs: Europe around the EU; America around the NAFTA; and the Pacific Rim around Japan. In the future the competition between these blocs is supposed to be real and it will be more economic than military by its character.[11]

It is necessary to make a clear distinction between new regionalization and continentalization. In our vocabulary regionalization is more related to co-operation between regions in different states than close co-operation between traditional state-connected actors on a continental level. We understand continentalization as a part of a wider globalization process which is also connected to a new struggle over hegemony on a world scale.

From our perspective the situation in Europe bears the most relevance. It has been a common assumption that the creation of the EC made it impossible to have any violent conflicts between the member states, most of all between France and Germany. The EC was also connected to a kind of universal movement from families to units larger than the nation-states. To some extent the same process existed in Northern Europe, where Nordic co-operation was already established in the 1950s.

In both of the above-mentioned cases, regional co-operation was explained on a theoretical level by common history, common political and cultural values, and so on.[12] To some extent this is correct. However, it is also possible to say that a common enemy in the East, the Soviet Union and the WTO, forced the EC as well as the Nordic countries to co-operate. It is possible to argue that threat has been a factor which has pushed states into co-operation and after the threat disappears there is liberty for pursuing more individual interests.

From the perspective of the nation-state it is also possible to say that the threat from the East kept states together. No region of any European state could freely pursue its own international policy. If this had been allowed, it would have affected the course of the cold war and it would have been exploited by the counterpart. This was evident in the cases of the Basque country in Spain or of Scotland in the United Kingdom. With the collapse of the Cold War system the hegemonic stability disappeared, too. And even further, the regions in the nation-states found it possible to extend their own (mostly economic) interests. This again has been visible in Scotland. The nationalist movement in Scotland expects the state authority to be, at least partly, moved from London to Brussels. This would increase Scottish autonomy.[13] Both aspects imply that after the cold war there is room for a new kind of organizing the international system. This is the point of departure which has given a possibility for regionalization in Europe.

There is also another element which has been the grounds for the restructuring of the international system after the cold war. In the sixteenth century states emerged between universalism, and localism. Catholic order demanded universalism, which went against the interests of the princes. There was left from the Middle Ages a tradition of local authority which was a hindrance for the development of the authority of the princes. A state which later became the nation-state offered a solution to the princes for both problems.[14]

The post-cold war international system faces the same situation, especially in Europe. The EU is taking a part of the state sovereignty on a higher level. On the other hand, states are not able to look after the interests of national peripheries or even economic centres in the framework of the nation-state approach. This and the collapse of the Cold War hegemonic order has given a push for regionalization. On a higher level, globalism is also a challenge for the state-centric international system.

The economy is the true global sector in the international system. All the different parts of the globe are interconnected by economic links. The infrastructure for the global economy was given by the transnational or multinational corporations. However, giantism seems to be over: during the last 10 years the most successful firms have been small enterprises with a low production capacity. The globalization of the market place has lead to a situation where manufacturing jobs glide to newly industrialized countries.[15] These changes require more flexible political organization than the states have been, which means that current economic trends create a space for regionalization. For instance, in the Baltic regionalization or in Euro-Region Via Drina the co-operation between wealthy and poor subregions is an economic advantage for both sides of the poverty curtain. In regionalization inequality can be used to improve positions in the world economy.

On the other hand, all states and even smaller regions like the Faroe Islands talk about integration into world markets. Somehow integration is seen as a solution for economic growth and for solving local economic problems. However, integration into world markets increases external dependence and marginalizes the small units. According to Zurn,[16] globalization of the economy increases inequality between and within nations. In that sense the global economy does not solve the local problems. This again manifests the need for regionalization. It is also necessary to bear in mind the close connection between these two: for instance, according to Rosenau[17] globalization and localization are interconnected phenomena.

In security issues globalism has also reached its limits. The more states became dependent on factors far beyond their borders, the more their security interests were globalized. This was already an important aspect during the cold war, at least in US foreign and security policy.[18] Global security has not lost its meaning after the cold war. The safer the international system is, the more secure is the economic development of the OECD countries and especially that of the USA. The problem, however, is that after the fall of the powerful Soviet threat it has become more difficult to maintain a military force capable of global operations. This means that global security is too expensive. After the withering away of the Soviet threat it has been difficult to motivate and to explain the huge military costs required by any kind of global security policy. Therefore, regional security scenarios have become interesting alternatives.

Finally, we would like to argue against the overemphasizing of the globalism approach by referring to environmental problems. It is true that in the 1980s and 1990s several international environmental agreements have been signed and some even ratified by various states.[19] This might stress the global character of environmental problems. However, there are good reasons for emphasizing that these are local by their character. The sources of pollution are always local, although the results cross borders. On the other hand, the effects are also local by their nature though the local authorities do not have any possibility of sovereign decisions to limit or stop the pollution. In this framework we come to conflicting interests of the polluter and the receiver.

REGIONALIZATION AS A PHENOMENON

As indicated above, regionalization might be a phenomenon which challenges the state-centric approach. In order to evaluate this we have to give some characteristics of regionalization: where it occurs, what forms it takes and how exactly it challenges the realist tradition. At the moment subnational regionalization is first of all a European phenomenon. Traditionally the Euro-centric system gives the essence to the entire international system. Therefore it is possible to say that if regionalism is a remarkable phenomenon in Europe, it might be essential to the future international system even on the global level. Besides this we can also find regionalization on other continents.

Currently there are different kinds of regionalization in Europe.

(1) *Regionalization emerges inside the EU framework*. The principle of subsidiarity means that an important sector of decision-making in the EU should take place on a substate level. This supports the strengthening of regions within nation-states. Simultaneously it weakens the role of the state and strengthens the position of the EU *vis-à-vis* the nation-state.

(2) *The EU supports cross-border regionalization inside the community*. In the EU the border regions have more chances of integrating their economy and politics while borders lose their meaning. This might create new power centres inside the EU, like the industrial centre along the French, German and Belgian border. Sometimes this area is called the 'Banana region' which stretches from London to Milan and is a future growth area of the EU.

(3) *The EU supports regionalization in its own border areas*. The EU is a member in the Barents region council. It is an observer at the Baltic Sea council. We also have to mention the Euro-region Via Drina, which connects parts of Eastern Germany and Western Poland to each other. All of these cases give a chance for the EU to connect nearby areas to its internal activities without permitting full membership with all burdens for the community. This co-operation in Northern Europe also connects Russia into Western Europe.

(4) *The EU supports regionalization beyond its current borders.* Co-operation in the Visegrád group (Poland, Czech Republic, Slovakia and Hungary) is supported by the EU. Regional co-operation became a precondition for aid from the community. This model is a kind of copy of American Marshall aid after the Second World War.

In all these four cases regionalization is a part of the policy of the EU. Regionalization is also related to states. Therefore, it is still in the frame of traditional international state-centric or integration politics. Further-more, it is possible to say that in the context of EU policy, regionalization comes from above and it is created by the EU or by the states. More interesting in this connection is regionalization from below:

(5) *The best example in the European context is the co-operation of the 'Four Motors of Europe'.* This is based on an agreement between Baden–Württemberg from Germany, Rhône Alps from France, Lombardy from Italy and Catalonia from Spain. The group has extended its co-operation beyond European borders. Ontario in Canada co-operates with the Four Motors. It is interesting to realize that all the four aforementioned European sub-regions are growth areas in their own countries. This leads to the conclusion that regionalization is probably a strategy for the well-off regions to sustain their economic development and to free themselves from poor regions. Indeed many scholars have emphasized this aspect of the 'Four Motors'. For instance, Christopher Harvie defined this form of co-operation as 'a potentially intra-European, high-technology cartel'.[20]

(6) *Another perspective is found, for example, in the Barents region co-operation.* Beside the regional co-operation created by the state there is also a local level in the Barents co-operation. Three Norwegian, one Swedish and one Finnish districts plus three Russian regions form a regional council in the framework of the Barents region council. All these regions are peripheral and live not on their own financial resources but on state sub-sidies. This leads to the conclusion that regional co-operation across state borders can also be a strategy for poor peripheral regions to survive or to avoid further marginalization.

In both of the two last mentioned cases co-operation brings new actors into international politics and it also creates a political forum where the states are not the most important actors. The interests of subregions differ from the national interests. There is a common motive for both types of substate-level co-operation. Economic survival is the reason for breaking the nation-state system: states cannot necessarily ensure the well being of all of their regions. The existing inequality within the states implies that national interests may be in contradiction with regional or local interests. From the point of view of economic development, cross-border co-operation could improve welfare on both sides of the border. However, the national security interest is at least a hindrance to this. Here we have an issue which is still evident along the Finnish–Russian border. Russian Karelia could improve its economy in co-operation with Finland. This requires an open border which is not in the interests of the Finnish authorities. From the Finnish point of view, Russia is still in many respects seen as a threat, though not necessarily in the military sense.

We have to add one more category of regions to the list we have already given:

(7) *Ecological regions have a political aspect which refers to some of the weaknesses of the state-centric approach.* In this connection we are interested in river basins which are related to environmental as well as economic problems of many countries. Ohmae[21] has mentioned the Mississippi basin as a potential economic region with common interests in the world economy. From our point of view river basins like the Jordan or the Nile are even more important. In the case that Ethiopia begins to develop its national economy by improving agriculture it needs a lot more water for irrigation. This water can be taken from the sources of Nile. However, 80 per cent of the Nile's water comes from Ethiopia and 80 per cent of the water of Egypt is taken from the Nile.[22] Here we come to the weakness of a state-centric and nationally-orientated approach. The problems of the Nile basin cannot be solved on the basis of national interests. Regional co-operation can be a precondition for a solution but it is not a solution in itself.

Co-operation on the sub-European level manifests and possibly also increases inequality in the EU and in the whole of Europe. It also increases inequality within the nation-states and therefore challenges the very existence and legitimacy of the nation-state. Even more important might be to point to the fact that regionalism changes the traditional state-connected and even monopolized security order. Security will be diversified in the nation-states since different regions are members in different coalitions and have also different security interests. However, this does not mean that armed security has lost its meaning. Certainly regionalization does not eliminate the very traditional reasons for conflicts between different international actors.

If we want to acknowledge the differences between different regions we have to assume that regionalization does not necessarily lead to a more equal and homogeneous Europe. Transactions between different regions will contain an aspect of inequality. This means that there will be a hierarchical structure even in the Europe of regions. This further means that core–periphery relations are not withering away in Europe. However, regionalization might create new cores in Europe, like the Four Motors of Europe or the Blue Banana. Therefore it is possible to state that regionalization does not mean the end of hegemony.

In regionalization we can also find different levels of integration. Some regions are in the first stages of their formation and some are developing towards autonomous subjects in politics. For our analysis it is important to realize differences in the level of the formation of regions. For us new regionalism means that a region will attempt to become a political subject in international politics. A region created from above as a geographic area where states organize co-operation does not belong to the category of new regionalism.

The variety of the development stages gives a very confusing picture of regionalism. It has also made some scholars argue that this is a typical postmodern phenomenon. No clarity is needed any more and regionalism can be based on informality but also in some cases on formal institutions. In the first case it is possible to talk about a new phenomenon and in the latter we can talk about old regionalism. It is true that the following forms of regional co-operation can be seen as co-existing, but they can also be seen as a historical development process:

- *geographical or ecological regions* – in which geography or ecology is the only common denominator which connects states or sub-regions to each other;
- *epistemic or identity regions* – in which people in general or just the elites have a feeling of belonging together or they share several common interests;

- *the region as a system* – in which the co-operating partners have concrete connections and transactions between each other;
- *the region as an organized system* – in which there is an agreement on co-operation between the partners and there are also regular meetings where the partners can at least discuss common problems and further harmonize their policies;
- *the region as a civil society* – in which people in the region have a real feeling of belonging together and partners have the same characters;
- *regions as political subjects* – in which the region has a political body capable of making authoritative decisions; in this case the region gets features familiar from the nation-states with the difference that heterogeneous regions can hardly develop into nation-states.[23]

The most important conclusion here is that we cannot talk about one single phenomenon when talking about regionalization. Regionalization is a major uniform trend in Europe only if we neglect the differences between different forms of regionalization. If we take seriously all the differences, we can no longer talk about one single process in Europe.

INTEGRATION THEORY AND REGIONALIZATION

Although most of the integration literature has to do with states, a lot of the concepts and basic issues can be utilized in subnational regionalization as well. For example, Nye's different levels of integration (economic, political and social) can be identified in subnational integration processes. Also, Nye differentiated between different forms of political integration that can also be found in subnational integration:

- institutional
- policy
- attitudinal, and
- security.[24]

Though the security aspect is absent from most forms of regionalization, this need not continue to be so. Regional formations can, in the transitional stage before becoming members of security institutions, start integrating their own security policies in order to strengthen their negotiating position and to gain credibility in security issues, and naturally to increase security and stability.

In other levels of political integration there are clear differences between different forms of regionalization: for example, in Eastern Europe co-operation is very close to traditional intergovernmental co-operation due to the transitional nature of the situation in this area, whereas regionalization in Western Europe is introducing truly new forms of regional co-operation, for instance, in the form of 'meso-regions'.[25] These new types of regions can be quite distant from each other but yet they are based on a common identity, mutual trust and on a common sense of belonging and common interests based on which they have been willing to create a common development strategy. An example of meso-regions is the 'European Blue Banana' connecting urban centres and stretching from London via Brussels and Frankfurt to Milan. Most of the urban centres in the 'Blue Banana' were growth areas already in the twilight of modernization in the sixteenth century.[26] Institutional integration of these types of regions is, however, fairly low: their integration is more functional and attitudinal.

In most forms of regionalization the level of institutional integration is fairly low, due to the conscious choice of the actors involved; regionalization is seen as something different from traditional intergovernmental co-operation and actors mostly try to avoid too strict institutional structures in order to keep co-operation closer to concrete activities and civil society. This can naturally also be interpreted as a way of avoiding too close engagement in these forms of co-operation: actors thus allow themselves the possibility of not abiding by the common decisions or 'rules of the game', or of 'opting out', so to speak.

Attitudinal integration can be said to be the most successful form of integration in subnational regionalization: it is clearly the base or the core of the whole phenomenon. Regionalization takes place for economic reasons: it is seen as a way of enhancing competitiveness in the changing global economy. However, attitudinal integration can also be seen as a *prerequisite* for any kind of regionalization. For instance, in Eastern Central Europe the need for new forms of co-operation was felt very strongly after the end of the cold war, and these countries (not regions!) felt the need to co-operate among themselves in spite of the obvious conflicts between them (minorities, territorial disputes)[27] because in spite of the apparent differences between them, they were after all facing a common plight of re-entering the European system and rebuilding their national economies.

The attitudinal aspect has also been important in Northern Europe: there are actually similarities between Eastern and Northern Europe in that both are trying to avoid (further) marginalization and regional co-operation is seen as a way of achieving this. However, what makes Northern Europe interesting is the fact that the level of attitudinal integration is high in spite of the apparently heterogeneous nature of the actors involved. For example, Baltic co-operation has been so successful that it is often considered the model case of European regionalization, and yet the regions (or countries) involved are very heterogeneous. Even though one might ask what countries like Sweden and Latvia could possibly have in common other than location by the Baltic Sea, it is obvious that they have at least enough common interests to be willing to make an effort to co-operate. As we saw earlier, it is also a question of inequality: whereas weaker states would cling to any possible solution to enhance their position, stronger states have a strong interest in accepting this because they can benefit from it.

OTHER ALTERNATIVE APPROACHES

In our view, integration and interdependence theories are not sufficient tools in explaining regionalization although they do contain some elements that help to conceptualize this phenomenon. More useful tools can be found in more complex models containing elements from different theories that may not be as efficient as paradigms but whose explanatory force is superior to that of the above-mentioned.

For example, models based on identities, new ways of thinking about nationality, regionality and territoriality can be useful in explaining regionalization as a phenomenon in international relations. In these approaches the most important point in our view is the fact that the ways of identification and the relationship between 'state', 'nation' and 'community' can be said to be changing, one might even say in turmoil.

In the state-centric approach identities are fairly clear-cut: nationality is the most important level of identification and the assumed 'national interest' is the main objective of policy-makers. Now the situation is changing, and this change contains some quite contradictory elements: interdependence and globalization are strong trends that exist parallel to growing nationalism and new states being born.

At the same time as nationalism is worrying the academic world and the person in the street, identities are not as easily identified anymore. When looking at regionalization from this point of view we must keep in mind that identities should not and indeed cannot be seen as a zero-sum relationship.[28]

However, if we consider 'European identity' crucial for integration in the changing European system, we are in our view misguided: more important than a single 'Pan-European identity' (especially when it is solely built on a West European base!) is the existence and recognition of different levels of identification; 'concentric circles of allegiance' (as Smith cites James Coleman[29]). This approach can be seen as the 'natural' solution for interpreting the European system from a regionalization point of view where national, subnational and supranational levels of identification exist simultaneously, each with different intensity. These levels of identification form networks where one single level of identification cannot be found. However, we think it is fair to say that subnational identities can be seen as more important than national or supranational identities since they are closer to the everyday life of people and civil society. Being aware of these *multiple belongings* of human persons is also necessary for those who not only analyse international relations but also make decisions at the international level, as for example Antony Black has argued: those who do for whatever reason possess the power to shape the international order can achieve better and more lasting results if they are aware of the multiple belongings of human persons.[30]

The community where identities and feelings of allegiance are formed can at the same time be state, subnational community or regional formation like the European Union and these intermingling feelings of belonging can be not necessarily exclusive but also *mutually reinforcing*. This has to do with the relationship between two types of regional co-operation: traditional forms such as the EC/EU and new, currently emerging forms of regionalization. These two types are different, but yet similar and they have a close relationship. Subnational regional co-operation can strengthen supranational co-operation and integration in emphasizing the multi-dimensional character of supranational integration and stressing diversity within, for instance, the EU. If the EU concentrates more on its pan-European character that allows for various layers of identity and co-operation, instead of stressing the need for unity, it can both legitimize its own existence and allow the creation of different subregional co-operative constellations to emerge that can benefit both levels – in this case the state would be the obvious loser when the other two levels would create mutually beneficial forms of co-operation. The state would not become obsolete, but it would suffer even more from the crisis concerning its legitimacy.

THE CHANGING ROLE OF THE STATE AND REGIONALIZATION

As we have already seen, the state is no longer the primary level of identification. The whole of Western thinking, however, is still strongly state-centric even though this seems to be changing, slowly but surely. We shall next look at the ways in which the role of the state is changing and how regionalization affects this change.

One important element of this change is the economic crisis that states (especially in Western Europe) are facing. Crisis of the welfare state needs not be solely negative: it can also bring out something positive by making people more aware of the necessity to act by themselves when less functions are performed by the state level. The crisis of the welfare state has brought out in the open one obvious change: the growing need for delegation and a new division of labour between state, regions and supranational level. This means, not only decentralization within the state but also more responsibility for the regions themselves.

Both tendencies are positive elements for the changing role of the state in that they are ways for the state to overcome the inherent problems of its own growth: they can serve as a way of restoring the legitimacy of the public policy when state is no longer single-handedly able to perform its old functions. Thus decision-making can also be brought closer to the citizen: more issues can be dealt with locally, and local initiatives can become more important. Naturally this development is not unproblematic in itself: the economic crisis is felt by all levels and all regions may not even be willing to expand their sphere of activity and autonomy. In some cases they may, however, be forced to do this.

In regionalization, *autonomy* will be a critical issue. All regions are certainly not willing to take over the traditional functions of states. On many occasions regions simply do not have the resources to run social security, education and health care systems. This implies a division of labour between states and regions. The Sami region in Northern Europe is a good case to show the discrepancy in autonomy demands.

Among the Sami people there is a movement towards independence. However, there is also an idea for a kind of confederation in which the Sami people would have autonomy only in their own issues. Otherwise, the states would still be responsible for education, health care and social security.

Widening supranational integration can also have both positive and negative elements for the regions: the state is bound to give up some of its authority but the transfer of authority is not a simple one-dimensional process: both supranational and subnational levels can profit from this transfer, and it can also be positive from the point of view of the state that can no longer perform all its traditional functions.

This change in the state's role stems from the two-fold development of *globalization* and *localization*: for a long time the globalization of the economic sphere has caused a sort of 'erosion' of the state. The trilateral constellation of the global economy (and the multinationals) have had a 'life of their own' where the state has had only a limited possibility for intervention and global issues have affected the local level in a way that the state has not been able to control. Now that especially Western Europe and Japan are faced with great economic difficulties and stagnation that have shifted the centre of economic activities in a greater degree towards new 'growth spots', especially towards Latin America and Asia outside Japan, the possibilities of intervention have weakened even more. This gives regions new possibilities for acting both locally and globally and causes change in local and global agendas which become more intermingled.

From the point of view of traditional realist thinking this means that domestic and international agendas and politics are even more difficult to handle separately: the whole distinction between the two becomes more and more irrelevant. The nature of most important global issues is also reinforcing this trend: economic, ecological and security issues cannot be limited to the territory of a state, and what once was a local problem is now global – and vice versa. Traditional military security issues are no longer *the* security issue and even they have to be seen in a wider environment (NATO being so far the only real security institution).

As we said earlier, the whole notion of security is changing. This applies to war as well. Whereas in traditional realist thought war was seen as a 'normal phenomenon' in international relations and interpreted in the Clausewitzian sense – war being the continuation of politics by other means[31] and peace being the result of balance of power – the post-Cold War situation presents new challenges. Growing instability within states, ethnic conflicts and the internationalization of conflict[32] imply that war and conflictuality in general are becoming more complicated. If regions were to substitute states, it would enforce this trend and possibly make the international system even more unpredictable. It can be argued that regionalization does not necessarily diminish conflictuality: it merely changes its form.

However, so far security has remained 'the monopoly of the state': regionalization has not even attempted to make real moves in this area and even at the supranational level the degree of integration in these areas is low. The EC has for a long time attempted to create a common security policy in one form or another but the fact remains that it is still far from being realized in practice and many problems remain. For example, problems concerning the division of labour between EU, WEU and NATO prove this point, and naturally even more so does the situation in Bosnia that has tragically shown the helplessness of all European security organizations. For example, in the case of the EU external expectations have exceeded its capability to act efficiently and in a unified manner.

Both the possible new solutions and those created so far, such as 'Partnership for Peace', have to find their place in the new European security system. The OSCE has also attempted to participate in the regional security issues, but it can be argued that it has focused too strongly on geographic expansion, on widening instead of deepening, and its role will probably be weakened even more by the new security solutions. The 'EU–WEU–NATO' triangle will most likely be the one within which the most important moves are to be made. In any case, the question remains whether sufficient political will does indeed exist in this area when most countries involved in new forms of regionalization face many different insecurities both externally and from within.

BACK TO REALISM?

Although the European system is undergoing changes that partly undermine the relevance of the traditional realist approach, we think it cannot be entirely replaced. The form of the traditional state system may have changed (and indeed has) but no credible alternative model has emerged.

There are several reasons for this relativity of change. Most forms of regionalization in Europe are still strongly influenced by the state;

especially in Eastern Europe, but also in Western Europe, state-level co-operation is still almost the only existing form of co-operation. There are very few exceptions from this rule: maybe the Carpathian Euro-region can be seen as such since it brings together subnational regions from different countries in this area (Poland, Slovakia, Hungary, Romania and Ukraine). Its role has however been limited partly due to the negative attitude of Russia concerning the participation of Ukraine. Even in Western and Northern Europe states there are important actors alongside subnational regions. As we have mentioned before, this is partly due to the fact that many regions are not even willing to replace states. They may want more influence over international issues but they are not willing (or able) to take over the state's position.

Supranational level has also influenced the way in which regions are developing. Regionalization first came up as a reaction to inefficient state and supranational regional policy that could not solve the problems of lagging and marginalized regions. Regions had potential for development that regional policy was not able to realise efficiently, and therefore regions saw the need to become more active themselves. This process has been both encouraged and limited by the supranational level. On the one hand, the European Community made it clear it was all for '*Europe de régions*' but on the other hand it has not so far been willing to make real moves towards establishing this goal. The Maastricht Treaty contained some elements for establishing a 'Europe of regions', but the real significance of the treaty remains low.[33]

The Maastricht Treaty falls short of creating a truly effective means of participation for the regions in the EU framework. Mostly the role of the regions is still more that of a 'lobbyists' than of independent and equal subjects on the European level. The same applies for the organizations created for and by the regions themselves, such as AER (Association of European Regions), AEBR (Association of European Border Regions) and CLRAE (Standing Conference of Local and Regional Authorities of Europe). Their role is that of pressure groups, and the extent to which they are able to influence policies of individual states or of the EU is dependent on the goodwill of these other levels.

So it can be argued that the state has by no means lost its authority, not to the EU nor, and even less so, to the regions. Whether this will remain to be the case is, however, questionable, since it would serve the interests of all these three levels to modify the division of labour between them. Even if this would (and it actually would) mean diminishing the authority of the state, it would be rational from the point of view of states, since they are bound to lose some of their authority due to the crisis they are facing for economic reasons.

A relevant question in the changing European structure is the true *nature and essence of realism*. Could realism be interpreted differently, in a way that substitutes states by different actors, for example by regions? This would mean that some core issues of realism would have to be seen differently, but (in our view) they would not have to be replaced or rejected. Politics among nations would be replaced by regions but the main issues would remain the same: competition, dicothomy between conflict and co-operation, struggle for power and so on would remain in the core of politics, even if actors did change and regions were to replace nation-states as the key actors in international politics (which does not seem to be happening in the near future even if regions are becoming more active and relevant from the point of view of international politics).

The biggest change would involve the notion of *sovereignty*. It is already apparent that sovereignty is indeed changing form in a way that makes it more difficult to name the level where it can be found. Transfer of authority is a complicated process and it seems that there is no longer only one single identifiable sovereign, but a multitude of authorities at different levels of aggregation and several centres with differing degrees of coercive power (not all of them public and governmental!). As we saw earlier, it becomes increasingly difficult to differentiate between public and private institutions, the state and civil society, domestic and international.[34] In our view sovereignty may not be as important as it was before and the change of the whole European system is both the reason for and the consequence of this. Yet, realism is definitely not becoming entirely irrelevant: it just needs to be adjusted to the changing environment in a way that takes into account new relevant actors and levels of international politics.

It looks as if states do get new competitors in international politics. However, this is true only in the case that regions are formed from below the state level and these regions also get an identity of their own and begin to act as subjects in international politics. An important aspect here is that regionalization from below breaks nation-states and creates new multinational units. If regionalization develops further, it is the nation-state concept which will be challenged. Otherwise regionalization changes the realist approach very little. Regions do not have common interests, not even in relation to environmental problems. Therefore competing interests and conflicts will still be a part of international reality.

According to our understanding of regionalization, competing interests will remain important even in the future. We have already argued that regional formations have contradictory interests. Rich regions try to free themselves from the poor regions and the poor regions try to get into the circle of prosperity. Therefore regionalization is not only an idealistic approach for peace in the way co-operation is understood in the tradition of peace research. Regionalization also implies exclusion of some actors. Regionalization has to be understood as politics which often includes action directed against others.[35] Therefore conflicts are a natural part in regionalization.

Another aspect of potential change concerns democracy. Regionalization can shift the traditional vertical democracy (vertical relationship between central authority and civil society) towards a more multidimensional process in which horizontal democracy and a wide variety of networks can emerge. This depends on the way regions develop in the future; if they attempt to create rigid institutions they will not introduce a new type of democracy but will instead replace states as centres of authority.

Finally, it is possible to argue that regions lead to a redivision of power. One result might be that the power is much closer to the grassroots level. Regionalization also creates more political subjects than the nation-state system has provided. Even this should lead to decentralization of political but not necessary of economic power. All these tendencies mean fragmentation instead of or in combination with globalization. Fragmentation resembles the Europe of princes in the Middle Ages.

Regionalization as a process which brings new actors into the political space, is a phenomenon which offers a possibility to develop the realist tradition further as a more general theory in the international studies, outside the Cold War context. Regionalization does not entirely undermine the realist approaches to a modernist script but it does challenge the essential role of the nation-state in this approach.

Notes

1. For an extensive (and provocative) view on the complexity of the research field and its current situation see James N. Rosenau, *Global Voices. Dialogues in International Relations* (Boulder, San Francisco and Oxford: Westview Press, 1993).
2. See for instance Björn Hettne and András Inotai, *The New Regionalism. Implications for Global Development and International Security* (Research for Action. UNU/WIDER, 1994).
3. John Vasquez, *The Power of Power Politics. A Critique* (London: Frances Pinter, 1983).
4. K. J. Holsti, *The Dividing Discipline. Hegemony and Diversity in International Theory* (London: Allen & Unwin, 1987).
5. Hedley Bull, *The Anarchical Society. A Study of Order in World Politics* (London: Macmillan, 1977) pp. 18–19.
6. Peter van Ham, 'The European Community after Hegemony: The Future of European Integration in a Multipolar World', *International Relations*, **11** (5): 451–67 (1993).
7. See, for instance, Raymond Vernon, *Sovereignty at Bay. The Multinational Spread of US Enterprises* (Harmondsworth: Penguin, 1973).
8. E.J. Hobsbawm, *Nations and Nationalism since 1780* (Cambridge University Press, 1990).
9. David J. Dunn has made the same conclusion and he went even further by referring to a plurality of identities. People do not identify themselves just as citizens of a certain state or according to their nationality but they identify themselves at the same time as European or members of the European Union or according to their religion. See David J. Dunn, 'Whither International Relations', a paper presented at the 1994 ISA Convention in Washington (28 Mar.–1 Apr.).
10. This is for instance the argument presented in several papers for the 1994 ISA Convention. See Grant T. Hammond and Bryant P. Shaw, 'The Rise of Nations and the Decline of States: The Decay of the State System', and James N. Rosenau, 'Fragmegrative Dynamics: Notes on the Interaction of Globalizing and Localizing Processes' papers presented for the 1994 ISA Conference in Washington (28 Mar.–1 Apr.).
11. See Paul Kennedy, *Preparing for the Twenty-First Century* (New York: Random House, 1993) Peace researcher Johan Galtung also sees the future as an economic power struggle between two continental blocks (Europe and North America) and a quartet consisting of Japan, China, Korea and Vietnam in the Pacific Rim. This was one aspect in his lecture 'The World after 1989. A Geopolitical Overview', given at the University of Tampere on 1 June 1994.
12. See, for instance, Ernst B. Haas *The Uniting of Europe* (Stanford, CA: Stanford University Press, 1958), Peter Wallensteen, Unto Vesa and Raimo Väyrynen, 'The Nordic System: Structure and Change, 1920–1970', Tampere Peace Research Institute, Research Reports, no. 6 (1973); or 'Norden, Europe and the Near Future', report from the Directors of the Nordic Peace Research Institutes, *PRIO Report*, no. 3 (1991).

13. In 1988 the Scottish National Party accepted the principle of an independent Scotland in an integrated Europe, in the EC.
14. Richard Mackenney, *Sixteenth-Century Europe. Expansion and Conflict* (Basingstoke: Macmillan, 1993).
15. See Brandley R. Gitz and Dirk VanRaemdonck, 'The Borderless World: Post-Industrial Economics, Industrial-Age Politics', a paper presented for the 1994 ISA Convention in Washington, DC (28 Mar.–1 Apr.).
16. Michael Zurn, 'The Micro-Level Responses to Inadequate International Governance', a paper presented for the 1994 ISA Convention in Washington, DC (28 Mar.–1 Apr.).
17. Rosenau, 'Fragmegrative Dynamics'.
18. Jyrki Käkönen, *Natural Resources and Conflicts in the Changing International System. Three studies on imperialism* (Aldershot: Avebury, 1988) pp. 147–53.
19. See Caroline Thomas, *The Enviroment in International Relations* (London: The Royal Institute of International Affairs, 1992).
20. Harvie 1994, op.cit. p. 65.
21. Kenichi Ohmae, (1993) 'The Rise of the Region State', *Foreign Affairs*, 43(1).
22. See, for instance Peter H. Gleick, (1993). 'Water and Conflict: Fresh Water Resources and International Security', *International Security* **18**(1).
23. See Björn Hettne, 'The New Regionalism: Implications for Development and Peace', in B. Hettne and A. Inotai, The New Regionalism, pp. 7–8.
24. Mansbach *et al.*, *The Web of World Politics. Nonstate actors in the Global System* (Englewood Cliffs, NJ: Prentice-Hall, 1976) p. 256.
25. On meso regions see, for example, Riccardo Cappellin, 'Regional Economic Development, Regionalism and Interregional Cooperation: the Role of Regions in a Policy for European Cohesion', report presented at the, University of Joensuu, Finland, 1993 European Summer Institute in regional studies (14–29 Jun.).
26. See Mackenney, *Sixteenth-Century Europe*, pp. 82–103.
27. Jeffrey Simon, 'Central Europe: "Return to Europe" or Descent to Chaos?' and William Bodie, 'Anarchy and Cold War in Moscow's "Near Abroad"'– both articles in *European Security Toward the Year 2000*, *McNair Paper* 20 (Institute for National Strategic Studies, National Defence University, 1993).
28. Anthony, D. Smith, 'A Europe of Nations – or the Nation of Europe?', *Journal of Peace Research*, **30** (2): 129–35.
29. Ibid.
30. Antony, Black, 'Nation and Community in the International Order', *Review of International Studies*, **19** (1): 81–9.
31. See for example Raymond Aron, *Paix et guerre entre les Nations* (Paris: Calmann–Lévy, 1962) p.69.
32. For example the case of the Gulf War, see Joseph Camilleri and Jim Falk, *The End of Sovereignty?* (Aldershot: Edward Elgar, 1992) pp. 139–70.

33. See, for example, Thomas Christiansen, ' "Interest Representation" Between Institutions and Identities: Regions in the European Community', EUI seminar paper *EC Law in Context: Interests, Policymaking and Law*, presentation on 25 March 1993.
34. On these issues see for example Roger Morgan (ed.) 'Regions, states and Europe: analyzing the territorial distribution of power in the European Community', EUI paper (Jun. 1992).
35. Vilho Harle, 'Conflict Studies and Political Theory: Incompatibles or Collaborators?' a paper presented for the 1994 ISA Convention in Washington, DC (28 Mar.–1 Apr.).

9 Regionalism and World Order After the Cold War

Richard Falk

This chapter seeks to assess the actual and potential contributions of regionalism to the achievement of such world order goals as peace, social justice, human rights and democracy.[1] This assessment proceeds by way of discussing, in an introductory section, several main features of the global setting that have become prominent in the early aftermath of the cold war. Against this background, four possible roles for regional actors are depicted:

(1) *containing negative globalism* – basically associated with the adverse impacts of global market forces;
(2) *mitigating pathological anarchism* – the breakdown of minimum order and decency in state/society relations arising from either extremes of excessive control and abuse by the state or of pervasive and dangerous chaos arising from the weakness or breakdown of governance capacity at the level of the state;
(3) *promoting positive globalism* – reinforcing the global capacity to achieve desirable world order goals; and
(4) *promoting positive regionalism* – achieving these goals at a regional level through the strengthening and orientation of regional structures of governance.

The intention here is to propose one type of research agenda with respect to the regional dimensions of world order. Necessarily, such an effort is preliminary, focusing on issues of conceptualization and offering a broad normative perspective that differentiates what is negative (to be avoided or overcome) from what is positive (to be achieved or enhanced), but, I hope, in a manner that usefully prefigures further and more detailed inquiry.

228

BACKGROUND CONSIDERATIONS

Of course, many of the fundamental tendencies reshaping world order were not derivative from the cold war, especially the complex dynamics of globalization. However, the preoccupations of the cold war, its East–West axis of interpretative logic, made it more difficult to appreciate the impact of globalization, including the various phenomena of backlash being generated. When the Berlin Wall was breached in November 1989 this ultra-stable geopolitical scaffolding provided by bipolarity, especially with respect to Europe since the Second World War, disintegrated before our eyes. The immediate reaction was to exaggerate the discontinuity, neglecting underlying forces for change that were having a transforming impact in any event, such as weaponry of mass destruction, technological innovation, environmental decay, economic integration, a global communications net, with accumulative effect of diminishing the functional competence and normative self-sufficiency of sovereign states.[2]

The end of the Cold War definitely encourages a greater emphasis on globalization, especially its human implications, and on such adverse reactions and contradictory trends as fundamentalism, a vehicle for religious and ethnic extremism. How regionalism of varying attributes fits within globalization is a central world order concern for which evidence and interpretation is necessarily inconclusive. This uncertainty is magnified by the unevenness of different regional settings and of the varying degrees to which economic, political, and cultural life has been regionalized. Almost any generalization about regionalism seems suspect, and must be qualified.

There is one important exception to these admonitions of conceptual caution. It is persuasive to claim that regionalism as a perspective in this historical period is a promising focus for both empirical and normative inquiry, that regionalism identifies emergent trends and structures and clarifies a distinct array of prescriptions and strategies. Following Hettne's assessment, the provision of world order in the near future is no longer likely to be provided to nearly the extent, as during the cold war, by hegemonic state actors;[3] indeed, I would go further, contending that the weakening of the state, in general, is producing various adverse types of societal vulnerability to the integrative tendencies in the global economy and is partly responsible for the intensity and incidence of pathological forms of anarchy that are of a different character from the type of structural anarchy that Hedley Bull has so influentially depicted.[4]

Thus, the regional alternative to statism seems potentially compensatory, in terms of the quality of world order, for both the erosion of hegemonic stability and the more acute forms of pathology that are afflicting the weak state. These background conditions are linked to the ending of the cold war, especially the collapse of bipolarity and the loss of a capacity to maintain order within bloc limits; also relevant is the inherently far more limited ordering role of unipolarity as a sequel to bipolarity has not lived up to expectations. This partly results from the contemporary perception by political leaders of a greatly diminished domain of strategic interests, but also the internal pressures exerted by the citizenry on government to address domestic priorities. More concretely, the Gulf War epitomized the post-cold war perception of the persistence of hegemonic stability; after all, here was a hegemonic undertaking, that succeeded fully in instrumentalizing the UN in the process, even generating illusionary claims of 'a new world order' legitimized through collective security mechanisms;[5] since 1991 it has become evident that 'the unipolar moment' was indeed of brief duration, and its idealistic embodiment in a serious commitment to collective security by way of the UN was quietly abandoned.[6]

Why were the crises in Somalia, Bosnia, Haiti, Rwanda treated as so much less deserving of a global community response than was the invasion of Kuwait? The paramount explanation is, of course, oil, but also the security threat posed by a militant Iraq, likely to possess nuclear weapons within years, to a strategic ally, namely Israel, as well as to a strategic region, the Middle East.[7] It is unlikely that the Gulf Crisis would have occurred in a bipolar world, the dynamics of mutual deterrence inducing greater prudence in relation to challenges directed at obvious strategic interests, as well as more effective control by superpowers over the initiatives undertaken by secondary states such as Iraq. But it is also unlikely that the internal tensions in Bosnia and Somalia would have spiralled out of governmental control as each country was of strategic importance within a Cold War setting, that is, warranting the expenditure of lives and resources by superpowers to maintain a given alignment. At the same time, the causal significance of the cold war is by no means uniform with respect to the collapse of minimum internal order; Lebanon spiralled dangerously out of control in the decade following the outbreak of civil strife in 1975, and superpower intervention failed in the major test cases of Vietnam and Afghanistan. There is a temptation, in other words, to exaggerate the ordering achievements of bipolarity and deterrence during the cold war era.[8] These achievements did seem considerable in Europe, but not necessarily elsewhere.

What is somewhat different, however, is the circumscribing of the domain of strategic interests on the part of intervening states in the North, particularly the USA. The outcome in Somalia, and even Haiti and Bosnia, has been widely regarded as a matter of virtual indifference, so long as the external effects are minimized. These external effects are associated with 'containment' in the post-Cold War senses, that is, not discouraging the expansion of the rival superpower/ideology, but the spread of disorder and violence via a wider war (Bosnia) or the massive generation of refugees (Bosnia again, but Haiti more centrally, where the prospects of even a relatively small number of black Haitian refugees coming to the USA is being resisted as strategically intolerable).[9]

The UN has been reinstrumentalized since its moment of prominence in the Gulf during 1990–1, resuming its role as marginal player, while being somewhat unfairly accused of 'failing.' Unlike the cold war, when failure was explained as a consequence of stalemate, it is now more damagingly seen as the expression of a feeble 'political will'. Yet it is here that enhanced roles for regional actors seem plausible, this possibility being highlighted, although ambiguously, by reliance on some military action by NATO in 1994 to curb the persisting excesses of the Bosnian Serbs. It is ambiguous as NATO had earlier floundered, and its temporary revival owed as much to the electoral success of Zhirinovsky in December 1993 (reminding Europe that the Russian bear might again prowl) as it did to the alleged moral shock of a mortar shell that killed civilians at a market on a February day in Sarajevo.

But security concerns are not the only world order context. The play of economic forces is at least as important even if not as visually captivating in a media sense. The transnational economic calculus is also being reshaped in contradictory ways by the ending of the cold war, above all by the weakening of alliance and bloc ties of bipolar variety as a result of the decline in global threat perception. Such a decline in globalization of security arrangements makes regional security and political economy factors generally more significant, yet not at all in a uniform manner. This decline is offset in a contradictory manner by the rising globalization of the world economy, stimulating tactics for participation and protection, both types of reaction bearing on regionalist prospects in this period. The patterns of differing influences and perceptions bearing on the role of regionalism is complex and confusing.

Europe and Asia–Pacific are currently the critical arenas for assessing the world order roles of regionalist configurations. In Europe, the collapse of the blocs, the widening of Europe, has definitely slowed the deepening of the European Union, and has possibly deferred indefinitely political integration. So many factors are at work that causal inferences will always seem argumentative and inconclusive. Yet there is an apparent contrast between Europe and Asia with respect to regionalist development. In Asia the USA is not needed as much as during the cold war, allowing economic priorities to gain precedence, especially being combined with new feelings of cultural potency and identity.[10] Similarly, the USA, no longer concerned with geopolitical alignment, is prepared to insist on more favourable trading and investment relations, creating special post-cold war tensions that invite a turn toward regional and bloc approaches. Whether this sets the stage for 'the clash of civilizations' is doubtful, but it does shift economic and political concerns from the old geopolitics of Westphalia to the new geopolitics of interregional relationships as mediated by the Group of Seven (reconstituted at Naples in 1994 as the Group of Eight, provisionally including Russia in their ranks).[11]

A focus on strategic considerations as explanatory ignores the complex and concealed politics of instrumentalization: who is instrumentalizing whom in relation to what? The Westphalian model of world order assumes that states are, more or less, the exclusive agents of instrumentalization. In a globalized world economy, states are themselves increasingly instrumentalized by concealed, external forces such as markets and profit margins, and their instrumentalization is expressed by way of the weakening of commitment to such foreign policy goals as human rights and environmental protection and to the reroutinization of tasks and capabilities entrusted to the United Nations. This reorientation of policy by states is accentuated by the weakening of organized labour as a domestic and transnational factor and by the discrediting of socialism (and its main operating modes) as a normative challenge to capitalism. Such an analysis supports an argument in favour of 'resituating the state' that is, strengthening its capacity to mediate between market drives and populist social forces.[12] The relevance of regional actors is evident, but far from consistent or *self*-evident: what is most uncertain can be phrased by reference to the theme of instrumentalization. Formal regional structures are still being constituted overwhelmingly by state actors as members, but to what extent are the regional approaches being taken by states themselves as the unacknowledged secondary effects of their instrumentalization by the global marketplace?[13] Within regional frameworks, hegemonic relations of varying sorts can be established, as seems the case with respect to Germany in Europe, and certainly on the part of the USA in the setting of NAFTA, and more generally, throughout the Western Hemisphere.

There are many dimensions of regionalism worthy of exploration and analysis at this time: four, in particular, seem to illuminate the character of the unfolding, yet still inchoate, post-cold war world order. In discussing these world order dimensions emphasis is placed on a distinction between 'positive' and 'negative' as pertaining to global and regional configurations of influence and authority. 'Positive' refers to desired objectives such as the reduction of political violence, the attainment of economic well-being, the promotion of human rights and benevolent governance, the protection of ecological diversity, the safeguarding of health and renewable resources. 'Negative' refers to the negation of these goals by way of warfare, poverty, racism, ecological decay, oppression, chaos, criminality. In the real-world positive and negative aspects are intertwined, and a given set of conditions associated, say, with global market forces or authoritarian government may generate positive, as well as negative outcomes. Economic growth, even if generating a non-sustainable consumerist ethos, may also be alleviating poverty and despair, as softer forms of authoritarianism, while cruel to its opponents, may nevertheless be providing effective leadership.

In the discussion that follows, for the sake of analytic clarity, this interplay of elements is put aside, and the discussion seeks to identify *four world order concerns*, two negative, two positive, that can be associated with the emergence of regional frameworks of political action alongside state and global frameworks.

(1) Clarifying the main links between regionalism and the *'containment' of negative globalism* – negative globalism refers here to the conjuncture of largely non-accountable power and influence exerted by multinational corporations, transnational banks and financial arenas, and their collaborators with the ideology of consumerism and a development ethos weighted almost entirely toward returns on capital mainly achieved by maximizing growth (no matter how often qualified, yet predominantly rhetorically, by the modifier 'sustainable'); in essence, the main regionalist tendencies are simultaneously both reinforcing this drift toward

negative globalism and creating resistance and alternative mitigating options, including the promotion of positive globalism
(that is, the democratizing of global institutions, creating
accountability and responsiveness to more democratic social
forces, and establishing procedures for wider participation by
representatives of diverse peoples; also relevant here is the promotion of human rights, including economic and social rights,
and a capability by the United Nations and other international
institutions to contribute more effectively to global security than
what is predicated upon a consensus among currently ascendent
geopolitical and geoeconomic forces).[14] It should be acknowledged that the neoliberal ideology informing global market
forces disseminates constructive ideas about freedom and the
rule of law, as well as destructive notions about greed and materialism.

(2)   Strengthening of regional frameworks to help meet the challenges being posed by several manifestations of *pathological
anarchism* – that is, breakdowns of order associated with political
normalcy and effective patterns of governance, leading to sustained violence that includes genocidal outbreaks and other
crimes against humanity, as well as chaotic conditions producing
massive displacements of people from their traditional places of
residence.[15] These geopolitical 'black holes' attract interventionary responses, but not of a reconstructive variety as the recent
tragedies in Somalia, Liberia, Sudan, Bosnia, and Rwanda illustrate in different ways; existing agencies of intervention, whether
under auspices of leading states or the UN Security Council, have
failed in both preventive and reactive modes, although some
reductions of suffering have been achieved to the extent the
intervening mission is defined in purely relief terms;[16] can regional frameworks make selective contributions?; under what circumstances? The failure of Europe in relation to Bosnia has had
the short-term effect of weakening regional sentiments, except
possibly through reviving, at least temporarily, the post-cold war
fortunes of NATO.[17]

(3)   Facilitating a *renewal of positive globalism as a world order project
through the medium of enhanced regionalism* – the implications of
(1) and (2) are essentially negative tendencies that can, to some
extent, be diminished or redirected by certain forms of regionalization. Positive globalism conceives of a governance structure for
the world that is of an aspirational character, one that promotes

sustainability, human rights, development (especially in relation to poverty and other forms of deprivation), and demilitarization (reducing warfare, arms races and sales).[18] Given concerns about homogenization, cultural diversity, and excessive centralization, the encouragement of stronger regional institutions might operate both as an alternative to and complement of positive globalism, thereby providing the peoples of the world with a vision of a desirable world order.

(4) Considering the normative achievements of regionalism in terms of its contributions to the well-being of the peoples living within its framework – this conception of *positive regionalism* as an end in itself is quite distinct from the evaluation of regionalism as a constituent element in a structure of global governance, and it has been most fully explored, of course, in the setting of Europe, especially by the encounter between Eurocrats of various hue and Eurosceptics, but has relevance, as well, to visions of a better future in Africa, Latin America, and Asia.[19]

Against this background, it is possible to explore in a tentative and preliminary manner the possible contributions of regionalism to an improved quality of world order, assessing improvement by reference to widely shared and explicitly specified world order values.

CONTAINING NEGATIVE GLOBALISM VIA REGIONALISM

Negative globalism refers to the adverse effects of economic and cultural integration at the global level. The integrative dynamic is not inherently negative, but it is having a series of adverse effects, given the current world order context. These effects include insensitivity to human suffering, insufficient attention to ecological sustainability, tendencies toward polarization (widening gaps between and within countries, and as among regions) and marginalization (virtual exclusion of countries, regions, ethnic minorities from developmental progress).

Negative globalism also instrumentalizes the state by mounting pressures to conform to globalizing priorities that give governments little political space. States are co-opted or subordinated, weakening impulses to regulate on behalf of the common good. In this regard the world economy, as a totality, bears certain resemblances to the early capitalist period when market forces prevailed to the extent that labour was exploited in a variety of ways (long hours, low wages, unsafe conditions, no job security, no protection in old age or in the event of emergencies). At the state level social movements helped to create a better equilibrium between state and market, corporate and banking power being balanced to varying degrees by organized labour and by a socialist option. Of course, the evaluation of this equilibrium was controversial, diverse, dynamic, varying from country to country and over time.

The state in democratic societies mediated between market and social forces until this role was partially superseded by the imperatives of 'competitiveness' in the wider settings of the regionalization and globalization of economic life. This process was complex and contextual, reflecting many factors, including the relative efficiency and productivity of the labour force and managerial methods, the extent to which labour protection was entrenched, the degree to which competition for markets was being mounted by low-wage societies, the overall impact of the Soviet collapse on the socialist option, and the shifting class and ideological composition of civil society.

What seems beyond debate are *two factors that underpin negative globalism*:

- the *successful resistance of market forces* in relation to the establishment of global regulatory regimes that restrict market and banking practices with respect to an enforceable code of conduct; the elimination of the UN Centre of Transnational Corporations in the late 1980s was an expression of the influence exerted by market forces; part of this success is associated with the instrumentalization of leading capitalist states, operating as agents of negative globalism, virtually taking the resistance option off the domestic political agenda despite its importance for the citizenry;

- the *downward pull on well-being standards* elsewhere exerted by the *comprador* market practices in the most dynamic sectors of the world economy, especially South Asia; this downward pull is accentuated by the increasing mobility of capital and by the relative failure of states with higher well-being standards to negotiate from strength and conviction. In other words, labour reforms in China, Indonesia and elsewhere, would reduce the incentives to relocate or invest on the basis of unevenness in the treatment of workers, thereby diminishing the downward pull on welfare and labour in countries with higher levels of business regulation. The issue is complex because unevenness in standards of living is being reduced by the capacity to increase exports from poorer countries, and may depend for a period on achieving competitiveness on the basis of lower production costs, especially labour.

Regionalism has not yet emerged as a counter to negative globalism. On the contrary, its main drive to date has been to facilitate more effective participation on a global level, either by protectionist policies or by achieving export competitiveness. The impact may again result in some levelling down of well-being and environmental standards, at least on an intra-regional basis. Sweden to prepare for its participation in the European Union has had to roll back aspects of its exemplary welfare system, reducing taxes, cutting some services. Regionalism has helped Europe aggregate capital and maintain technological parity with the USA and Japan, and therefore avoid the fate of moderate marginalization in relation to the globalized market.

In Asia–Pacific, although the experience varies from country to country, and over time, regionalism has been seen almost exclusively as a means to accelerate growth of trade and investment, avoid marginalization, and combine capital, resources, labour, and market without regard to statist boundaries. The 'regionalism' of Asia, especially recently, has not been based on the whole region or even on whole countries, but on privileging high growth segments of society, leading to the emergence of so-called 'regional states'.[20] Of course, it is misleading to assimilate the reality of states in the full Westphalian sense into the terminology of regionalism. The analogy is suggestive, but only if critically assessed in terms of its actual properties of control over a territorial domain that encompasses a clearly demarcated region. The notion of state implies an effective governmental centre, clear and generally accepted boundaries, and a status that is accepted beyond the region in diplomatic relations. Europe, as the most developed region institutionally, has not yet clarified its boundaries: will Turkey be part of Europe? Surely, the East European countries will be included, but what of Russia and the Ukraine? And does 'Europe' include the space of countries that remain formally separate as Switzerland and Norway have chosen to do?

The economic achievements of regional arrangements of different sorts are impressive in many respects, but *not* in relation to the containment of negative globalism, at least not yet. Indeed, the contrary conclusion is more illuminating, that regional formations, especially with respect to the three main trading/investing blocs, has served to consolidate the negative feature of global economic integration.

This consolidating role has been played out by removing economic policy from the realm of domestic politics, an aspect of weakening the state as a mediating actor between territorial concerns, especially of those being marginalized, and global market forces. It is confirmatory, as well, that regionalism has not taken hold in those settings that are being most marginalized by the world economy, and further that religious extremism in Islamic countries has produced a partly voluntary, partly involuntary delinking from the world economy.

There are additional kinds of evidence. The recent efforts by the US Government to build support in the citizenry for NAFTA was distinctively bipartisan at the level of elite politics. President Clinton was able to mobilize all five living presidents for the signing ceremony, a show of bipartisanship that would neither be possible (degree of consensus), nor necessary (extent of societal opposition) on any other issue of policy significance. Also, it seems anomalous that a president representing the Democratic Party would so unconditionally support NAFTA, despite its Republican lineage, and given the hostile attitude of almost every labour union and of most liberal constituencies (environmental, church, social activist). But it is not a true anomaly. It is an expression of the instrumentalization of state power in the strongest of states in relation to the priorities of economic globalism. Such an assessment is confirmed by the timing of the Zapatista revolt of Mexican indians, centred in Chiapas, and time to coincide with the effective date of NAFTA, expressing this awareness that economic regionalism and negative globalism were being reinforced at the expense of the most vulnerable ethnic and economic sectors of Mexican society.

Negative globalism is also, possibly pre-eminently, embodied in the WTO arrangements of the Uruguay Round of GATT, which creates the institutional and political foundations for what has been described as the basis for an 'economic autocracy' by its critics.[21] Both the modes of negotiation, and the efforts to avoid full constitutional review, as would be appropriate if the latest GATT arrangements were regarded as a treaty requiring ratification, are expressive of this dynamic of instrumentalization. Within the USA the executive branch is most responsive, by and large, to these globalist pressures, while the Congress remains more influenced by local and territorial factors, more resistant as a result to the pure allure of non-territorial influences. Such a GATT framework, elevating the priority to be accorded unencumbered trade, also operates to ensure conformity at the regional level, making an electoral choice of social democracy almost impossible to implement in practice.

MITIGATING PATHOLOGICAL ANARCHISM

Labelling internal deformations of state power as 'pathological' implies a conception of normalcy in the relations of state and society that has broken down; to associate this normalcy with the anarchy of international relations is to stress the structural point that institutions of global governance are very weak.[22] Pathological anarchism refers to acute political disorder: genocide, severe crimes against humanity, large-scale famine, substantial breakdowns of government.

In the long Westphalian period of international relations, pathological anarchism was essentially ignored unless the strategic interests of leading states was seriously threatened. Such threats were rarely perceived unless the governmental actor in question embarked upon expansion at the expense of the existing distribution of power informing world order. The response to Nazi Germany and Stalinist Soviet Union are paradigmatic in both respects: appeasement or, at most, containment, with respect to the pathological behaviour, but willingness to risk everything to prevent territorial expansions that seek to revise the hierarchy of relations that inform world order. It is not that the pathological dimension is irrelevant. Indeed, especially in relation to democratic societies, the pathological character of a rival is relied upon to mobilize resources and commitments needed to conduct warfare or to practise containment credibly.

The corollary point is that if the pathology does not pose external threats it will be tolerated.[23] This has been again demonstrated in the period since the end of the cold war in the much discussed instances of Somalia, Bosnia, Haiti, Rwanda. Perhaps, the situation is more ambiguous: the historical memory of the Holocaust has encouraged the sentiment of 'never again', particularly in Europe, and this has generated interventionary pressures in relation to Bosnia; the CNN factor selectively lifts the veil of ignorance from the occurrence of acute distress, and induces public support for constructive responses; the entrenchment of human rights in international law has eroded the sovereignty arguments that abuses within states are of no concern externally. As a result, there have been responses to the recent instances of pathological anarchism, but of a half-hearted character as compared to the response mounted to reverse Iraq's aggression against Kuwait. These responses, collaborations between the UN and leading states, especially the USA, have provided a measure of relief for elements of the afflicted populations, but have not challenged the core pathologies. What has been relied upon has been diplomacy, sanctions, relief operations, and pinprick assertions of military power. The sum of these efforts is *less* than its parts!

To the extent that responses have moved toward more serious levels of commitment it has resulted from boundary-transcending impacts: the prospects of a wider war in the Balkans, the outflow of refugees causing destabilizing effects in important state actors (the USA, Germany, France). These possible developments convert pathological anarchism into an occasion of strategic concern (justifying large allocations of resources and risks of loss of life), raising the stakes in the event that containment fails. Also, in relation to refugees the alternatives of repatriation or deterrence may both fail, leaving only the option of military intervention. Such an interpretation of the situation in Haiti during the summer of 1994 has made some commentators write of intervention as 'inevitable'.

Enter regionalism: both states and the UN have failed to address pathological anarchism effectively. Could this failure be overcome, in some circumstances, by the empowerment of regional institutions? Could NATO act in the former Yugoslavia to challenge Serbian 'aggression', restoring order and a unified, multi-ethnic Bosnia? Could the OAS bring constitutional democracy to Haiti? Could the OAU act in relation to Somalia, Rwanda, Burundi, Sudan and Liberia?

These questions return us to the theme of instrumentalization. To the extent that regional actors are effective in peacekeeping or peace enforcement it is because they are carrying out the policies of their leading members, states, especially, of course, hegemonic states. And further, to the extent that these leading states have themselves been instrumentalized by negative globalism, there is not much prospect that the pathological challenges posed within an organized region will produce a response different in kind from that issuing forth from the global level. In essence, the conception of strategic interest will not be very different, except for its geographical and cultural proximateness. If regional capabilities include impressive military assets, then if strategic interests are deemed present, as has from time to time seemed weakly to be the case in relation to Bosnia, then the availability of NATO to act is definitely a potential factor in any move to challenge the core pathology. Nullifying this potentiality is the extent to which proximateness may fracture collaborative possibilities, each major state perceiving its interests in handling the crisis in a distinct manner and being distrustful of its rivals; such rivalry has been operative in relation to Bosnia from the outset, varying in intensity over time.

The major conclusion to be drawn is that regional communities have not evolved to the point where their institutional ethos or capabilities are sufficient to address pathological anarchism in a manner comparable to the efforts made by competent and constitutionally moderate states in relation to pathologies embedded within their own polities. States, too, are not always effective, sometimes accommodating, containing, collaborating, and sometimes being instrumentalized from below by the pathology or even having the pathology capture legitimate state power (as Hitler did in Germany, 1933). Can (should) regional actors be encouraged to take on these ordering tasks, especially the protection of those most victimized by pathological anarchism, as part of the mixture of a commitment to implement human rights and to maintain regional peace and justice?

The dilemma posed here seems quite fundamental: to be effective and autonomous (that is, non-instrumentalized), regional institutions would have to become cohesive and capable of commanding loyalty, thereby coming to resemble in certain respects a state of Westphalian lineage, but such an evolution would seem likely on a global level to stimulate interregional conflict among regions of greatly different resource bases and civilizational identities, making it more credible that 'a clash of civilizations' would indeed ensue as the sequel to the cold war.

PROMOTING POSITIVE GLOBALISM

There are two intersecting traditions at work: first, the anxiety that effective global governance cannot avoid encroachments on human freedom unless it avoids centralism; a regionalized world order is one approach to reconciling the quest for global governance with a concern for constitutional equilibrium, and to a lesser extent with the preservation of cultural diversity.[24] The overriding goals in this outlook are so ambitious – transforming statism, ignoring globalization – in relation to the flow of events and horizons of aspiration, that little serious evolution of this possibility has been under consideration in academic circles. A more moderate expression of this view is somewhat more influential in the form of an *advocacy of 'subsidiarity' via regional institutions* as a way of allocating downward from the UN, particularly with respect to security issues, and thus in the context of delimiting the UN role. Such an approach, borrowing from the

European experience, which evidently borrowed from a Vatican doctrinal tradition. Such an approach is meaningful, of course, only to the extent that meaningful regional institutions exist, which is not the case with the possible exception of Europe, and in extremely limited respects, Central and South America and Africa.[25]

The second approach here is to view *regional institutions as complementary and subordinate tools of global governance*, being shaped within the UN, contributing in various settings to either effectiveness or legitimacy, or some combination. The UN Charter in Chapter VIII seems to envisage such a relationship.[26] Since effective regional governance has so often in international history meant interventionary diplomacy by a hegemonic state, and thus geopolitics, it has been viewed with suspicion by those disposed toward more law-governed modes of governance. The revival of practice and advocacy of spheres of influence is suggestive of a post-cold war pattern that acknowledges the failures of the UN in the setting of pathological anarchism, but it can hardly be properly identified as a variant of 'positive globalism.'[27] Conservatives give some credibility to the view that international institutions add elements of constitutional moderation to traditional modes of interventionism and discretionary geopolitics, conceiving of recourse to the UN or a regional actor as confusing, hypocritical, and superfluous.[28]

At this point, it is difficult to credit regionalism with being more than an occasional instrument for the assertion of hegemonic control that depending on circumstances can be viewed as either legitimated by collective procedures or not. The US intervention in Panama in 1989 was carried out despite the refusal to accord it legitimacy at either the regional or UN level, whereas a prospective intervention in Haiti enjoys both regional and UN blessings. There is some difference, yet in both contexts intervention is essentially a hegemonic initiative (shaped in Washington, with respect to time, goals, modalities, battlefield control).

Regionalism in relation to the emergence of positive globalism remains a latent potentiality. The Charter gives ample space for complementary regional roles in peacekeeping settings, and does in Article 52(3) express a favourable disposition toward resolution of disputes at a regional level, thereby seeming to endorse subsidiarity. Again, context matters; Castro's Cuba is under more intense hegemonic pressures as a regional pariah than it is in the UN setting.[29] It would seem that the virtues of regionalism in relation to positive globalism are, at present, mainly speculative. Its more serious relevance would arise as a derivation from the emergence of positive globalism, not currently in the offing.

PROMOTING POSITIVE REGIONALISM

Regionalism has achieved positive results in relation to specified world order values in several substantive sectors and various geographic settings, most significantly, of course, in Europe, but also in Asia/Pacific, Latin America, Africa, and the Middle East.[30] The most impressive of these achievements involve promotion of human rights, including revolutionary sovereignty-eroding procedures, as embodied in the European framework, and to a lesser extent within the inter-American setting;[31] mitigation and resolution of conflicts via diplomacy, mediation, and regional linkages; promotion of environmentalism; innovations in transnational co-operation and institutionalization; experimentation by way of the Maastricht Treaty with innovative extensions of political identity by way of the conferral of European citizenship.[32]

European regionalism has demonstrated that it is possible to extend the Rule of Law beyond the state, and often promote further human rights gains within generally democratic states by asserting grievances at a regional level. This has been impressively demonstrated with reference to the extension of gay and lesbian rights, which provides a model for other concerns, including the protection of resident refugees and foreigners generally.[33] There is a school of Eurocrat thought, most prominently associated with Jacques Delors, that further economic integration will depend upon parallel moves to strengthen the political facets of the European Union, and that such a momentum needs to be maintained to consolidate the economic results in terms of increased trade and investment so far achieved.

Perhaps, most significantly, regionalism has protected the peoples of Europe against deteriorating standards of living, and the prospects of gradual marginalization. This protection has been somewhat controversial because of its tendency to build pressure by way of competitiveness to conform to the requirements imposed by negative globalism. The latter has contributed both to high levels of unemployment and to static, or even falling, real wage levels in Europe and North America. An assessment is not a simple matter. To the degree that regionalism has been instrumentalized by negative globalism then it forms part of an overall global structure of dominance that is leading to acute marginalization for certain nations and regions, sectors deemed inefficient and uninviting if considered either as producers or consumers. The geographic distribution has some North–South features, but the burdens of marginalization are not so neatly configured, given the rise of South and East Asia, and parts of South America. This disregard of marginalization is accentuated by the ideological consensus in support of neoliberal economism in elite circles, and reinforced by the abandonment of socialist and welfare-orientated perspectives by even the leading social democratic parties in Europe.

With respect to economic regionalization, the most important recent steps have involved Europe, North America, and Asia–Pacific. The cumulative impact on peoples within and outside these more integrated trading blocs is, as yet, conjectural and intensely contested. Whether the characterization 'positive regionalism' is at all appropriate cannot be determined at this time until more evidence on effects has been gathered. A worst-case assessment would suggest that regionalism is serving as a cover for the re-entrenchment of relations of privilege and domination that had been challenged during the revolt against colonialism. A best-case scenario would attribute unevenness in benefits and burdens to the short-run, with a more equitable, sustainable, and democratic global economic order emerging in responses to grassroots and other challenges mounted against negative globalism.

In the Asia–Pacific region, the internal dimension of regionalism is to take early, mainly informal and *ad hoc* steps toward economic co-operation and co-ordination, viewing especially ASEAN as possessing a potential for expansion and further institutionalization in the post-Cold War era. These steps are reinforced by a new Asian cultural assertiveness, which both moves toward the affirmation of a regional identity, but also represents a deepening of the decolonization process by its implicit repudiation of Eurocentrism.

In this regard, *Asian–Pacific regionalism* resists any renewal of Western hegemonic projects, and helps explain Asian unity with respect to opposing doctrines of humanitarian intervention to correct several abuses of human rights or to remove military rulers from power. As such, Asian–Pacific regionalism, even more than its European counterpart, may be moving toward limiting the Western, especially the USA's role, thereby encouraging a defensive dimension of regionalism.

A CONCLUDING NOTE

More particularistic inquiries may help to clarify the impact of regionalism on world order values. This chapter has tried to conceptualize
several main contexts in which regionalism has seemed dynamic in
this post-cold war period, taking especial account of hegemonic pas-
sivity on a global level (the disappearance of strategic, zero-sum
rivalry, inducing a shrinking of perceived strategic interests; a rising
sense of domestic opposition, increased realization that power-projec-
tion is expensive and often inconclusive in relation to 'black hole'
challenges), of the disappointing capacity of the United Nations to
provide a less hegemonic, yet still effective, world order, and of the
overbearing reality of globalization with respect to markets, money,
and information. Little ground for optimism has been found with
respect to regionalism as either a counter-hegemonic democratizing
influence or as a source of a new kind of benign hegemonic order
(although the trend toward the reactivation of spheres of influence is
clearly evident in Russia's effort to provide leadership and exert
control over the new states that were formerly Soviet republics; and
by the USA in relation to the Western Hemisphere, especially Central
America, through a reassertion of the Monroe Doctrine as an ingre-
dient of foreign policy; and by France in relation to Francophone
countries in North and sub-Saharan Africa).

From a world order perspective the role of regionalism is to help
create a new equilibrium in politics that balances the protection of the
vulnerable and the interests of humanity as a whole (including future
generations) against the integrative, technological dynamic associated
with globalism.[34] One kind of balance is being promoted by transnational social forces connected with human rights and the environment,
but regionalism could be another. Both phenomena are, in part,
reactions to the displacement of the state, from without and within,
and the decline of sovereign territorial space as a domain of unconditional political control. Regionalism, if democratically conditioned,
might yet provide, at least for some parts of the whole, a world
order compromise between statism and globalism that has indispen-
sable benefits for the circumstances of humanity, as well as some new
dangers.

A recurrent theme of postmodern thought is the stress upon unde-
cidability. The rational grasp of reality does not resolve difficult issues
of choice. The cynical view is that such a circumstance ensures that
interests will prevail, and there is support for such a reading of the

Regionalism and World Order After the Cold War

times, particularly given the rise and spread of crime, even the danger of the gangster-co-opted state. A more hopeful view is that the tendencies toward democratization and human rights can be focused in the years ahead on the menaces of negative globalism and pathological anarchism, and that regional arenas will be important as sites of struggle, and as exemplification of the play of opposed forces.

Notes

1. For elaboration see R. Falk, *A Study of Future Worlds* (New York: Free Press, 1975); *Explorations at the Edge of Time: Prospects for World Order* (Philadelphia, PA: Temple University Press, 1992); and *On Humane Governance: Toward a New Global Politics* (Cambridge, UK: Polity, 1995).
2. The European focus of several early influential analyses of the end of the cold war reinforced these perceptions of discontinuity. See Jack Snyder, 'Averting Anarchy in the New Europe', *International Security* **14** (1990): 5–41; John Mearsheimer, 'Back to the Future: Instability in Europe after the Cold War', *International Security* (1990) 14: 5–56
3. Björn Hettne, 'The New Regionalism: Implications for Development and Peace', UNU/WIDER, (1994): 4–5; see Robert Gilpin, *War and Change in World Politics* (Cambridge University Press, 1981) for a clear presentation of hegemonic stability as the basis of world order, and of its erosion.
4. See. Bull, *The Anarchical Society: A Study of Order in World Politics* (New York: Columbia University Press, 1977); for assessments of post-statal world order see James N. Rosenau, *Turbulence in World Politics: A Theory of Continuity and Change* (Princeton University Press, 1990); Falk, *The End of World Order* (New York: Holmes & Meier, 1983).
5. Consider George Bush's neo-Wilsonian rationale for resisting Iraq: 'What is at stake is more than one small country. It is a big idea: a new world order where diverse nations are drawn together in common cause to achieve the universal aspirations of mankind – peace and security, freedom, and the rule of law.' Quoted in *The Round Table* (Summer 1994) p. 5.
6. See Charles Krauthammer, 'The Unipolar Moment', in Graham Allison and Gregory F. Treverton (eds) *Rethinking America's Security* (New York: Norton, 1992) pp. 295–306.
7. What made Israel 'strategic' is somewhat elusive, but it was so perceived by Western leadership, especially in the United States, and reflected domestic pressures via Congress and the media, as well as calculations about stability in the Middle East.

8. For instance, John Mearsheimer, 'Why We Will Soon Miss the Cold War', *The Atlantic* (April 1990).
9. But note that what was accepted by Washington for two years as tolerable was either the return of a populist leader like Aristide or the stabilization of military rule provided the refugee problem is 'handled', even if handling meant forcible repatriation, brutal means to discourage the outflow, and resettlement in already over-burdened countries in Central America and the Caribbean; in the background is the view that restoring democracy is not worth a single American life; also, from a progressive perspective US intervention has been coherently opposed; see Joanne Landy, 'Born-Again Interventionists', *The Progressive* (September 1994) p. 23; for a mainstream analysis of hegemonic caution see Michael Mandlebaum, 'The Reluctance to Intervene', *Foreign Policy*, **95** (1994): 3–18. For recent assessments that have taken account of the successful restoration to power of Aristide and a peacekeeping presence by US/UN forces see James Morrell, 'Haiti: Success Under Fire', International Policy Report, Center for International Policy, Washington, DC (Jan. 1995)
10. What is called 'Asia's "Asianization"' in a recent article. Yoichi Funabashi, 'The Asianization of Asia', *Foreign Affairs*, **72** (1993): 75–85.
11. Samuel P. Huntington, 'The Clash of Civilizations?', *Foreign Affairs*, **72** (1993): 22–49.
12. For extended argument along the lines of this paragraph see Falk, 'The Political Economy of World Order', Portrack Seminar Paper (June 1994).
13. A relevant datum here is the extent to which nominally socialist or welfare-orientated political leaders are led to adopt unconditional capitalist orientations once in power; Blair, Mitterrand, Clinton, Mauryama are clear examples.
14. The distinction between negative and positive globalism is itself a reflection of recent developments, especially the globalist character of the world economy; earlier, globalism, at least on the surface, seemed motivated almost exclusively by idealistic ambitions to overcome war by creating effective mechanism of collective security, with the eventual objective being the achievement of a disarmed world administered by a government of federative structure, that is, a mixture of the Wilsonian effort to supplant the balance of power approach to stability and the more utopian pursuit of the Kantian notion of 'perpetual peace'. This latter notion has in its weak form resurfaced in the latter stages of the cold war, and subsequently, as achievable by the spread of market-orientated constitutionalism, premised on the argument that liberal democracies do not go to war with one another. See Michael Doyle, 'Kant, Liberal Legacies, and Foreign Affairs', *Philosophy and Public Affairs* **12** (1983): 205–35, 323–53; Bruce Russett; this positive globalism can also be criticized as naïve, hypocritical, insufficient. For a classic treatment see E.H. Carr, *The Twenty Years' Crisis: An Introduction to the Study of International Relations* (London: Macmillan, 1939); for a more recent argument applied to recent world developments, see Henry Kissinger, *Diplomacy* (New York: Simon & Schuster, 1994) esp. pp. 804–35.

15. See *Human Development Report 1994* for an analysis of antecedent conditions.
16. See Thomas Weiss, 'UN Responses in the Former Yugoslavia: Moral and Operational Choices', *Ethics and International Affairs*, 8: (1994) 1–21.
17. This revival must also be connected with the reappearance of a Russian threat to Europe in the form of a more assertive foreign policy and by way of the rise of ultra-nationalist challenges to Yeltsin's leadership (the Zhirinovsky factor).
18. For earlier lines of specification see Falk, *A Study of Future Worlds* (New York: Free Press, 1975); Falk, *Explorations at the Edge of Time: Prospects for World Order* (Temple University Press, 1992).
19. See Dusan Sidjanski, *L'Avenir Fédéraliste de L'Europe*, (Paris: Presse Universitaires de France, 1992).
20. Kenichi Ohmae, an articulate champion of such regionalism, 'Political leaders, however reluctantly, must adjust to the reality of economic regional reality if they are to nurture real economic flows.' In effect, such leaders must subordinate claims on behalf of the marginalized sectors of their own societies: 'Resistant governments will be left to reign over traditional political territories as all meaningful participation in the global economy migrates beyond their well-preserved frontiers.' See Ohmae, 'The Region State', *Foreign Affairs* **72**: (1992) pp. 78–87, esp. p. 85.
21. This paragraph owes much to a conversation with Ralph Nader, consumer activist, on 5 August, 1994; for a range of views along these lines see collection of essays by Nader and others, *The Case Against 'Free Trade': GATT, NAFTA, and the Globalization of Corporate Power* (San Francisco: Earth Island Press, 1993).
22. See Raymond Aron, 'The Anarchic Pole of World Order', *Daedalus*, (1966); note that this weakness may disappear under the aegis of negative globalism, which is, as argued in the prior section one of the features of the WTO dimension of the extension of GATT now under consideration.
23. There are some alleged exceptions by way of 'humanitarian intervention', but none stand close scrutiny as real exceptions; for exposition see R.J. Vincent, *Nonintervention and International Order* (Princeton University Press, 1974) esp. pp. 344–9.
24. See proposals of University of Chicago under the aegis of Robert Hutchins: Hutchins and others, *Preliminary Draft of a World Constitution* (University of Chicago Press, 1948).
25. For a sustained argument along these lines see W. Andy Knight, 'Towards a Subsidiarity Model of Global Governance: Making Chapter VIII of the UN Charter Operational', paper presented at Annual Meeting of Academic Council of the United Nations System, The Hague, Netherlands (June 1994).
26. For support of this notion of a complementary relationship, as an aspect of an effective UN, see Boutros Boutros-Ghali, *An Agenda for Peace* (New York: United Nations, 1992) pp. 35–8.
27. Russia in 'the near abroad', the USA in most regions, but especially in the setting of Haiti and Central American policy, France in relation to

Francophone Africa, especially Rwanda. See Kevin Fedarko, 'Back to the USSR?', *Time* (25 Jul. 1994) pp. 40–3; an editorial, 'Russian Interventions', *Wall Street Journal*, (8 Aug., 1994); Charles William Maynes, 'A Workable Clinton Doctrine', *Foreign Policy*, 93: (1993–94): 3–20

28.   See assessment in the context of authorization for use of force to oust the Haitian military regime. Charles Krauthammer, 'Goodbye, Monroe Doctrine', *Washington Post* (2 Aug., 1994).

29.   Compare South Africa in the apartheid period under comparable pressures at both regional and global levels.

30.   See Hettne's overview in 'The New Regionalism'.

31.   See evaluation by David Held, *Political Theory and the Modern State* (Stanford University Press, 1989) esp. pp. 214–42.

32.   For assessment of these tendencies as pertaining to citizenship and political identity see Bart van Steenbergen (ed.) *The Condition of Citizenship* (London: Sage, 1994); also treaty provisions reprinted under the rubric 'A Citizen of the European Union', in Paul Barry Clarke, (ed.) *Citizenship* (London: Pluto, 1994) pp. 188–90.

33.   See L. Helfer, 'Lesbian and Gay Rights as Human Rights: Strategies for a United Europe', *Journal of International Law*, **157** (1991).

34.   Hettne's formulation of 'the proper balance' between such ideas and forces being 'the crucial issue' does not explicitly signal any particular concern for those social and environmental elements of society that are being most victimized by the phenomena of globalization, see p. 5, n. 3, possibly, this concern could be brought in by way of 'regionalism and world order values'. See Vol. 4 in this subseries.

Table of Contents of Titles in the WIDER New Regionalism Series

Index

competitiveness
  and flexible specialization 38
  global 120–1, 140
  and regionalism 236, 237
  and technology 40, 46, 107
  Third World 69
comprador practices 68, 70, 73, 163, 236
computers *see* telecommunications and computers
conflict
  'clash of civilizations' 193, 232, 241
  and globalization 46–7
  interregional 18, 241
  regional xxiii–xxiv, 9–10, 16
  and regionalization 203, 208, 220–1, 224
  resolution xxiii–xxiv, 9–10, 16
  social 47, 66–7, 70–1
Confucianism 22, 193, 194
  industrial neo-confucianism 195
constructivism 94
continentalization 208
core regions xv–xvi
corruption 119
costs
  global production 120
  of investment capital 140
  social 121
Côte d'Ivoire 69
Cox, Robert xiii, xxxii, xxxiii, 22–3
cross-border co-operation 206, 213
cross-regional coalitions 95
Cuba 69, 94, 242
cultural identity 48
culture
  as factor in civil society 39
  pluralist 22–3
  and regionalism xix, 9, 12, 244
currency blocs 27, 138
currency, international 64–5
Czech Republic 71, 212

debt crisis 78, 125
degenerate regionalism 36–7, 46
deglobalization 6–7
delinking 57, 62, 157, 238

democracy xix–xx, 13, 84, 163–4, 224
  communitarian 194–5
  democratic deficit xxxiii
  market forces and 118–19
denationalization 36
Denmark 90
deregionalization 186
deregulation 36
Deutsch, K.W. 100
devaluation 36
developing countries 108–9, 125, 133–4, 135, 139–40, 144
  see also NIEs; Third World
development xxii, xxiv–xxv, 5, 67–71
  core–periphery 38
  Eastern or Western models of 195
  flying geese 27, 109–10
  neoliberal 44–6
  and new regionalism 5, 16, 18–19, 107–11
  polarization 72
  uneven 67–71
  see also industrialization
Development Bank of Southern Africa 34
development integration model 32–3, 44, 46, 47–8, 169–70
devolution 147
dichotomy, globalism and regionalism 181–200
  and gender issues 187–9
  limits and costs 182–98
  and Pacific Europe 196–8
  and postmodernism 182–3, 198–9, 200
  statist 183–4, 185–6
  Western globalism–Asian regionalism 189–92, 196
disarmament 77
disintegration, state xx, xxiii, xxiv, 15–16, 18, 234, 239–41
distribution of power
  global 117–19, 126–7
  and regionalism 224
division of labour 4–6, 37–40, 44, 45, 46
  and centre–periphery polarization 58